CW00971423

Piers Plowman Studies VII

A GAME OF HEUENE

WORD PLAY AND THE MEANING OF *PIERS PLOWMAN* B

Piers Plowman Studies

ISSN 0261–9849

A Game of Heuene

Word Play and
the Meaning of *Piers Plowman* B

MARY CLEMENTE DAVLIN, O.P.

D. S. BREWER

First published 1989 by D. S. Brewer, Cambridge

D. S. Brewer is an imprint of Boydell & Brewer Ltd
PO Box 9, Woodbridge, Suffolk IP12 3DF
and of Boydell & Brewer Inc.
Wolfeboro, New Hampshire 03894-2069, USA

ISBN 0 85991 272 8

British Library Cataloguing in Publication Data
Davlin, Mary Clemente, 1929–
    A game of heuene : word play and the
    meaning of Piers Plowman B. – (Piers
    Plowman studies ; 7)
    1. Poetry in English. Langland, William.
    Piers Plowman. Critical studies
    I. Title   II. Series
    821'.1
    ISBN 0-85991-272-8

Library of Congress Cataloging-in-Publication Data
Davlin, Mary Clemente, 1929–
    A game of heuene: word play and the meaning of Piers Plowman B /.
Mary Clemente Davlin.
        p.   cm. – (Piers Plowman studies, ISSN 0261-9849 ; 7)
    Bibliography: p.
    Includes index.
    ISBN 0-85991-272-8 (alk. paper)
    1. Langland, William, 1330?–1400? Piers the Plowman.   2. Play on
words.   3. Christian poetry, English (Middle) – History and
criticism.   I. Title.   II. Series.
PR2017.P54D38   1989
821'.1–dc19   88-22195
                                                                           CIP

∞ The paper used in this publication meets the minimum
requirements of American National Standard for Information
Sciences – Permanence of Paper for Printed Library Materials, ANSI
Z39.48–1984.

Printed in Great Britain by
St Edmundsbury Press, Bury St Edmunds, Suffolk

for 'Mercy ... and hire sone' (V.635, 636) and
for John and Marguerite

Contents

Acknowledgements

Each of us who studies *Piers Plowman* owes the text not only to Langland, but also to Skeat and the editors who have followed him; we owe the basis of our understanding to those who have loved, analyzed, and taught the text before us. In particular, my thanks are due to Professor Charles Muscatine, with whom I began the study of *Piers Plowman* and who has helped me ever since, most recently by reading and criticizing an early draft of this study. I am grateful to Professor John Lawlor, Professor Robert W. Frank, Jr., Sisters Jeremy Finnegan, Mary Paynter, Philip Mary Reilly, and Gretchen Hessler, Professor Chinosole, Professor M. T. Tavormina, and Saundra Becker who have also read drafts and helped me with suggestions and encouragement; to many librarians, especially those at the Rebecca Crown Library, Rosary College; the University of California, Berkeley; and the Regenstein Library, University of Chicago; and to Ms Pru Harrison, friends at St Leo's, Oakland, and Sister Marie Grant, Rosary College, for technical assistance.

A sabbatical leave from Rosary College enabled me to begin this book. The National Endowment for the Humanities through a Summer Stipend; the Newberry Library and the British Academy through their joint fellowship; the Board of Crosby Hall, Chelsea, through the Bosanquet Bursary; the University of Chicago Midwest Faculty Seminar through Lilly and Mellon occasional fellowships; the Vatican Film Library, St Louis University, through Mellon grants; the Department of English at the University of California, Berkeley, by furnishing study space; and the administration and community of Rosary College in countless ways have made it possible for me to complete it.

I have many other happy debts to those who have generously shared time, encouragement, scholarship, and life with me, particularly my teachers, including the late Sister Mary Aquinas Devlin, O.P., who introduced me to Middle English, and my family, colleagues, students, and friends, especially my Dominican sisters.

Chapter One

Word Play in Piers Plowman: *An Introduction*

In Passus IX of *Piers Plowman*, Wit calls human speech 'a game of heuene' (104).[1] This phrase, I believe, is a clue to the nature of *Piers Plowman*, 'one of the most difficult poems ever written, ... a work that continually challenges but evades interpretation' (Woolf, 'Tearing' 50). As the phrase 'game of heuene' suggests, language in *Piers Plowman* is something with which one plays, and the play is 'of heuene' at least in the sense that it is for Will and for Langland a way to truth. The purpose of the following chapters is to explore some of the modes and effects of this 'game' by analyzing passages of verbal play and by discussing some of its implications.

All poetry, in its tension, delight, and supra-logical character, is a form of play, as Huizinga has shown. He stressed the play of the author in 'poetic creation' (119),[2] and V. A. Kolve, in demonstrating that medieval vernacular 'drama was conceived as a *game*,' i.e., as 'pley' (16, 20), emphasized the play of author and actors. Recent critics have used game-theory

---

[1] The phrase 'game of heuene' itself is a pun, and I discuss it in Chapters III and VI. Here I am stressing its meaning as 'heavenly sport, game,' without prejudice to its other meanings. David Aers observes, 'For Langland the play, the game, is a saving game and its medium is speech, particularly the remembering and creating speech of the makers' (*Piers* 67). See also John Burrow, *Ricardian* 45, 84. With a very few exceptions, I am concerned here only with the B-text, and the text used throughout, unless otherwise noted, is the Kane and Donaldson B-Text, by permission of The Athlone Press, London.

[2] See Huizinga 3–13, 119–135, esp. 32, on play and on poetry as play. He quotes R. Guardini's 'Die Liturgie als Spiel' from *Spirit of the Liturgy* (Freiburg: Ecclesia Orans 1), 1922. See also Barthes, 'From Work to Text' 162–3, and Curtius on 'Jest and Earnest in Medieval Literature' 417–428 and 'Poetry as Entertainment' 478–479. Cassirer speaks of Shakespeare's 'game of the pure self-activity of the word' (176). Wittgenstein's study of *Sprachspiel* is important in his philosophy of language (*Brown Book; Philosophical Investigations*). Barbara Herrnstein Smith defines literature as 'among other things, verbal structures that have been designed or discovered ... to invite and reward ... "cognitive play"' (121), and Ong notes that reading is play: 'Readers over the ages have had to learn this game of literacy ... And they have to adjust when the rules change ... even though the changes in the unpublished rules are themselves for the most part only implied' ('The Writer's' 12).

in analyzing many works of medieval literature, stressing the games which characters themselves play. The Canterbury pilgrims with their tale-telling game are the most obvious example; Harry Bailly says to them, 'Ye shapen yow to talen and to pleye' (A 772). Donald Howard traces uses of 'game' in 'Troilus ' and 'Gawain,' and notes that in *Piers Plowman* 'the dreamer's wandering itself has the random, unreal, repetitious character of game' (285).[3]

Some works of literature may be seen as games in the further sense that they are designed to be played not only by author, actors and characters, but also by readers or audience through interaction of some kind, including active play with language in which audiences may 'make' or 'discover' meaning. Thus Louise Mendillo argues that 'Pearl' is a language-game, in which one is 'to pull apart these networks [of language] slowly, to work at restoring the full range of associations possible for the words of 14th-century English ... to pursue ... verbal ambiguities' ('Word Play' 7).

Piers Plowman may be seen as a game, not only because it has to an extreme degree the tension, delight, and supra-logical character of play of which Huizinga speaks, but also because, as an enigma or puzzle, it requires its readers to participate actively in the poem.[4] Although, as John Bowers points out, Langland minimizes certain 'play-elements' popular in other poems of the time, namely 'rhyme, fixed meter, stanzaic composition, decorative imagery' (211), he cultivates other elements such as shifting symbols, parallels and echoes, errors, conversions, other unexpected changes and deceptions, and especially word play, all of which elicit and require play of mind in the reader. Uncertain and tantalizing, these elements and especially verbal play invite readers to seek more meaning through allowing their minds to play upon possibility and probability.

The unfinished quality of a poem filled with verbal play as *Piers Plowman* is, the possibility or probability of two or more meanings in many words, is part of what makes the text enigmatic and turns the act of reading it into a game. The reader not only reads the poem, but 'plays' it actively

---

[3] For some of these studies, see Olmert, 'The Parson's' 167–8. As he says, 'The analysis of literary works [in medieval literature] from a ludic viewpoint has become a staple of twentieth-century interpretation' (158). See also his 'Game-Playing,' on *Pearl*. All Chaucer quotations are from the Riverside Chaucer.

[4] Chamberlin says, 'It is not that there are too few strands of continuity, but too many – multiple, simultaneous concatenations that spin out from the words of the text. ... Having to attend to and keep track of surface repetitions in order to interconnect the text can monopolize the reader's concentration and reduce intelligibility. But words themselves seem to be a unique resource of meaning for Langland in the richness and multiplicity of their interrelatedness within the language system; it is this that the poet is exploring in his poem.' Allen calls *Piers Plowman* 'a general hermeneutic puzzle,' (*Ethical* 112, n. 46), and Baker argues that 'Langland deliberately creates this enigma [of Truth's pardon] to engage his readers with the issues of the poem' ('Pardons' 470). Cf. Schmidt, *Clerkly* 88.

and 'finishes' it, especially by participating in puns through solving them as puzzles, enjoying the pleasures of surprise and of intensified verbal awareness.[5] In addition, each of the two or more meanings of any pun relates in its own way to other words in context so that these words seem to come alive in surprising ways. There is still further 'game' in the possibilities of relationship between referents, which each pun suggests.

Repetition of words in the text works in a similar way.[6] If, in reading *Piers Plowman*, one remembers a word, phrase, or line when it is repeated and then compares the contexts where it occurs, meaning often blossoms. One occurrence often seems suited to be a commentary on the other; the use of a word in one place opens up unrealized possibilities of meaning for it in another context. Such 'concordance' (Alford, 'Role' 81–83) has an effect like that of puns extended through the entire narrative, an effect which Nevill Coghill called echo and foretaste ('Pardon' 333–4). Although the narrative does not depend upon such echoes, awareness of them is part of the game.

Not only particular words and passages, but the poem as a whole demands the reader's participation in completing, discovering, or creating its meaning. The demands which *Piers* makes upon its readers are extreme, and we play a game, work a puzzle, enter a competition with the poet when we study it. The very act of reading such a long work is an investment. The sudden changes in the narrative from one level of consciousness to another, from one sort of time to another, and from one interlocutor and psychological setting to another, as well as shifts in the text from the literal to the figurative mode and from one language to

---

[5] On the pleasures of puns see especially Baum, 227. Ong explains that the reader of word play becomes involved on several levels as word play evokes both 'the manipulation of thought on an abstract level and ... operations on a physiological, muscular level which engage the whole organism in relevant perceptions and feelings' ('Wit' 318). Burnley distinguishes between 'connotational and cognitive meaning,' the latter being 'that meaning which at any given moment is considered to be central and essential' (208).

[6] As Josephine Miles says, 'Quantity is not alien to art. In its form of repetition it is a primary organizing as well as substantiating force. Art uses quantity just as it uses quality, to make the effect it chooses' (*Continuity* 535). On repetition in *Piers*, see especially Spearing 'Verbal'; Salter *Introduction* 9, 48; Alford, 'Role'; and Chamberlin. In 'Figural,' Salter notes that foretastes and echoes are 'a very clearly recognized feature of typological or figural compositions ... [and that] repetition is at the very heart of Langland's poem as it is at the heart of his faith' (88–89, 92). Kirk notes the 'echoing of image' through the poem (*Dream* 196). Studies of various image patterns, such as those by Robertson and Huppé (44, n. 52), Kellogg (32–44), and Debs are relevant to the study of verbal repetition, showing how repetition develops themes, links episodes, and creates emphasis and sometimes irony. See also Middleton, 'Narration,' on 'episodic units whose arrangement seems somehow reiterative rather than progressive' (92). Vinaver shows the use of repetition through 'interlacement' in the Arthurian romance (*Form* 15–16).

another, require attention and interpretation; its shifting symbols, parallels, figural types, dreams within dreams, ironies, errors, lies, conversions and hypocrisies challenge the most sophisticated efforts of its students.

Terms which Frank Kermode uses for the analysis of narrative suggest the importance of these challenging peculiarities, especially word play, as clues to the meaning of *Piers Plowman*. Kermode distinguishes two elements in narrative, 'narrative sequence ... and what I shall loosely, but with pregnant intention, call "secrets"' (81) ...

> My immediate purpose is to make acceptable a simple proposition: we may like to think, for our purposes, of narrative as the product of two intertwined processes, the presentation of a fable and its progressive interpretation (which of course alters it). The first process tends toward clarity and propriety ('refined common sense'), the second toward secrecy, toward distortions which cover secrets. The proposition is not altogether alien to the now classic *fabula / sujet* distinction. ... Secrets ... are at odds with sequence ... resisting all but abnormally attentive scrutiny, reading so minute, intense, and slow that it seems to run counter to one's 'natural' sense. ... We have hardly, even now, found decent ways to speak of these matters. ... It is a question of the form of attention we choose to bestow; of our willingness to see that in reading according to restricted codes we disregard as noise what, if read differently, patiently, would make another and rarer kind of sense
> (82, 83, 84, 96).

Kermode proposes that abnormalities in any text (he mentions, for example, 'dislocated narrative sequence,' even 'gross distortions,' and 'the unreliable narrator' 87, 92, 85), are in fact 'secret invitations to interpretation' (89).

On its simplest level – the level, in Kermode's terms, of sequence and the proprieties – *Piers Plowman* is an education-fable, a wisdom-narrative, an imaginative imitation of a human life from youth to age, not as life ought to be, but as one experiences it, with false starts, failures, and new beginnings. It is comic in form despite its lack of a happy ending because it promises ultimate happiness for the human race. Yet no *schema*, however medieval, really explains *Piers Plowman*. Nor does any single genre, for although the poem includes several recognizable genres,[7] 'it is finally controlled ... by none of them' (Muscatine, *Poetry* 74). It still reads like 'a commentary on an unknown text' (Bloomfield, *Apocalypse* 32). Will learns something in *Piers Plowman* and so do we, but the poem does not end in victory or full understanding. For that matter, it does not really end at all. These facts, as well as the enigmatic characteristics mentioned above,

---

[7] The classic treatment of the genres in *Piers Plowman* is Bloomfield's (*Apocalypse* 10 and passim), but as he suggests, no one of the genres which influenced the poem wholly explains it. See my *'Piers'* on the possible influence of wisdom literature.

make it appear that the poem defies or fails to observe the proprieties of 'connexity, closure, and ... the receipt of a message' (Kermode 81, 84). Readers, therefore, who give *Piers Plowman* what Kermode calls 'a straight reading' – one which values 'the proprieties (as to connexity, closure, and character)' (81) – may judge the narrative to be seriously flawed.

But disruptive elements and aspects of form may be, in Kermode's terms, 'secret invitations to interpretation' (89), invitations to a deeper 'form of attention' which will enable us to discover a 'rarer kind of sense' in the 'secrets' of a narrative. The 'secrets' of *Piers Plowman* are surely the *'sacra mysteria,'* the central Christian mysteries of the nature of God, Christ, and human life, which the text invites us to contemplate and which it sometimes enables us to 'taste' through such devices as puns, irony, metaphor, pun-like symbols and echoes – devices which require almost 'abnormally attentive scrutiny' (Kermode 84). Kermode's insights enable us to see that an apparent discrepancy in the text between argument and form may be a necessary result of the presence of meanings which cannot be expressed through 'connexity, closure, and character,' and which, if they are to be perceived at all, must be discovered by 'abnormally attentive scrutiny.' Kermode has shown that in some narratives, abnormalities of form point to secrets. It is my belief that *Piers Plowman* is such a text, designed to draw readers into wisdom, i.e., into the contemplation of divine mysteries as they impinge upon and irradiate ordinary experience; its enigmas, including its word play, invite and demand that readers learn attentive, contemplative, active reading – a new 'form of attention' (Kermode 96; Baker, 'Pardons' 470–471). In a game of discovering and creating meaning, readers may discover coherent 'secrets' which do not appear on the surface. In this respect, *Piers Plowman* is like liturgical texts, which exist not to be read or heard passively, but to be participated in, played out, worked and played with over and over; their purpose is experience, both aesthetic and religious, and in this experience they release an increasing fullness of connotative meaning. No liturgical text is meant to be heard simply for entertainment or information; neither is *Piers Plowman*. The reader must participate in *Piers*, play with it, so that its purpose – a particular kind of experience at once aesthetic and religious – can be achieved.

It is not unusual for medieval poems to have as their purpose some religious or moral change in their readers or audience; Judith Ferster has shown that such change was a conventional expectation, and that readers were expected to read actively to the point that 'reading can be a kind of rewriting' in 'a dialectical relationship between authors and audiences' (10–11).[8] Thus a Wycliffite sermon quoted by Kolve speaks of miracle plays

---

[8] The most obvious example is the *Commedia* of Dante, who writes in the letter to Can Grande that he desires *'removere viventes in hac vita de statu miserie et perducere ad*

which 'assayen to convertyn the puple by pley and gamen' (Kolve 18). This expectation is congruent with medieval 'rhetoric in accord with the meditational principles of active involvement ... [which] invites active contemplation and interpretation' and 'stresses the active participation of the auditors in the process of understanding the Word' (Hala, *'Signum'* 319, 325).[9]

Meditative study of texts, especially of Scriptural words, their root meanings and the ways in which their various occurrences illuminate one another was an established and important way to seek wisdom in medieval society. Jewish and Christian exegetes were aware of the importance of word play in Scripture, and the words of Scripture were believed to be, as Peace puts it, 'lettres' from 'Loue' (XVIII.182). For Christians, moreover, Christ, the Wisdom of God, is 'the Word,' and contemplation not only of scriptural words, but also of Christ, in his life, in sacrament, in others, in all nature and experience, is perceived as a means of entering into the revealed but inscrutable mystery of God. In the monastic practice called *lectio divina*, scriptural passages were to be learned 'by heart' until the nun or monk would find words resonating in the memory, so that a particular word would recall other passages with the same or similar words, and each would serve as commentary on the others. This method of reading and remembering by 'concordance' has an obvious relationship

---

statum felicitatis: 'to remove those living in this life [his readers] from a state of misery, and to lead them to a state of happiness' (Cecchi and Sapegno II: 67); cf. *Par.* II: 1–15. Josipovici points out that 'Chaucer's art in *The Canterbury Tales* can be seen as a game, but, no less than Dante, he aims at a redirection of the reader's will. His game is not a "mere" game. It has designs on the reader ... [who is] to acknowledge ... folly and learn from the game' (196). See Mendillo on *Pearl*, 'Word Play' 7.

[9] In this quotation, Hala is writing of a Middle English lyric, but in 'For She,' he implies that an 'active poetic' of the same kind informs *Piers Plowman*. He distinguishes the context of classical rhetoric, one 'of audience passivity,' from the Christian context 'stressing the active role of the percipient' (*'Signum'* 319). Kolve's quotation is from 'A Sermon against Miracle-Plays,' ed. E. Mätzner, *Altenglische Sprachproben* I: 2. Berlin, 1869: 222–242. Tompkins states that 'most critics before the twentieth century' were concerned with '[reader-] response conceived as action or behavior' (206), 'strategies designed to ... make [the reader] enact in his responses the very subject matter of the poem. ... [For them,] the text is not a spatial object but the occasion for a temporal experience' (Fish 345). Allen, too, argues that 'Medieval poetry is, in the modern sense of the word, constantly rhetorical' (*Ethical* 289), and says that in *Piers* 'the activity of language as such is carried on without ever being allowed to be self-existent or independent' (281); cf. 298–300. On theories of reader-response criticism, see, for example, Scholes 8–14, 126; Fish 343–347; Barbara H. Smith 123, 153; and Tompkins 201–206. Quilligan, *Language* 70–79, 162, 222–3; Simpson, 'From Reason' 14; Schleusener 81; Baker, 'The Pardons' 470–472; and Allen, 'Langland's' 359, see *Piers Plowman* as designed to cause readers to change their reading habits, to discover, to 'move ... [toward] true belief' (Schleusener 81, 163). See also Middleton, 'Idea' 98, 103–4 on poet, persona, and audience. Schmidt emphasizes the desirability of close, sensitive reading, (*Clerkly* 3–4, 112, 126, 128).

to the echoes and foretastes which Coghill pointed out in *Piers* and is another of the ways in which Langland seems affected by monastic spirituality.[10]

Throughout *Piers Plowman*, as we shall see, the poet treats his own words and the words which he quotes and interprets from Scripture, liturgy, and proverbs as if they are a 'tresor' which yields wisdom, precious 'lettres' which can, if played with and savored, yield life-giving insights.

Moreover, the poet says explicitly in various passages that attention to words, even playing with words, is a way to wisdom, and I think we must take these passages very seriously since they accord so exactly with his practice. For example, Holy Church's first lesson to Will is that 'truþe' 'wolde þat ye wrouȝte as his word techeþ' (12–13); this demands loving attention to the 'word.' In Passus XII, Will excuses himself for writing poetry by explaining that playing with words will teach him what he needs to know:

> '... of holy men I here', quod I, 'how þei ouþerwhile
> [In many places pleyden þe parfiter to ben].[11]
> Ac if þer were any wight þat wolde me telle
> What were dowel and dobet and dobest at þe laste,
> Wolde I neuere do werk...'   (XII.23–27)

Lines 23–24 are not simply an apology for recreation; they define and defend an attitude toward poetry. The 'werk' (27)[12] of which Will speaks so diffidently is a kind of playing (with language), an imitation 'of holy men [that]... pleyden the parfiter to ben' (24), which makes him a better person ('parfiter') by giving him knowledge he cannot otherwise attain ('What

---

[10] Cf. Bloomfield, *Apocalypse* 75–77 on the influence of monasticism on *Piers*. On the importance of words, see Deut. 30: 14 and Rom. 10: 8: 'For the word is very near to you, on your lips and in your heart.' On word play in the Bible, see, for example, Caird 96–108 and Payne. See Rahner on religious symbolism. On *lectio divina* see Alford, 'Role' 81–85; Leclercq *Love* 89–96; Rousse 471, 476, 481; and Leclercq et al, *Spirituality*: 'By an understanding of the words themselves, by a yielding to the word of God, vocal prayer becomes mental prayer, as St. Benedict wished' (119). Brewer associates Langland's thought with *lectio divina* in *English Gothic* 192, 207.
[11] For K-D's line 24, Skeat gives: 'Pleyden, the parfiter to be – in many places'; the Schmidt ed. gives 'Pleyden, the parfiter to ben, in [places manye].'
[12] 'Werk' is used in Passus IX to connote labor which is not merely manual, but creative and artistic, like God's creation of the world; see Chapter III. Middleton sees the reference to 'werk' here as one of the ways in which Langland suggests that Will is '*homo faber* ... [and] his work ... the serious work of a fabricator' 'Narration' 102, 121; cf. her 'Idea' 103. Salter notes 'the dreamer's rather surprising identification of "makynges" with "bokes ... to telle men what dowel is, dobet and dobeste bothe ..." and even, perhaps, with "werk" itself ...' 'Langland and Contexts' 21. Chaucer's Harry Bailly sees the telling of tales as both work and play: 'to pleye ... to werken' (A 772, 779). For an excellent discussion of the writing of the poem as play/work, see Bowers 192–4, 211. Schmidt speaks of word play as 'word-*work* for poet and readers alike' (*Clerkly* 128).

were dowel and dobet and dobest at þhe laste' 26). 'Makyng,' then, precisely as a form of play/work, is for Will a way to wisdom (cf. Schmidt, *Clerkly* 18).[13]

In Passus XIX, writing or speaking – 'lelly to lyue by labour of tonge' (232) – is described as one of the direct gifts of God: 'tresor/ And wepne to fighte wiþ whan Antecrist yow assaileþ' (225–226). 'Wordes' are a way to truth, but not an easy way, since by using words, one must 'wynne' truth:

> Some [wyes] he yaf wit with wordes to shewe,
> [To wynne wiþ truþe þat] þe world askeþ,
> ...
> And by wit to wissen oþere as grace hem wolde teche.   (229–230, 233)

The narrator claims here that Grace (God) teaches others ('wissen oþere' 233) through the words of the writer or speaker. The intelligent, truthful use of words is therefore a means of divine wisdom not only for the one who works and plays in composing them, but also for 'oþere,' readers or listeners.[14]

---

13 Scholars do not agree about the strength of Will's defence at XII.23–7, which I think considerable. Martin says, 'Will's reply is at best a non-sequitur, a comment on his spiritual condition rather than his role as a poet. At worst, it capitulates to the most narrowly didactic view of literature' (*Field* 57). Burrow calls the reply 'not convincing' ('Words' 117). Kane writes, 'Under rebuke ... the Dreamer makes a perfunctory excuse, as if for all the charge being well-founded, he does not take it seriously and means to continue in his way' ('Music' 45). Boitani believes that 'Langland ... doubts his very right to write' (87). Salter, however, says that 'the defence he offers is honestly thoughtful [;] ... the answers to the questions that trouble him must be processed through his poetry' (*Introduction* 28). Kirk points out the unusual character of Will's argument that poetry is 'his only means of finding out what he has to know' (*Dream* 140–145), and gives another view of 'pleyden' from mine. Minnis believes that Will's defence 'can be recognized as deriving from a typical late-medieval justification of exempla technique and "imaginative writing,"' but rejects the idea that Will is advocating 'an individualistic means of reaching truth' ('Langland's' 87, 91). Middleton points out that 'play' is his defence ('Narration' 117–119; see also her 'Idea' 111). Olson establishes that in the middle ages, 'literature for pleasure rather than profit was acknowledged, if not venerated' (31). See also Olson 94, 101–102; Godden, 161; Economou, 'Self-consciousness' 190; Coleman, *Medieval* 125; Bowers 199–211; Schmidt, *Clerkly* 15–20.

14 Since the poet's game consists in telling the truth, it is significant that Piers' work is 'to tilie truþe' (XIX.261). The phrases are similar in more than sound (Huppé 168, Robertson and Huppé 17–19, 221–222). In the gospels, 'The seed is the word of God,' meant to blossom and bear fruit (Luke 8. 11; cf. Matt. 13, Mark 4). Thus Piers' work is to 'sowe and sette' (V.541), to 'tilien þe erþe' symbolically (VII.2), i.e., 'to tilie truþe' (XIX.261). Word play especially is both telling and tilling. Thus the agricultural imagery which dominates the poem through its title-character is also relevant to the poem as game, and the pairing of tilling with telling, work with play, captures the nature of learning to read, its difficulty and delight. Simpson, commenting on 'pleye with a plow' (III.309), notes 'The work of plowing is transformed into a kind of spiritual play' ('Transformation' 165). On medieval uses of agriculture as symbol, see Barney, 'Plowshare.' See also Bowers 214–5, and the forthcoming book by Ordelle Hill: *The Manor, the Plowman and the Shepherd.*

In IX, as we shall see, Wit speaks with horror of spilling (wasting) speech because it '[spire] is of grace / And goddes gleman and a game of heuene' (103–104), and he refers to the speaker or writer or his words as a 'fiþele' (105). The puns in this passage are discussed in Chapter Three; the point here is that words – surely including poetry – are something to *play* (both as music and as a game). One plays either an instrument or a game 'þe parfiter to ben' (XII.24), perhaps in order to play better, which in this case, as XII.24 actually says, is also to *be* better. Three of Wit's metaphors imply some form of participation by 'oþere': the 'gleman' and 'fiþele' will have listeners who may also sing and dance, and a 'game' has players. The poet not only 'plays,' then, 'þe parfiter to ben' but engages others in play as well, 'to wissen oþere as grace hem wolde teche' (XIX.233), and the play is heavenly, for speech is '[spire] ... of grace, goddes gleman and a game of heuene.'

Some characters within the poem demonstrate this playful use of speech and reading; others demonstrate the difficulty of reading or speaking well. Lady Meed does not even turn the page (III.336–347). The priest in the pardon scene (VII.115–118), and Righteousness, Truth, and Faith in XVIII interpret narrowly, restricting the meanings of words by their own pre-conceptions, not realizing what words might mean if interpreted with generosity. Holy Church, Mercy, Peace, and Christ, at the other extreme, give words their fullness of meaning, allowing all the potential richness of words to become operative, and opening up the possibilities of redemp-tion. In between, Piers and Will (and the reader) try to learn to read texts and events in such a way as to understand their secrets. In the pardon scene, for example, Piers does not yet know how to reconcile the priest's reading with his own understanding. Yet Piers already 'reads' – i.e., in-terprets – more truly than the scornful priest, as Schmidt points out (*Clerkly* 86). The process of learning to 'read' or to search for a 'kynde knowyng' is difficult for the characters in the narrative. At every step, truth is hard to grasp and impossible to control or to comprehend fully.

The personal engagement which the poem requires of its readers and, in particular, the mental process experienced in attending to continual word play, parallel the personal engagement and the mental process required of characters in the poem; both of these experiences model the way to a 'kynde knowyng' of 'treuþe.' For 'kynde knowyng' seems to encompass the ability to find the secrets not only in texts (Baker, 'Pardons' 470–71) but also in all those cryptic realities which Will learns so slowly to read: the world, the liturgy, Scripture, oneself, the poor, the 'vncristene creature,' even a corrupt society – and somewhere within them, to find the Word, to see Truþe – or 'no truþe' (I.198). Wisdom is the ability to shell the walnut and find 'a kernel of confort' (XI.262), to see the Christ 'In a pouere mannes apparaille' (XI.186), to read God's poetry of wit (IX.39–44) (cf. Simpson,

'From Reason' 6–7). Word play in particular requires and enables the reader to begin to read in this way. It leads to surprises, intuitive 'tastes' of truths that cannot be fully grasped by inference, in a process like the non-inferential mental processes of faith and wisdom. Since many of the puns are about divine mysteries or include a religious meaning, playing with them leads the mind to play upon those central Christian mysteries and to glimpse and experience them in the imagination. As Hala says, puns 'become examples of the way in which God's word, signified by his creation, is to be read' ('*Signum*' 326). Thus in a quasi-sacramental way, playing the 'game' of the poem, especially by entering into its word play, both signifies and effects imaginatively the purpose of reaching a 'kynde knowyng' of 'truþe.'

The following chapters will show that word play in *Piers Plowman* is not an occasional or fortuitous device but a characteristic way of writing and thinking, a clue to the way the poet saw the world. They will propose that it is also a 'secret invitation to interpretation' (Kermode 89) of the purpose and enigmatic structure of the poem, since as the most characteristic and frequent element of 'instability' in the texture of *Piers Plowman*, it is para-doxically the vehicle of some of its most important intimations of stable meaning.

Thus, careful, active reading with attention to word play is essential in *Piers Plowman*, and not only because 'the pregnancy of its language' is the source of much of its meaning and beauty (Spearing, 'Development' 252; cf. 'Langland's' 182–3). It is true that if we ignore this richness we misread or half-read important passages and lessen our understanding and plea-sure. But as I shall try to show in the last chapter, attention to word play is essential for another reason as well: the form of the pun and the mental process of perceiving puns are models of the nature and purpose of the whole poem.

Before analyzing particular passages, it is necessary to clarify some terms and premises. No single term for Langland's manner of playing with language, his 'game,' seems entirely satisfactory. 'Word play' is the most natural term and one which I use, although it is difficult to define exactly.[15]

---

[15] In a thorough bibliography (the first of its kind, so far as I know), Franz Hausmann (1974) cites some 250 works on various aspects of word play. I have found Ong (1947), Muir (1950), Brown (1956), Mahood (1957), Heger (1963), and Ducháček (1970) especially helpful. A smaller number of articles and parts of books on words and word play in particular Middle English works has been steadily building, including works by Tatlock (1916), von Soden (1927), Heraucourt (1936), Silverman (1953), Kökeritz (1954), Baum (1956), Richardson (1970), Leyerle (1974), Stock (1981), Burnley (1983), Joseph (1983), Tkacz (1983), Hahn (1986), and Prior (1986), on Chaucer; Speyser (1981) on drama; Manning (1962), Woolf (1968), Weber (1969), Oliver (1970), Gray (1972), Reiss (1972), and Hala (1984) on lyrics; O'Brien (1982) on 'King Horn'; Johnson (1953),

Word Play in Piers Plowman

Word play in general has been described as 'continuous subtlety of design at the purely verbal level' (McAlindon 129), and more specifically, by Ducháček, as 'très variés[,] étant inspirés par divers phénomènes linguistiques tels que homonymie, paronymie, polysémie, antonymie, association d'idées, conscience étymologique, tendance de motivation, attraction lexicale (morphématique et sémantique), contamination, euphémisme, dysphémisme, ironie et sarcasme, éventuellement par la combinaison de deux des phénomènes cités' (117). Most of these forms of verbal play are used frequently in *Piers Plowman*.[16] Langland plays continually upon the repetition of words, phrases, synonyms and whole lines; he plays with every form of contrast and irony, and with sound. Indeed, Langland's play with the sound and meaning of words may be coextensive

---

Rupp (1955), L. D. Benson (1965), Wilson (1971), Muscatine (1972), Borroff (1973), Mendillo (1976, 1977), and Arthur (1987) on the Pearl Poet; Mendillo's dissertation includes a summary of previous research on word play in 'Pearl.' 'Pun' is sometimes taken to be coterminous with 'word play': 'Play on or upon words: a sportive use of words so as to convey a double meaning or produce a fantastic or humorous effect by similarity of sound with difference of meaning; a pun' (*OED* 'Play' II.7.b). I use 'pun' in the more restricted way explained in the text. See also Bennett, *Poetry* 95. It is perhaps unnecessary to note that puns need not be trivial though they are playful; see Donaldson, *Piers* 174.

[16] In 1939, Morton Bloomfield called for a study of 'the meaning of Langland's words and lines' as one of the needs of *Piers Plowman* studies ('The Present State' 232). Kaske's study (1951) of figures of speech focuses attention on the language of the poem, as do Spearing's articles (1960, 1963, 1983), and Bloomfield (1961) notes Langland's 'delight in word play... his love of puns, half-puns, repetitions, and word play in general' (39). Lawlor (1962) discusses word play (264–277). Although Kean (1965) does not speak of word play, she demonstrates 'the poet's own exploration of different alternatives in the complex' of images and allusions in the plant of peace passage, and thus emphasizes words and their relationships (360). Hieatt (1967) notes 'dreamlike' ambiguities, including puns (90–91). Middleton (1972) argues that the poem aims 'to make human language eschatologically adequate' (172). In an important book, the first to make the language of the poem its central concern, Mary Carruthers (1973) argues that 'analysis of words as ambiguous tools of thought, capable of revealing a true cognition but also of generating a corruption of understanding, is the basic concern of the poem ... [which is] an epistemological poem, a poem about the problem of knowing truly' (4, 10). She sees its action as the search for a 'redeemed speech' (20). Anderson (1976) emphasizes the importance of play in the poem; though she calls it the play of mind rather than of language (5), she notes particular examples of word play (e.g., 13, 19), and comments 'Words mean, of course, for Langland – indeed, mean more than for us – but they mean gradually, fluidly, and fully only in the fullness of time and of the person' (208, n. 8). P. Martin (1979) explores various plays on abstract and concrete language (71–90), and Quilligan (1979) discusses some puns and shows their centrality (58–61, 72–79, 160–162), as does Alford (1982). Spearing (1983) sees 'the tendency to pun, in Langland as in Shakespeare, [as] ... one sign of the poet's reliance on the multi-dimensionality of language itself' (190), and James Simpson discusses puns in his study of figures of thought in *Piers* ('Transformation' 1986, e.g., 163–4, 169–70, 182, and 'Et Vidit' 1986, 10). Schmidt (1987) notes Langland's 'unusual fondness for word play' (112) and analyzes its effects in many passages (108–141).

with that semantic process in poetry which Barfield calls 'the making of meaning' (136). Within this context, the pun is of particular interest; it is, as Huppé argued and as recent explications of particular examples continue to show, a central device in the poem's development, important to its meaning, texture, and form.[17] Yet although important articles and sections of books have made its presence obvious and although it is becoming more and more a focus of interest, no full-length study of the pun or other forms of word play in *Piers Plowman* has yet been made.

The pun (sometimes called *paronomasia*) is 'the use of a word in such a way as to suggest two or more meanings or different associations, or the use of two or more words of the same or nearly the same sound with different meanings...' (*OED* 'pun'), whether the double or triple meaning derives from shared etymology or from coincidence. That is, sometimes a single word, used once, has more than one meaning. Or sometimes the pun is a form of repetition, the same or a similar word being used twice (or more often) with two or more different meanings. These two sorts of puns have been classified in different ways by rhetoricians and linguists. Classical and medieval rhetoricians called the first sort of pun (one word with two meanings) *significatio*. It is also sometimes called *double entendre*, *double entente*, or a play on meaning. Rhetoricians named the second sort of pun (with two or more words) *traductio* and *adnominatio* (or *annominatio*); it is sometimes called a play on sound. An example of the one-word pun may be seen in Passus XX, where Contrition asks Conscience to admit 'frere Flaterere' to Unity as a confessor. Conscience replies:

> 'I may wel suffre', seide Conscience, 'syn ye desiren,
> That frere flaterere be fet and phisike yow sike' (XX.322–323)

'Suffre' is a pun (*significatio*), meaning primarily 'permit, allow [it]' but also 'suffer'; the pun is ironic, since Conscience will certainly suffer because of allowing the friar to enter. It is possible that there is also a pun (another use of *significatio*) on 'syn' as 'since' and 'sin': the primary meaning is 'I may well allow [it] / suffer, since you desire that...' but an elliptical secondary reading is possible, as well: 'I may well allow / suffer the sin you desire, [i.e.], that...'

---

[17] Besides works noted in n. 16, studies of particular words have included Quirk's (1953) on 'kind wit' and 'inwit', Vasta's (1965) on 'treuthe,' S. Mary Jeremy Finnegan's (1964) on 'Leggis a-lery,' Harwood's (1973–) on 'liberum arbitrium,' 'clergye,' 'Imaginative,' 'kynde wit,' 'kynde knowyng' and other psychological terms, Kaulbach's (1979, 1985) on 'Inwitte' and 'Ymaginatif,' and mine (1971, 1981) on 'kynde knowyng.' Recent analyses of word play in particular passages include Mann (1979), Dillon (1981), Donaldson (1982), Schmidt (1983), Stokes (1984), Hala (1985), Hill (1987), and Shoaf (1987). Josephine Miles laid the groundwork for study of Langland's vocabulary in *Renaissance* (1960), with addenda in the introduction to the 1965 edition of *Continuity* (ii).

In Passus XIX, in the description of Pentecost, the line 'And as alle þise wise wyes weren togideres' (166) contains an example of the two-word pun or play on sound. 'Wise' and 'wyes' sound almost the same, and in this case the likeness in sound supports the description of the apostles as wise; but it is probably ironic, because they have just been described as refusing to believe the women who saw Christ: 'For þat womman witeþ may noȝt wel be counseille' (162), and the next line describes them as locked in for fear. The juxtaposition of 'wise' with 'wyes' requires us to consider the suitability of likeness in sound and whether it expresses harmony or ironic contrast of meaning.

Linguists classify puns from a different perspective, to distinguish word-forms and kinds of similarity which make a pun possible. They explain that it can be based either on a polysemous word (one word with two or more meanings) or on coincidence of homonyms (two words that sound alike but have different meanings). In practice, as Ducháček points out (109), it is difficult (and for our purposes unnecessary) to distinguish between these two, though Heger does so by defining a polysemous word as one with two meanings and a single syntactic function (noun, verb, etc.) (e.g., 'suffre,') and homonyms as words with two meanings and two syntactic functions (e.g., 'syn,' 'wise/wyes') (484). A single-word-pun (*significatio*) on homonyms thus demands ambiguous syntax (as in the line with 'syn ye desiren').

Piers Plowman has dozens of puns of these various kinds, simple and elaborate, traditional and original, one-word puns and puns of repetition, based on both polysemous words and homonyms.[18] Some of them are self-contained and some are part of a thematic pattern. They are some-

---

[18] As Kökeritz and Baum both point out, there is disagreement among rhetoricians about the meanings of the terms '*traductio*' and (especially) '*adnominatio.*' I have tried, therefore, less to classify examples than to explicate them. Skeat found twelve puns in *Piers Plowman* (14 instances II: 482), and B.F. Huppé, in the seminal article which proclaimed the centrality of word play in *Piers Plowman* (1950), increased the list to over 100 instances of puns as a 'sampling and list of additional references' in addition to over 50 plays on sound and other instances of thematic and verbal repetition. 'At the heart of the great poem, its unifying principle, is a play on words. God may be known only through Will, that is, the will, instructed by Piers, *Petrus, id est, Christus*' (Huppé 190). William Ryan (1968) lists over 100 'sample puns of special merit or interest' in *Piers Plowman* and over 150 additional 'common and largely repetitive puns' (100–122, 131–141), and (1969) he estimates 1000 examples of *annominatio* in *Piers* (265), without discussing them. Besides *annominatio* and 'matched pairs which appear twice or more' (W. *Langland* 143–145), Ryan has counted particular kinds of words in the A, B and C texts (e.g., words for poverty and riches) and made some observations about their meanings and about additions and deletions in B and C. H. Tristram's work is of the same type. Schmidt (1987) speaks of 'over 180 examples . . . in the B-text' (113); he also points out 'the *quasi-pun*, or chime,' proximity of two words not exactly alike (114); this includes what he calls 'pararhyming' words or half-rhymes (68). For puns he uses the term 'amphibologies' from Alexander of Villedieu (115).

times amusing, often ironic, and usually vehicles of significant meaning. They seem to embody important characteristics of the poet's sense of reality, especially his sense of freedom, 'treuþe,' and the inwardness of what is most precious. Even if explication of these puns may sometimes threaten to become tedious, the pun itself is always an economy and discovery, and often a surprise.

A word like 'sonne,' for example, is a homonym with two etymologically unrelated meanings: 'sun' and 'son.' It was commonplace in English in the middle ages to take advantage of this circumstance and of the liturgical prayer which names Christ *'sol iustitiae,'* the 'sun of justice,' by punning, and in at least three passages, Langland does this.

The first examples occur in the prayer of Repentance, recalling the death of Christ:

> Ther þiself ne þi sone no sorwe in deeþ feledest,
> But in oure secte was þe sorwe and þi sone it ladde:
> *Captiuam duxit captiuitatem.*
> The sonne for sorwe þerof lees siȝt [for] a tyme.
> Aboute mydday, whan moost liȝt is and meel tyme of Seintes,
> Feddest wiþ þi fresshe blood oure forefadres in derknesse:
> *Populus qui ambulabat in tenebris vidit lucem magnam.*
> The liȝt þat lepe out of þee, Lucifer [it] blente (V.489–494)

In line 489, 'sone' is used without punning:

> Ther þiself ne þi sone no sorwe in deeþ feledest (V.489)

Then in 491 it is a pun, meaning the sun, and also the Son:

> The sonne for sorwe þerof lees siȝt [for] a tyme. (V.491)

This pun causes the delight that comes from the discovery of a second possible meaning: for a time, the sun goes under a cloud of sorrow; the Son dies of sorrow, for a time. It also causes the pleasure of paradox, as it probes an apparent contradiction, since 'þi sone no sorwe in deeþ feledest' but 'for sorwe ... lees siȝt' by dying; the paradox, of course, is that of the incarnation, since the Son feels sorrow as man but not as God. The pun associates Son with sun – the sun stops shining as the Son dies, implying that in some sense the Son is a sun or is like the sun. This gives the double meaning of line 491 its depth, and the pun 'works.' It also gives pertinence to a line which follows:

> The liȝt þat lepe out of þee, Lucifer [it] blente (V.494)

This line, in turn, strengthens and develops the association of Son/sun suggested in the pun of line 491.

In another passage (XVI.92) with the same pun, the word 'sone' is used only once, and recognition of the pun depends upon a knowledge of the phrase 'sun of justice' from the office of matins: 'for out of thee [Mary] arose the sun of justice, Christ our God' (Huppé 178).[19] In this passage, *spiritus sanctus* speaks in Gabriel's mouth, telling Mary

> That oon Iesus a Iustices sone moste Iouke in hir chambre   (XVI.92).

The phrase 'a Iustices sone' presents the incarnation as a simple story of village hospitality, as Gabriel tells Mary that a judge's son is to rest in her chamber (*OED* 'jouk' v. 2). But it echoes and seems to mis-translate the sublime liturgical formula, '*sol iustitiae*,' with its image of the blazing glory of divinity. The Latin phrase is awesome; the English one, earthly and human. Thus the phrase is an emblem of the incarnation itself. As Schmidt says of another passage, 'the deft collocation of the two registers ... functions to activate our sense of the mystery ...' (*Clerkly* 107).

Again in Passus XIX the 'son/sun' pun is used. A cleric speaks of God:

> *Qui pluit super Iustos & iniustos* at ones
> And sent þe sonne to saue a cursed mannes tilþe
> As brighte as to þe beste man or to þe beste womman.   (XIX.431–433)

Here the pun on 'sonne' accompanies the use of 'tilþe' as both literal and metaphorical. Thus, 'a cursed mannes tilþe' is at once the farm saved by sunshine and the 'cursed' fallen human being saved by the Son, who is brilliant, healing, and life-giving like the sun.

One of the effects of a pun is to make the reader aware of the potentialities of a word, so that wherever it occurs, that word is perceived as a *possible* pun if context, history, grammar, syntax, and tone make a pun probable.[20] In this case, for instance, the Son is always at least potentially associated with light, and this association is developed in many passages about Christ, especially in the episode of the harrowing of hell.

Some polysemous words, called analogous or analogical terms,[21] are

---

[19] Margaret Goldsmith gives similar uses of the phrase *sol iustitiae*, concluding that Langland took 'the conjunction of thoughts and images in this scene' from St. Bernard ('Piers' Apples' 317–320).

[20] As both Frost and Blake warn, it is important not to assume the presence of a pun if this does violence to syntax, context, tone, or custom, even when 'poetic or literary language can possibly sustain more than one simultaneous implication' (Frost 555).

[21] '*Analogia*' was the name given by medieval logicians to Aristotle's third form of predication, between the univocal and equivocal (*Organon* 106–108b). See Aquinas, *Summa* Ia, 13, 5; Bonaventure *Itinerarium*; Klubertanz; Mondin; and Burrell 222–223, 240. Theologians explain that the name 'truth' for God, for example, is taken from the name for human faithfulness to indicate that human faithfulness is an image, though imperfect, of God's perfect fidelity. This concept of 'analogical' or 'analogous' terms is to be distinguished from analogy as a form of comparison and also from the analogical argument or argument from fittingness mentioned below, Ch. IV, n. 15. Vasta notes the analogical nature of the word 'truth' in *Piers Plowman* ('Truth' 21, *Spiritual* 59–60). Simpson discusses ironic and 'transforming' uses of this kind of language in 'Transformation,' e.g., 163, 183. See also Griffiths 23–25.

susceptible of a particular kind of word play frequently used by Langland. Neither univocal (with a single meaning) nor equivocal (with two unrelated meanings), such terms have different meanings which are related by degree: 'their meaning is proportional to the subjects of which they are predicated' (Klubertanz 463). Many of the most common and important terms in *Piers Plowman*, like 'truþe,' 'loue,' 'word,' are analogical. That is, 'truþe' as the name for God ('The tour on þe toft ... truþe is þerInne' I.12) does not mean exactly the same thing as 'truþe' when it is a term for human rectitude ('truþe þat trespased neuere' XII.287). Yet neither are its meanings as different as those of 'meene' (the noun 'mediator' and the adjective 'poor') or 'good' ('goodness' and 'goods'). The meanings of 'truþe' are neither wholly alike nor wholly different, but proportional to one another. Thus when used in puns they bring together meanings with a peculiar likeness-in-difference. For example, in I.131, when Holy Church promises heaven to all who 'enden, as I er seide, in truþe,' 'truþe' means simultaneously 'faithfulness' and 'God': one who ends 'in faithfulness' goes to heaven, and so does one who ends 'in God.' Here the double meaning suggests that perhaps one who ends 'in faithfulness' is already in some sense 'in God.' It is possible for the same word to be used in either analogical or equivocal ways, as 'kynde' is: it is predicated analogically when it means 'nature' in proportional ways, i.e., *natura naturata* (nature) and *natura naturans* (God); it is predicated equivocally when its operative meanings are semantically very different (though they may be etymologically related), like 'kind,' 'thorough,' 'natural.'

Some puns are chiefly ironic, playing upon homonyms or polysemous words to clarify ironic gaps where harmonious likeness should be. For example, Symonye knocks Conscience down, causing Good Faith to flee 'and fals to abide,'

> And boldeliche bar adoun wiþ many a bright Noble
> Muche of þe wit and wisdom of westmynstre halle.   (XX.132–133)

'Many a bright Noble' is a troop of splendid aristocrats bearing down upon the Commons at Westminster Hall; at the same time, 'many a bright Noble' is a pocketful of the coins first minted by Edward III and capable of bribing 'much of þe wit and wisdom of westmynstre halle.'[22] The first reading fits the violent allegorical context of the passus, the uprising of Antecrist and 'a greet hoost al agayn Conscience' (XX.113). The second reading, comically realistic, is the 'sentence' of the allegory. The 'nobles' that overcome many of those in Westminster Hall stand only for noble (but ignoble) coins, coins named aristocratically and meant, like all good things, to be used nobly, but here used in a way that belies their name and

---

[22] Cf. 'the noble yforged newe,' Chaucer, Miller's Tale, A 3256.

makes it ironic. Moreover, the pun with its two meanings suggests the mercenary motives which bring followers to Antecrist. The pun is a light, neat, ironic expose of bribery, and it shows with what economy puns can work.

Another kind of ironic pun balances a meaning intended by the speaker with a quite different meaning perceived by the reader and presumably intended by the poet. Mahood, in her study of Shakespeare's word play, sees this as 'The chief function of the pun ... to connect ... the primary meanings of words in the context of a person's speech and their secondary meanings as part of the ... underlying pattern of thought' (41). Langland uses it as Shakespeare does, as a form of dramatic irony, with two different purposes. In some passages, the irony lies in the contrast between two sorts of values, those expressed and those implied, or those of the character acting and those quite different values implied in some way by the words themselves. For example, in XI, Concupiscence of eyes says to Will, 'Haue no conscience ... how þow come to goode' (53). 'Goode' is a pun, meaning 'goods' ('Don't worry about what means you take to accumulate goods') but also 'goodness,' so that the line has an ironic second meaning ('Don't even think about how to reach goodness') which neatly spells out the implications of the first meaning.

A second sort of dramatic irony arises from meanings unintended and not perceived by the speaker, which have implications for other parts of the poem. Such irony often occurs with interjections or polite social terms which have their intended meaning and also another literal, ironic and more far-reaching one. For example, when Will asks Holy Church initially to 'kenne me kyndely on crist to bileue' (I.81), he means simply, 'Teach me to believe accurately, thoroughly, in Christ,' (*MED* 'kindeli' 3 a, d). But when one has read the poem many times, the phrase also resounds with implications which Will does not yet know but which the poet and habitual reader do know, 'Give me a "kynde knowyng" – in all senses of that phrase.' This is not to say that all meaning attached to a phrase anywhere in the poem is everywhere present, but that once one knows the poem, certain phrases do become, as Coghill said, foretastes and echoes ('Pardon' 333–334), just as they do in Shakespeare's plays, and one of the possible effects of this is dramatic irony.

There is a similar ironic use of words, also a form of dramatic irony, not quite a pun but producing an effect very much like that of the ironic pun. It is very common, especially in the Mede episode (II–IV), the Land of Longing episode (XI), and the last two passūs (XIX–XX). It, too, suggests a disparity between the values of poet and character, almost between language and character. It occurs when a polysemous word, usually one capable of a wide range of meaning, is used with the meaning which has the least emotive or ethical value, its 'thinnest' or 'weakest' meaning, in a context

17

where the full meaning could (grammatically and syntactically) be operative, but is not. Only the 'thin' meaning is operative, so there is no actual pun, but the ironic gap between what is meant and what might in other circumstances be meant by the same word has an effect like that of a pun. Schmidt, quoting Christopher Ricks, calls this an 'anti-pun' (*Clerkly* 111), 'which creates its double meaning by evoking but excluding' (Ricks 174). Both meanings are in play within the mind – one because it is operative, and the other, ironically, because it is inoperative but suggested by the word itself, for example, in Mede's words to the mayor:

> 'For my loue', quod þat lady, 'loue hem echone,
> And suffre hem to selle somdel ayeins reson.'   (III.91–92)

'Loue,' noun and verb, here connotes greed, graft, and passive agreement not to prosecute, for the sake of personal gain. The irony lies in the euphemism; in another context, spoken by another character, line 91 could be the words of a great lover or saint. Then line 92 makes Mede's meaning explicit and the passage ironic. Alone, either line would be unremarkable; together, they are purest satiric irony, as all the potential altruism of the word 'loue' mocks the greed which it denotes. This irony is achieved through the simultaneous presence in the mind of the meaning Mede intends and the meanings she does not intend, the latter showing up the tawdriness of the former.[23] In such passages, the words themselves are haunted by echoes of their ordinary meanings which flow from etymology and from previous uses. So liars and hypocrites are exposed by irony, which acts as a testing for truth (I.85–86).

As I argue in Chapter Five, such irony exists not only in comic passages like Lady Mede's or in the obviously erroneous speeches of Truth and Righteousness in XVIII, but wherever there is inappropriate emptiness of language. Like a counterfeit coin (XV.349–353), a word is false when it retains only its surface meaning and is short of its full value, like 'blisse' in Fortune's speech (XI.26) or 'kyn' in Book's (XVIII.257), its surface meaning working against its normal range of meaning and etymological associations. False words are not always lies, nor are they always intended to deceive. They may be signs of relatively innocent self-deception, of shallowness, blindness brought on by infidelity to truth, or simply human error. But their use is always a sign of some flaw in perception, some falsity of perspective which limits and distorts language. Words that do not matter very much to their speakers, words that are used without attention to their root-meanings, their possible analogical meanings, their potenti-

---

[23] C. David Benson treats this irony in an interesting way, arguing in a more extreme view than mine that in this passage Mede is 'a parody of Christ' (199). Hala's unpublished paper, 'For She is Tikel,' explicates ironic word play in the Mede episode.

ality for puns, all take revenge, through irony, on their speaker or referent. If a word cannot be fully itself because of the speaker's or the referent's ignorance, carelessness, malice, or foolishness, it parodies itself and resonates with irony that implicates the speaker or the one spoken about. One criterion for discrimination between true and false in *Piers Plowman*, therefore, is linguistic. The sign of truth in the language of the poem is its openness to free, full word play; the true meaning of a word is the one which is 'trewe' to the word's etymology and harmonious with the various meanings of its cognate forms. Thus, irony is important in the wisdom-game, because words used in a 'fals' way ironically evoke the fullness of meaning they lack.[24]

Something else not quite a pun but very like it happens when speakers (especially but not exclusively Holy Church) use personal or demonstrative pronouns (especially 'it,' 'that,' and 'this') in an ambiguous way where the context can bear two or more interpretations. For example, when Holy Church begins to tell Will how to save his soul, she says,

'Whan alle tresors arn tried treuþe is þe beste;
I do it on *Deus caritas* to deme þe soþe.
It is as dereworþe a drury as deere god hymseluen.   (I.85–87)

The lines are cryptic, and I discuss them in detail in Chapter Two. Here I wish to point out that in 87, 'It' could refer either to 'treuþe' or *'caritas'* and has been interpreted in both ways. But the indefiniteness itself has the same effect as a pun, and it is important, I think, not to choose too easily between antecedents. For the ambiguity makes us aware that 'treuþe' is like *'caritas,'* and that either is as 'dereworþe a drury as deere god hymseluen,' both being his names. Often this kind of ambiguity adds meaning rather than confusing it, because the unclear reference causes the reader to consider relationships between or among possible antecedents, which tend to 'overlay' one another like the meanings of a pun.

Many puns are developed as the 'sun' / 'son' puns are, i.e., the same pun is repeated in separate passages. Other key polysemous and analogous words and phrases, like 'kynde' and 'treuthe,' have a slightly different development, and properly exemplify *traductio* (repetition with various meanings) as well as *significatio* (one-word puns). In separate passages, separate meanings of the same word are established singly; then in other passages, the word is used as a pun, a fact which can affect earlier uses retrospectively, making them seem foretastes as one rereads.

---

[24] On irony, see Martin, e.g., 'Christianity depends as much upon profound ironies as on direct analogies' *Field* 108–109. Lawlor points out the presence of irony when one use of a word is mistaken for another ('Christian'), and Burrow notes irony where 'poeticisms in Langland's work are applied ... as if within marks of quotation, to unworthy subjects' (*Ricardian* 34). See Schmidt, *Clerkly* 10–11.

The pun has been called a 'prismatic' device (Mahood 10). A means of poetic economy (Huppé 168) and of multiplying meaning, it has many functions. Its primary purpose is obviously the linking of meanings, since a pun by definition means two things at once. By calling up the various potentialities of a word, its possible denotations, connotations, and etymological associations, punning links ideas and images with great emotive and intellectual power.

The most magical thing about a pun is that in linking ideas it also makes assertions or at least suggestions about the relationship of its referents.[25] The pun proves nothing, demonstrates nothing about the 'real world.' Yet it leads the reader to look at possible associations, analogies, and relationships between the realities to which the pun refers.[26] Often the sense of identity or analogy created by a pun is only momentary, humorous, ironic or fictitious, and perhaps, as Ducháček suggests, those puns based on homonyms especially tend to be ephemeral and purely entertaining.[27] But often a pun does reveal an underlying relationship so that we see genuine and permanent though unexpected harmony. John Lawlor, commenting on Owen Barfield's work, speaks of 'the coinherence of multiple "meanings" in any one "word" as expressive sometimes of "ancient unities." '[28] Walter Ong, too, stresses that 'Puns are [sometimes] used where semantic

---

[25] People 'do not *invent* those mysterious relations between separate external objects, and between objects and feelings, which it is the function of poetry to reveal. These relations exist independently, not indeed of Thought, but of any individual thinker. ... The second principle is ... operative in individual poets, enabling them ... to intuit relationships which their fellows have forgotten – relationships which they now express. ...' (Barfield, commenting on Shelley's 'Defence,' 72, 73, 74). In his study of medieval grammars, Bursill-Hall comments that '*partes orationis* were in fact considered correlatives of things in the world of external reality' (115). This view held by the *modistae* and others (in sharp contrast to that of nominalists) accords with Langland's practice. 'Grammar reflects the structure of mind, but, more important, the relation of concepts in the human mind corresponds to relationships of real entities in the universe, to what eternally is' (Middleton, 'Two Infinites' 185). Shoaf speaks of Dante's and Chaucer's 'faith which assumes that word and thing do ... tally' (*Dante* 14). Cf. Donaldson, *Piers* 178; Allen, *Ethical* 281; Alford, 'Grammatical' 737, 739, 754; Schmidt, *Clerkly* 81, 90–91, 109.

[26] James Brown writes, 'The pun makes both meanings apply; accepting the ... [pun] as meaningful forces one to accept the assertion of identity permitted by accidents of lexical ambiguity and context, even though common sense reality may thereby be violated[;] ... we cannot refuse to find the disparate reconciled. This startling state of affairs is the source of the pun's power, the cause of its peculiar effect' (15, 17). Caird notes that 'Some deliberate uses of ambiguity must be called exploratory, because the speaker has not made up his mind between two senses, but is discovering a new truth by investigating the interconnexion between them' 105. See also Borroff 13.

[27] 'Ceux [jeux de mots] qui sont fondés sur l'homonymie ou la paronymie sont, comme nous avons vu, de simples récréations philologiques tandis que les calembours qui s'appuient sur la polysémie sont parfois des mots spirituels, des maximes même qu'on aime à citer à l'occasion' (110).

[28] I thank Mr Lawlor for this observation.

coincidence penetrates to startling relations in the real order of things … word play can be more than mere phonetic tinkering and become a fertile ground for intellectual activity when the criss-cross of sound represents a genuine complexity of real relations' ('Wit' 315, 319). Many of the non-ironic puns in *Piers Plowman* that reveal such relations might be called existential or experiential puns, because they give insight into the fact that in the real life of an individual things may or do exist together which are theoretically quite distinct, for which we therefore have different concepts and different names. For example, the concept of human faithfulness is distinct from the concept of God, but Langland's puns on 'treuþe' suggest that there is meaning in the fact that they have the same name and that existentially, wherever faithfulness is, the faithful God is.

It is important to note that the mode of signification proper to word play, the way it makes such 'assertions,' is not logical, but intuitive and associative.[29] Sometimes word play enriches the sequence of thought by forming a web of supra-logical associations difficult to paraphrase. To use I.85 again as example, 'Whan alle tresors arn tried treuþe is þe beste,' the word 'tried' is a pun meaning 'refined, proved.' As 'refined,' it has semantic and historical associations with 'tresor' as 'precious metal,' and etymologically it is connected with 'treuþe' which means 'that which has been tried and found faithful.' As 'proved,' 'tried' has an affinity with 'beste,' a superlative which therefore implies judgement. The vital, supra-logical character of word play – the fact that it does not in fact *assert* in so many words, that it does not prove and cannot be proven, is perhaps the secret of its power. For the possibility of more and more meaning is one of the things which make the text enticing and draw the reader into it as into a game.

Thus word play is ideally suited to express the experience of gradual, partial vision and to draw the reader into the process of knowing intuitively. It causes the mind partially, restlessly, but really, to intuit what it cannot prove, to search for more and more meaning, to catch a glimpse of two things existentially coinhering and to hold them in tension, even though it can never understand how they coinhere. Thus it engages the mind in contemplation of what cannot be grasped by logic. Like his characters Mercy and Peace (XVIII), the poet plays with words not in order to relativize or escape truth, but to tell it as fully as possible, to make available truths beyond the ordinary range of language but susceptible of being suggested by word play. Such word play reveals Langland's 'capac-

---

[29] In his study of the serious pun, Kenneth Muir stresses the 'illogical' nature of puns and observes that they 'seem to shoot out roots in all directions, so that the poetry is firmly based on reality – a reality which is nothing less, if nothing more, than the sum total of experience' 483.

ity to see a situation simultaneously under different aspects, each independent and existing on its own level, in its own right, but at the same time
forming part of a transcendent order in relation to which alone its complete
meaning is to be ascertained' (Traversi 135). Playing with a word can yield
partially and gradually the wisdom of insight into this transcendent order.
Such play is perhaps the only way to get through the density of a polysemous word, to find again 'the ancient unities.'

If non-ironic word play in this vital, tantalizing way invites the reader to
find an analogy, reconciliation, or identity between disparate referents,
and ironic word play insists on the ironic gap between referents often
thought to be mutually inclusive, word play is continually paradoxical and
always related to the theme of appearance and reality. Both the realization
that what appears acceptable may be false, i.e., that what appears 'trewe'
may be 'no truþe of þe Trinite but tricherie of helle' (I.198), and the awareness that what appears wretched or routine may have meanings not
immediately perceived, lead to that sense of shifting and ambiguity so
familiar to readers of *Piers Plowman*. [30]

The language of *Piers Plowman* is most precisely 'a game of heuene' in its
verbal play on sound and meaning, ironic and non-ironic, which functions as a central source of meaning and coherence, leading the reader/
listener into the experience of the Christian mysteries, toward a 'kynde
knowyng' of 'treuþe.'

This study is obviously based upon certain critical assumptions. The most
basic is that style has meaning, which the reader can hope to decipher by
working with its words, structures and various devices in the light of
historical and linguistic knowledge. Such an assumption and the close
reading which I am advocating are elements of formalist and stylistic
criticism. Another idea that underlies this analysis, i.e., that the mean-
ing(s) of a text may depend for actualization and completion upon the
reader's play of mind, is an assumption both of medieval rhetoricians and
'makers' and of modern reader-response critics.

Another kind of assumption is that although 'no amount of supplying of
the historical and intellectual context of Langland's work is likely to be
profitable in the absence of a concern with his habits as a poet, a meddler
with makings' (Spearing, 'Langland's' 183; cf. 193), yet concern with 'his

---

[30] Huppé notes that puns may set a tone of ambiguity (186) and Bloomfield says that
Langland's 'delight in word play ... reveal[s] an intellectual perplexity and at the same
time a fascination with that perplexity' (*Apocalypse* 39). For other comments on
Langland's general habit of ambiguity and 'shifting,' see especially Muscatine, *Poetry*
102–106 and 'Locus' 121; Carruthers, *Search* 22–23; Burrow, 'Words' 121–123;
C.D. Benson 199; Salter and Pearsall 7, 19; Coleman, *Medieval* 117; Pearsall, 'The
"Ilchester"' 192; Bowers 33–34.

habits as a poet' can contribute to our understanding of his historical position. Important recent readings of *Piers Plowman*[31] in relation to medieval grammar, logic, and metaphysics, especially to the Speculative Grammarians or *Modistae*, the *Moderni*, and Ockham in particular, make progressively clearer the difficult intellectual history of late 14th-century England and the range of world-views and critical attitudes possible at that time. Yet because we have no external evidence of the poet's positions with respect to other thinkers, it is all the more essential to continue to study his poem from the inside out, as well as studying its historical context.

More specifically, I believe that recognizing word play is not very important unless it helps us to understand and enjoy the text, and that puns cannot be 'found' in violation of grammar or the history of the language.[32] Moreover, although we would like to know Langland's intentions, we have no external evidence of them, and therefore I treat the distinction between deliberate and accidental puns as ultimately irrelevant: the question is whether the pun is present or not. Nor, in my view, does the presence of word play depend upon the ability of a particular audience to perceive all of it.[33]

My premise then is that the presence of verbal play must be deduced neither from authorial intention nor audience-interpretation but from context. If a particular pun is possible historically and grammatically, one must judge its probability from the passage as a whole – its subject, structure, characterization, setting, tone, and other elements of style. Such judgements will always be a matter of more or less likelihood, not certainty, so that not all readers can be expected to agree upon the presence or genuineness of particular examples of verbal wit (Baum 229). Particular instances, in any case, vary in probability. But the very frequency of word play and the added meaning and coherence which it reveals in the text argue the importance of verbal play in *Piers* and the advantages of being attentive to it.

[31] For example, Adams, 'Piers's'; Alford, 'Literature'; Birnes; Bowers; Coleman, *Piers*; Gradon, 'Langland'; Middleton, 'The Idea'; Minnis, 'Langland's' and *Medieval*; Muscatine, *Poetry*. Cf. also historical works, not about *Piers* but bearing upon it, by Bursill-Hall; Leff; Oberman; Olson; Tierney. Cf. Ch. IV, n. 10, and Ch. V, n. 23.

[32] Lawlor warns against 'dispensing with all warrant in the text [through] the ingenuity of the exponent' (*Piers* 268). Blake argues that 'words in Middle English lacked the same clear-cut significance or connotative associations of modern words,' since, he says, there had been no opportunity yet in the fourteenth century to build up a body of literature commonly known in English (99). His argument does not apply, I believe, to connotations built up within the course of this long poem.

[33] As Ong says, it is not necessary to suppose 'that all these details were to be apprehended in full consciousness and in all their minuteness [by an original audience]. But there they were. And the medieval affection for etymologies, real or fanciful, certainly made a great mass of such detail quite assimilable' ('Wit' 319–320). On Langland's audience, see Burrow, 'Audience,' and *Ricardian* 33–34 and Middleton, 'Idea.'

Since analysis of puns takes so much longer than punning, commentary on the whole poem is impossible, and I have chosen to analyze examples of word play in four passūs scattered through the text. Passūs I and XVIII are both essential and irresistible. They begin and in a real sense end the action,[34] demonstrate puns with the greatest fullness of meaning, and contrast in two different ways 'false' or 'empty' language with 'true' or 'fulfilled' language, thus best defining the 'game.' Passūs IX and XI are near the center of the poem, rich in word play, different from one another and from both Passūs I and XVIII. Passus IX is about words and 'game'; XI (with its related passage from XII) contains a pun which is also a famous crux in *Piers Plowman* studies. Other passūs might have been chosen, and I have used examples from some of them in this chapter and Chapter Six. There are puns and other forms of word play throughout *Piers Plowman;* their frequency varies from place to place. Since verbal play is only one element of style, and since its presence in any passage is to be judged by context, it has seemed useful also to analyze and describe briefly the style(s) of each of the passūs to be discussed. Where other plays with sound, word games, or other forms of word play seem particularly interesting, I discuss them as well as examples of puns.

The following chapters, therefore, advocate and demonstrate a way of reading *Piers Plowman*: a way which supplements other ways by clarifying and complicating passages and drawing attention to linguistic brilliance. This reading sheds some light on the most difficult problems with which *Piers Plowman* scholars are faced, by offering some clues to the nature, purpose, structure, and progress of the poem, not only as a text to read, but also as a puzzle to solve and a game to play: 'a game of heuene.'

---

[34] 'In its typological significance, the Harrowing is the true end of the poem' (Bloom-field, 'Allegories' 32); see also *Apocalypse* 124–125. By 'end' I mean not the cessation of action, but its final cause and its vision and promise of the end of the world. See Chapter V, n. 26 and Chapter VI.

Chapter Two

Passus One

Although it has been analyzed more often than other parts of *Piers Plowman*, Passus I remains extraordinarily difficult – both puzzling and seemingly inexhaustible in meaning. It has been studied more than other passūs not only because it begins the action of the poem, but also and especially because in a sense it contains the whole poem within itself.[1]

The plan of Passus I is simple and its orthodoxy is familiar. It is a reverse catechesis in which Will questions Holy Church and is instructed by her; its two hundred lines are made up of a four-line introduction followed by six questions and answers.[2] Yet in spite of the simplicity of its structure, the passus is very difficult because of the style of Holy Church. Her speech has an allusive quality; she seems to say everything at once. Besides employing irony, she consistently uses analogous language and puns; the result is a puzzle which Will is unable to work out. This is the initial situational irony of the poem: that despite the fact that she represents and expresses the wisdom and experience of fourteen centuries, Will cannot understand her and cannot be expected to, because her words are fuller than he knows. The failure of communication between Holy Church and Will is absurd, amusing, and pathetic,[3] and besides setting the action of the poem in motion, it suggests in a challenging yet comic way the demands the poem will make upon the reader.

---

[1] Though, as Kirk warns, 'the Church is the opener of the way, not a substitute for the journey' (*Dream* 32), still, as Bloomfield has pointed out, Passus I 'sets out clearly the object of Will's search and really gives him the answers later to be made detailed and fully clear' (*Apocalypse* 25; 152–153). 'In some sense Holy Church's speech throughout this passus is an epigraph to the whole poem, an epigraph which we will not understand until the very end' (Knight 288); see also Salter *Introduction* 96 and Kaske 'Holy Church's.' For a contrasting view, see Harwood, 'Langland's *Kynde Knowyng*' 243.

[2] The Holy Church episode continues, of course, to II.52, with two more questions and answers. Holy Church's style does not change in II, so I have chosen to restrict my analysis to Passus I.

[3] Significantly different views include C. D. Benson's description of her as 'a remote, even hostile, figure to the Dreamer ... [who] never loves in fact' 195–196; to Harwood she seems 'imperceptive of his [Will's] plight' which Harwood sees as lack of faith and

Holy Church's style[4] appears so simple that Will is deceived, not realizing that her language demands any effort of understanding. Her words are plain, like her costume. She often repeats single words, clusters of words, and whole lines, as if to clarify. Her diction and sentence structure are colloquial and, except for frequently ambiguous pronouns, her words are easy to understand. Her tone is familiar and fits the plainness of her language. Thus she speaks familiarly of God – 'deere god hymseluen' – and familiarly to Will, whether in gentleness or anger. Her diction, including expletives, and the directness of her questions reinforce the familiarity which 'thou' implies – 'sone, slepestow?' (5); 'Thow doted daffe!' (140).[5]

Plain and familiar as it is, her language creates a rich semantic texture, one of the richest in the poem. A number of her frequently repeated words are puns. Other words become heavily connotative as she repeats and interweaves them in their various denotations. Yet her tone is neither playful nor clever, though in one passage she jokes heavy-handedly to ridicule falseness. Words are a 'tresor' to her. She turns them over and over, and speaks as if she is passionately inimical to their misuse.

A personification herself, she makes abstractions seem familiar by personifying or making metaphors of them.[6] Thus, 'Mesure is medicine' (35),

---

of intuitive knowledge of Christ ('Langland's *Kynde Knowynge'* 244–245). Carruthers describes their failure in communication as a 'dramatic indication of what the poem sees as the failure of the orthodox rhetoric of the Church to make meaningful statements about the world to those who live on the field of folk' *Search* 35; see also 5–6, 36; I am more in agreement with her later observations ('Time' 186). Bloomfield suggests that one reason Holy Church never appears again in the poem as a personification may be that 'Perhaps ... he felt that the voice of the true Church was so hard to hear in his time' (*Apocalypse* 21). I think this must be true, and perhaps the poem shows how to hear her. Martin discusses the irony of Will's use of questions (*Field* 48) and the contrast between 'practical' and 'idealistic' perspectives in the scene (113).

[4] Kirk effectively describes a number of its qualities: 'The air of chaotic and idiosyncratic association of ideas that Lady Holy Church imparts to a speech that is, in fact, quite effectively structured. ... Her terse and executive tone, her habit of hitting the nail on the head apparently quite at random, and her association of ideas ... her high-handed and brisk disposition of explosive material and her snappy style of exegesis' (*Dream* 30, 31). See also Griffiths 19, 21 and Norton-Smith's analysis of Langland's style in I (30–33). As Anderson points out, Holy Church's statements are 'sequentially more difficult to follow, perhaps more associative than most other sections' (16).

[5] Bennett comments, 'As a superior [she] uses 2 sg. forms in all remarks addressed to the dreamer alone, while he uses the respectful plural' (ed. 105). Cf. Norton-Smith 31.

[6] Holy Church and other personifications are of course not realistic characters; each is rather, in Lawton's words, an 'embodied universal' or 'grammatical first person subject,' yet some, like Holy Church, have a 'literary idiolect' (Lawton 11, 5, 8), 'language that is appropriate to ... character function rather than character portrayal' (Britton 2). On style in general as an expression of speaker, see Borroff 3, 4, and 8, and Middleton, 'Idea' 100. On personifications in *Piers*, see especially Griffiths; Frank, 'Art'; Kaske, 'Use' 589; and Salter and Pearsall ed. 3. Spearing notes the use by Holy Church of 'common life and the common language ... more metaphors than similes ... [including] local metaphors' ('Langland's' 186).

'þe wrecched world [is] ... a liere' (38, 39), 'loue is triacle' (148). Many of the images in her metaphors and similes are familiar, homely ones from vill-age, countryside, or city: a needle, spice, a well, a linden tree, chains, a lamp, a road, the mayor. Her versions of Bible stories, too, are filled with concrete objects like wool, linen, wine, water, feet, a penny, an elder tree, swords and a throne. She is usually practical and sometimes earthy and blunt in her figures and admonitions. Obvious examples are her reference to Malkyn's 'maydenhede þat no man desireþ' (184) and her pronounce-ment: '[Al is nouȝt] good to þe goost þat þe gut askeþ' (36).

She speaks with the didactic, authoritative tone of a teacher or preacher. Some of her lines read like proverbs or platitudes. Many are rules ex-pressed in the imperative mode, and others are instructional identifica-tions, like 'truþe is þerInne.... he is fader of feiþ' (12, 14), 'That is þe castel of care' (61). She is unhesitant about making value judgments: 'He is lettere of loue, lieþ hem alle' (69), 'who is trewe ... He is a god' (88, 90), 'That is no truþe of þe Trinite but tricherie of helle' (198). Holy Church has no doubt that she knows 'þe beste' – 'I wisse þee þe beste' (42).

Her tone sometimes descends to scolding and sometimes rises to a tender lyricism, for the poet gave her his own 'capacity to express the most elevated of religious feelings in the simplest terms ... the "incarnational" style, the *sermo humilis* that reaches sublimity of feeling without elaborate dependence on the "high style" of rhetorical tradition' (Muscatine, *Poetry* 94). She can also be ironic, vituperative and impatient, and her last line in Passus I has the slightly rushed tone of the busy person with another appointment: 'I may no lenger lenge; now loke þee oure lord' (209).

Yet her style has peculiar difficulties for Will and for the reader. Her key words shift in meaning from one referent to another without warning and often have more than one meaning at once; thus, for example, 'loue' denotes at various places affection, good will, God, and Christ. It is fre-quently difficult to tell what the antecedents of her pronouns are meant to be. The pronoun 'it' is frequently ambiguous in her speech, as 'that' and 'this' sometimes are. Her argument is also sometimes puzzling because transitions between sentences, if present at all, are often vague coordinat-ing conjunctions ('And,' 'For'). She moves from one thought to another by hidden means, as, for example, in lines 85–86, where there is no explicit connection between a statement about 'treuþe' and a statement about 'loue,' so that she seems to change the subject when in fact she is develop-ing relationships between one subject and another. She frequently ap-pears to define terms, yet her definitions are cryptic, like '*Deus caritas*' (86), 'This I trowe be truþe' (145), or 'loue is triacle of heuene' (148). They are difficult to decipher because of course they are not logical definitions at all, but figures, puns, perhaps emblems, their meaning implicit, not ex-plained (Schleusener 173; Griffiths 22–23). Her answers to Will appear as disconnected fragments which logic cannot easily put together. They are a puzzle to Will and to the reader.

Why begin a long narrative with such a puzzle? Why fling down such a challenge before a reader?

For one thing, the style of Holy Church reflects the best and most difficult aims of what she personifies: an attempt to express faith and the wisdom of love[7] though they can perhaps barely be communicated in words at all, and then only by formula, implication, analogy, antithesis, irony, or figure (Ong, 'Wit' 337). The gap of understanding between Holy Church and Will suggests the poet's painful awareness of the difficulty of such communication.

Surely the puzzling quality of Holy Church's style is also an instructive game, devised by the poet to teach the audience how to hear or read the whole poem. The difficulties of the beginning are a clue to the method of listening or reading which is necessary throughout; solving the initial puzzle teaches the rules of the game, the methods of understanding style and finding meaning through style. These methods are not arcane, but familiar: active, intuitive attention to words and to word play and to all the devices of poetry.

Holy Church begins with a light irony that has a touch of sadness, as she shows Will the folk of the field:

> ... 'sone, slepestow? sestow þis peple,
> How bisie þei ben aboute þe maȝe?
> The mooste partie of þis peple þat passeþ on þis erþe,
> Haue þei worship in þis world þei [kepe] no bettre;
> Of ooþer heuene þan here holde þei no tale.'   (5–9)

Various meanings of her word 'maȝe' (maze) fuse in a pun to suggest an ironic situation: 'confused medley of people' (Skeat II: 21), 'a source of confusion or deception, ... confused or useless activity, ... labyrinth,' (*MED* 'mase' a, c, d). Thus, 'people caught in the labyrinth of the search for worldly gain' (Bennett ed. 105) are also caught in the delusion of useless activity and are unaware that they are passing to a place 'ooþer ... þan here' (Martin, *Field* 76).

The same sort of irony satirizes the people's sense of values. The statement, 'Haue þei worship in þis world þei [kepe] no bettre' (8), not only means, 'If they have honor in this world they want nothing better'; but also, since 'kepe' is a pun meaning 'keep' as well as 'want,' it means, 'they keep nothing better, i.e., they fail to retain and protect their more valuable possessions.' One of the things the people neglect is suggested by the

---

[7] As Anderson points out, 'she perceives love as a continuing process ... a continuous act[;] ... love exists, takes form, in her words ... in the word' (19).

word 'worship,' which can also mean honor paid to God (*OED* 8) and is used as a verb a few lines later (16) with this religious meaning. In what Ricks calls an anti-pun (100, 174; cf. Schmidt, *Clerkly* 111), an obviously untrue but syntactically possible meaning hovers ironically over Holy Church's words: 'If they have worship – a chance to honor God – in this world, they want nothing more,' and the inapplicability of this meaning to the folk on the field suggests the gap which exists between a holy life and that of 'this peple.'

There is a similar ironic gap between literal and figurative meanings of 'heuene' in line 9. Holy Church refers only obliquely to its literal meaning, 'heaven,' since to the folk, heaven seems so distant; they have their 'heaven' here. This is effective verbal irony, since the life of the field would not seem so empty if it were not compared to a heaven, nor would 'this peple' seem quite so foolish and pathetic if they did not consider it to be one (cf. Simpson, 'Transformation' 172).

But when Will asks, 'mercy, madame, what may þis bymeene?' Holy Church abandons irony and begins to pun:

> 'The tour on þe toft', quod she, 'truþe is þerInne,
> And wolde þat ye wrouȝte as his word techeþ,
> For he is fader of feiþ, and formed yow alle   (12–14)

'Truþe'[8] in line 12 is not a personification but a proper name for God the creator, who 'is fader of feiþ and formed yow alle' (14) (Griffiths 18). 'Truþe,' Langland's favorite name for God,[9] is a common Biblical name

---

[8] The word 'truþe,' here first used by Holy Church, occurs with its cognates fifteen times in I and over 150 times in the poem (by my count). According to the *OED*, 'faithfulness' and 'covenant' are its oldest meanings. 'Veracity,' 'a statement in accordance with fact,' and 'reality' are first recorded in the 14th century, when the meanings of 'truþe' broadened to take on these cognitive meanings which had previously been carried by the words 'soþe' and 'soþfastnesse.' (See note 18 below.) Certainly the chief denotation of 'truþe' in *Piers Plowman* is 'faithfulness,' though many other meanings are used in word play. This 'faithfulness' is also feudal loyalty, as Stokes shows 81–86. Derived from OE 'tríewþ, tréowþ, trýwþ' (*OED* 'truth'), 'truþe' is akin to Gothic 'triggwa faith, covenant' (*OED* 'true'), and ultimately to Sanskrit '*dāruna* hard, *dāru* wood' (*Webster's Third* 'true'), and is therefore etymologically related to 'troth,' 'truce,' and 'tree.' In the 14th century, according to the *OED*, 'truþe' could mean: faithfulness or constancy (*OED* 1), a covenant (2), faith, trust, or confidence (3), veracity or sincerity (4), a statement which is in accordance with fact (8), true religious belief or doctrine (9), abstract reality (10), or the name of Christ (10). 'Truþe' is among the words mentioned by Kaske ('Use') and by Huppé; Vasta has analyzed its uses, especially in I–III, 'to determine the meanings of this term from its context in order to elucidate the passage itself and Langland's view of salvation' (*Spiritual* 59); see also his 'Truth,' 17–29. He does not, however, emphasize etymology or word play, though he points out that 'truth' is used analogically. Stokes notes (as Anderson does, 18) that 'the many meanings of that central medieval abstraction "treuthe" are all operative in this first Passus' (81), and points out the puns at lines 76, 85, 130–131 (82–87).

[9] Except for the standard names, 'God,' 'Lord,' 'Jesus Christ,' the name most often used for God in *Piers* is 'truþe'; it occurs over 50 times. The next most common names, 'king' and 'fader,' occur only 11 and 10 times respectively, by my count.

(Schmidt ed. 307), Hebrew '*emet*,' 'faithfulness, that which has been tried and found reliable.'[10] But the proximity of 'truþe' to the cognitive words 'word' and 'techeþ' (13) suggests that 'truþe' also means 'something/ someone knowable.' Thus God's name may be a pun meaning 'he who is faithful' and 'he who is knowable.' 'Word' is also a pun, and, like 'truþe,' a conventionally analogous term; it usually refers both to a text and to the '*Verbum Dei*,' the Son of God (John 1; Ong, 'Wit' 314–318). Here, both meanings are operative at once, the revealing person and the revealed teaching present in the same word:

> ... truþe is þerInne,
> And wolde þat ye wrouʒte as his word techeþ.
> For he is fader of feiþ ... (12–14)

The fact that the word is Truth's word, 'his word,' may also suggest that God is not a single person, but that, as John's gospel proclaims, 'the word was with God, and the word was God,' and this notion is echoed in the word 'fader' in 'fader of feiþ' (14). 'Feiþ,' too, is a pun, and its meanings fit exactly with the meanings of 'truþe': 'feiþ' can mean 'doctrine,' 'belief,' and 'faithfulness' (the latter including feudal loyalty, Stokes 81–82) (*MED* 'feith'). Thus 'truþe' as 'the faithful one' is father of faithfulness, and as the truth to be known, he is father of revealed truth and of belief.

In these three lines, we have Holy Church's most characteristic pattern of speech: sentences simple on the surface, made up of polysemous words whose various denotations and connotations relate to create complex but coherent sets of meanings.

Holy Church sometimes plays on sound as well as meaning, as she does in two examples of *adnominatio* in 37–38:

> [Al is nouʒt] good to þe goost þat þe gut askeþ,
> Ne liflode to þe likame [þat leef is to þe soule.
> Lef nauʒt þi licame] ... (36–38)

That which is dear or pleasurable ('leef') is contrasted here with that which is materially lifegiving or sustaining – 'liflode'; one might expect them to be alike, and their consonance (repetition of final consonant sounds) together with alliteration make them sound somewhat similar.[11] There is an even more obvious likeness in sound between 'leef' and the pun 'Lef'

---

[10] '*emet* designates ... the very sources of ... faithfulness, the essential solidity of a being. ... Truth, for a Hebrew, is that which has been put to the test and has revealed itself to be solid' (Guillet 34–5). In the Bible, God's faithfulness is shown especially in his keeping covenants, and since in other contexts 'truth' means 'covenant, troth,' this connotation also reinforces the sense of God's fidelity in line 12.

[11] In the 14th century, 'lef' was associated with the first syllable of 'liflode' in a term of endearment, 'lef liif' (Will of Palerne, 1879: *MED* 'lēf' adj., adv. 1 a (b); and 'Sir Orfeo' 78, 382.)

which means both 'Believe [not thy body]' (*MED* 'leven' v. (4) 1(a)), and 'give not permission [to thy body]' ((3)(b)). In both cases, the discrepancy between the meanings of words which sound alike underscores the surprisingly disjointed character of our sinful world where soul and body, trustworthiness and pleasure, can be at odds.

When Will asks the meaning of the dungeon, Holy Church contrasts it with the tower of truth:

> 'That is þe castel of care; whoso comþ þerInne
> May banne þat he born was to bodi or to soule.
> TherInne wonyeþ a [wye] þat wrong is yhote;
> Fader of falshede, [he] founded it hymselue. (61–64)

'Falshede' in line 64 is a pun whose meanings are antithetical to the meanings of the puns 'feiþ' and 'truþe': it means both 'falsehood,' i.e., lies and error (*MED* 3, 4) and 'falseness,' i.e., unfaithfulness and treachery (1, 2). As its second syllable suggests, we are here at the very 'head' of the nature of 'fals' as Holy Church understands it: negative, destructive, unreliable, deceptive.[12] Even what Wrong 'founded' (or 'built,' Norton-Smith 32) is ambiguous and ominous. What is the 'it' which he founded – 'falshede' or the castle whose inhabitants curse their birth? Surely the two meanings are meant to play upon one another, for in founding 'falshede' he also initiated 'care.'[13]

A mention of Wrong's treasure in line 70 – 'That trusten on his tresour bitrayed are sonnest' – connects an earlier exchange about money (44–5) to Holy Church's central explanation of truth in lines 85–89:

> 'Whan alle tresors arn tried treuþe is þe beste;
> I do it on *Deus caritas* to deme þe soþe.
> It is as dereworþe a drury as deere god hymseluen. (85–87)

As we have seen, the juxtaposition of 'tried treuþe,' words similar in sound, with a common etymology, tightens line 85 by stressing the principal meaning of 'treuþe' itself as that which has been tried and found reliable or faithful. 'Tried' is also part of the 'tresor' metaphor, since it is the verb used for refining gold and silver (*OED* 'tried' 1).[14] The words 'deme,' which means 'judge,' 'beste,' which implies judgment, and 'soþe,' which

---

[12] 'The False has no real form of its own, and works to negate and empty coherent structures of all kinds, cognitive, moral, and verbal' (Carruthers, *Search* 40).

[13] Cf. IX.157: 'And þus þoruȝ cursed Caym cam care vpon erþe,' and *Wisdom* 2: 24: 'It was the devil's envy that brought death into the world, as those who are his partners will discover.'

[14] Holy Church has biblical precedent for her metaphor of Truþe as treasure: see especially Matt. 13: 44–46 and Luke 12: 32–34. She uses the metaphor at I.85, 87, 135, 137, 207, 208. Cf. Robertson and Huppé, 41–42, n. 48 and Simpson, 'Transformation' 163–4.

denotes an absolute,[15] also relate to a process of 'trying' truth for its experienced genuineness.

Even with these implications, line 85 looks simple; but – what is 'treuþe'? It may still be a name for God, but it need not be. It could mean human faithfulness, justice, or obedience (Pearsall ed. 46, Kirk, *Dream* 29–30), or it could mean faith, (i.e., belief, *OED* 'truth' 9). Each of these translations is feasible in context. Which of them and how many of them are meant? In order to find out and to see all that Holy Church is saying in 85–87, it is necessary to look at each phrase separately and to 'try' various readings and combinations of readings until the puzzle fits together. The techniques of word play used here are the same as those used in 12–14, but they are used in a fuller, more extreme way.

First of all, there is no explicit transition between lines 85–86; they appear to be discrete statements, one about truth as treasure, the other about love. Yet there are several subtle but clarifying connections between them in syntax and word play. Line 86, a reference to I John 4. 16, 'God is love, and one who abides in love abides in God, and God in her or him,' is usually given Skeat's translation, 'I appeal to the text God is love ... as my authority.'[16] However, another translation which is complementary and punning is also possible. 'I do it' may refer to 'Whan alle tresores arn tried' in 85, meaning, 'I do try (test) treasures [including truth] on [the touchstone of John's principle], "*Deus caritas*."'[17] In the pun, both meanings work together. Holy Church does appeal to John's text as to her authority for all that she says; that is how she tries each treasure, (including each truth that she encounters), to see whether it meets the test of charity. She will illustrate the results later, in 179–199.

'To deme þe soþe' is another pun. It can be taken as a filler, meaning something like 'to tell the truth,' or it can be taken literally. If it is taken as a filler, the line means, 'I appeal to the text, "God is love," and test treasure on it, to tell the truth.' But taken literally, 'to deme þe soþe' means 'to judge the truth,' so that one may also read 86 as: 'I appeal to the text "*Deus caritas*" and test treasure on it in order to judge the truth, the ultimate reality.'[18] 'To

---

[15] See note 18 below.

[16] As Skeat pointed out, 'I do it on the king' at B III.187 (K–D 188) means 'I appeal to the king' (II: 23, n. B. I.82).

[17] As Carruthers observes, 'These early passus of the Visio seem to me to present a test of language ...' (*Search* 52); however, she seems to say that the test shows language to be 'corrupt.' I do not think that it does.

[18] 'That which really is' is the usual meaning of 'soþe' in *Piers*. See, for example, 'hire workes ben yhudde / In þe hondes of almy3ty god, and he woot þe soþe' X.437–438. The *OED* shows 'sooth' from the time of *Beowulf* and 'soothfastness' from c. 825 bearing the cognitive meanings of '*veritas*,' i.e., that which is, or that which conforms to reality, meanings which 'truth' does not bear until the 14th century. However, it indicates that as early as the 9th century, the adjective 'soothfast' overlaps in meaning with the

deme þe soþe' reinforces 'Whan alle tresors arn tried, treuþe is þe beste,' 'deme' pairing semantically with 'tried' and 'soþe' with 'treuþe.' Yet since 'treuþe' and 'soþe' are not absolutely the same in their meanings, they play upon one another here as they often do in Middle English texts; they both mean 'truth,' but only 'treuþe' means 'fidelity,' and 'soþe' (more than 'treuþe') means 'the ultimate reality.' If both 'treuþe' and 'soþe' in 85–86 are read as names for God, still another dimension of word play is present in the use of three 'true' but different names for the triune God ('treuþe,' 'soþe,' '*caritas*') who is being found true, ironically, by being tried and judged (cf. Moske 66).

Line 87 begins with a metaphor, 'It is ... a drury ...' The grammatical antecedent of 'It' might be 'treuthe,' '*Deus caritas*,' or '*caritas*,' and, as usual, this lack of clarity makes semantic overlapping among these words more obvious. 'Drury,' which means 'treasure' or 'token of love,' can also mean 'love' or 'beloved,' (*MED* 'druerie' 3,1,2), and in several ways the line develops these possible meanings and makes them all operative. The adjective 'dereworþe,' as a word for assessing material value, has affinity for the meaning of 'drury' as 'treasure.' The assessment, 'It is a treasure worth as much as ...' ends with the paradox, '... as God': 'It is as dereworþe a drury as deere god hymseluen,' an ending which would be metaphysically violent in tone were it not for the familiar, personal adjective 'deere.' 'Deere' gives emotional meaning to 'dereworþe,' suggesting that God is 'dereworþe' not only because of his value – his essence, power, beauty, worthiness – but also because he is 'deere' – beloved and loving.

---

adjective 'trewe' in its ethical meaning, 'faithful.' 'Soothfast' means '1. Of persons: speaking or adhering to the truth; veracious, truthful; true, faithful, loyal.' In 1936, Heraucourt pointed out that 'truth' acquired new meanings ('verity,' 'facts,' 'that which is') in the 14th century and tried to clarify the differences in meaning between 'sooth' and 'truth' in Chaucer, drawing heavily from a study by von Soden, 1927. He concluded that as the meaning of 'truth' expanded in the 14th c., it was used especially for that which is known *by experience or empirical evidence*, while 'soothfastnesse' continued to convey the abstract idea of truth, that which is known to be in accordance with reality through authority, proverbs or philosophy. Although the *OED* seems to contradict this thesis when it gives 'That which is true, real, actual (in a general or abstract sense); reality' as a 14th c. meaning for 'truth,' all its 14th c. citations which exemplify this are Biblical, and it is arguable that Biblical 'truth,' even if it appears general or abstract, always has the experiential sense of the Hebrew original, i.e., 'that which has been tried and found faithful.' (On the Hebrew sense of 'truth' see also Boman 165–166.) The scope of Heraucourt's research was limited to Chaucer, and the results are, I think, inconclusive though interesting. A study of the linguistic development of these two words would be most useful. The use of 'truth' in *Piers* is ambiguous enough to be of little help in such a study. Although it is likely that 'experience' is one of the connotations involved in some of the word play with 'truth,' I find no single instance in the poem where the primary denotation is unequivocally 'that which is known by experience.'

Thus the pun on 'deere' brings together two standards of value[19] and allows 'drury' to mean 'beloved' and 'love' as well as 'treasure.' Both 'drury' and 'deere god hymseluen,' (a plain English paraphrase of *'Deus caritas,'*) thus reinforce line 86: God, Treuþe, is love, and love is the test of all truth (virtue, faith). Unless truth is loving, it is not true.

Yet, except as a name for God, how can even loving truth be 'as dere-worþe ... as deere god'? The equation seems irresponsible, and leads to a prior question. Whose treasure is Holy Church talking about in 85–87?

All the readings of 85–87 explored so far present truth as treasure which belongs to or dwells within true human beings: God, their faith, their own faithfulness. But both of the Latin texts[20] to which Holy Church has referred in this passus suggest that she may be talking not only about a treasure possessed by true human persons, but also about a treasure possessed by God. Her first text, in fact, spoke of God's treasure:

'*Reddite Cesari*', quod god, 'þat *Cesari* bifalleþ,
Et que sunt dei deo or ellis ye don ille.' (52–53)

Her second text, *'Deus caritas,'* suggests the nature of this treasure, since those who love not only have God abiding within them, but also 'abide in God.' Thus 85–87 may express a divine perspective upon human life, about which Holy Church might be expected to speak. From this perspective, human truth (and by metonymy the true person)[21] is God's best treasure, 'dereworþe' enough for 'deere god hymseluen' to offer, as he does in XVIII: "lo! here my soule to amendes / For alle synfulle soules' (327–328). Since he gives his soul for this treasure, it is from his point of view 'as dereworþe a drury as deere god hymseluen.'

The seemingly disparate strands of meaning in these lines come together and are intertwined in the cryptic text, *'Deus caritas,'* and Holy Church's words are likely to be ambiguous in just the way John's are. As he equates God with love, so she has equated God with 'treuþe.' As he speaks of abiding in the virtue of charity, she speaks of being true in tongue and work. John explains the real connection between the two referents of the analogous term *'caritas'* when he says that one who is in charity is in God and God is in her or him. Presumably this statement of coinherence applies to truth as well; although Holy Church does not say so explicitly until later, she comes close to doing so when she says:

[19] Huppé points out a play on 'God'/'good' with the same effect: 'the verbal connection between treasure and love [is] made in the phrase, *dereworth as dere god,* with a play on *dear God* and *dear good,* that is, treasure' (*'Petrus'* 181). Stokes notes the pun on 'dereworþe' and 'deere' as a connective between 85–86 (84).

[20] On the importance and possible structural purpose of the Latin quotations, see Alford, 'Role' esp. 82–83.

[21] Sellert (109–115) lists many examples of metonymy in *Piers*, though not this one. Murtaugh (6) notes the pun on 'treuþe' in 85.

[For] who is trewe of his tonge, telleþ noon ooþer,
Dooþ þe werkes þerwiþ and wilneþ no man ille,
He is a god by þe gospel … (88–90)

Paradoxically, then, human truth is God's best treasure, not only because 'deere god' 'suffrede to be sold' (XVIII.214) to buy it, but also because human truth implies the abiding presence of divine truth.

And so the pieces of the puzzle come together. The simple word 'treuþe' in 85 means 'God' and 'faith' and 'human faithfulness' (Griffiths 20) and the pun is possible because, as the *'Deus caritas'* text says, the full presence of one implies the presence of the others. 'Deere god' who is *'caritas'* as well as 'treuþe,' is the best treasure, but so are loving fidelity and loving faith, which imply the presence of God; and the true, loving person who possesses God is possessed by him as his treasure. All these meanings in Holy Church's words, like the meanings in John's, depend upon and support one another, as if each meaning 'abides in' the others and is their treasure, so well does style express meaning.[22]

In the next forty lines, as Holy Church turns to social ethics, insisting on the centrality of truth in an ordered society, her word play is simpler but based upon the technique and meanings established in 85–87. She plays, for example, on 'cleymeþ' when she says that clerks who know truth should teach it:

The clerkes þat knowen [it] sholde kennen it aboute
For cristen and vncristen cleymeþ it echone.
Kynges and knyȝtes sholde kepen it by reson (92–94)

'Cleymeþ' may mean 'clamor (for), ask (for),' (*MED* 'claimen' 1 (a)), so one reading is that clerks should teach truth since everyone is asking for it. 'Cleymeþ' may also mean 'claims' or 'claims to know,' (2), so in another reading both Christian and non-Christian claim to have the truth, a claim that Holy Church neither affirms nor disputes.

The meanings of 'treuþe' in its next four uses (96, 99, 102, 109) are all social: two or three of them are also puns. Knights should 'holden wiþ hym and with here þat [asken þe] truþe' (102): in asking a knight for 'truþe,' people seem to have a right to expect faithfulness as well as justice, and in seeking these, they may also be seeking God, consciously or not. The same possibility is present in 99, where David's knights swear 'to seruen truþe euere.' And when Holy Church says that Christ taught the angels '[þoruȝ] þe Trinitee [þe] treuþe to knowe' (109), she puns on at least four meanings. He taught them to know what was actually the fact, to know fidelity by

---

[22] 'God is both Truth and Love and Truth is both the ruler in the "tour on the toft" and the treasure man seeks' (Kirk, *Dream* 30); see also Kean, 'Langland' 349. This fullness of meaning is present again in 'truþe' in I.135 and 137.

being obedient ('To be buxom at his biddying ... Lucifer ... lerned it in heuene' 110–111), and hence to know the law or covenant; he also taught them to know God and through their knowledge of God to know the truth of created things (Dunning, *Piers* 48).[23]

These uses of analogous terms, which bind together 'the means and the end, morality and theology' (Ames 197), come to a climax at 133:

> And alle þat werchen with wrong wende þei shulle
> After hir deþ day and dwelle with þat sherewe.
> [Ac] þo þat werche wel as holy writ telleþ,
> And enden, as I er seide, in truþe þat is þe beste,
> Mowe be siker þat hire soule shal wende to heuene
> Ther Treuþe is in Trinitee and troneþ hem alle.　　　　(128–133)

Just as 'wrong' in 128 means both the character named 'Wrong,' 'þat shere-we' (129) and also sin or wrong-doing, so 'truþe' in 131 means both God and moral goodness, honesty, or faithfulness (Stokes 87), as noted above. There is another ambiguity in the same line, since 'þat is þe beste' may be taken as either restrictive or non-restrictive. Its last phrase is repeated from Holy Church's earlier line 'Whan alle tresors arn tried treuþe is þe beste' (85) and is repeated twice more in the passus (135, 207). Similarity to these passages suggests that a non-restrictive reading of 131 is primary: 'And end, as I said before, in truth, which is the best [treasure].' However, it is possible also to read the line, 'And end, as I said before, in truth that is the best [they can find or do]'; this relates to the reading of line 93 discussed above, where Holy Church shows that she is aware that Christians and non-Christians claim the truth, and is harmonious with Imaginatif's words about Trajan's salvation, XII.280–284. (See Chapter Four). The syntactic and semantic ambiguity creates a counterpoint between objective and subjective achievement, suggesting the value of both: 'the beste.' Thus line 131 by its tantalizing ambiguities implies what the *'Deus caritas'* text says, that those who end 'in truþe,' in a state of goodness, even those who do the best they can to be faithful, are already dwelling in God, in Treuþe.

Holy Church concludes this section, weaving together words which have been enriched by mutual interaction:

[23] The pun, as Dunning shows (*Piers* 34), illustrates the theology of angelic knowledge as a vision of all truth in God; it also suggests a necessary relationship between their faithfulness and their knowledge. Perhaps, however, this vision in God (109) is meant to be the knowledge of the Trinity by faith which the angels had before the fall, rather than the eternal beatific face-to-face vision, since Langland seems to say that they sinned after having this knowledge.

> Forþi I seye, as I seyde er, by siȝte of þise textes:
> Whan alle tresors arn tried truþe is þe beste.
> Lereþ it þus lewed men, for lettred it knoweþ,
> That Treuþe is tresor þe trieste on erþe.' (134–137)

But Will misses most of the richness; hearing the words 'lereþ' and 'knoweþ,' 'lewed' and 'lettred' so close to 'truþe,' he seems to understand 'truþe' in its cognitive rather than moral senses, and asks how to know and learn it:

> 'Yet haue I no kynde knowyng', quod I, 'ye mote kenne me bettre
> By what craft in my cors it comseþ, and where.' (138–139)

Here he first uses the phrase 'kynde knowyng' which will become an important theme in the poem. Previously, he had asked Holy Church to 'kenne me kyndeli on crist to bileue' (81). Will's complaint here, 'ye mote kenne me bettre' expresses the sharp desire for a 'kynde knowyng' which will drive him in one way or another throughout the poem.[24] Holy Church responds, however, as if he has insulted her teaching, and as if the answer were self-evident (Martin, *Field* 112):

> 'Thow doted daffe!' quod she, 'dulle are þi wittes.
> To litel latyn þow lernedest, leode, in þi youþe:
> *Heu michi quia sterilem duxi vitam Iuuenilem.* (140–141)

Her display of anger at his ignorance of Latin is generally taken as a joke, but it seems to me a significant joke. Given the richness of meaning in her word play, Will's inability to understand what she has told him may in fact point to ignorance about language, not simply ignorance of theology.[25] In the 'game' of the poem, this is another clue to the importance of language.

She continues with what look like two definitions:

> It is a kynde knowyng þat kenneþ in þyn herte
> For to louen þi lord leuere þan þiselue.
> No dedly synne to do, deye þeiȝ þow sholdest,

---

[24] See my '*Kynde Knowyng* as a Major Theme' and '*Kynde Knowyng* as a ME Equivalent' and for a somewhat different view, Harwood's 'Langland's *Kynde Knowyng*.' Harwood sees 'faith [as] problematic for Will' (243) and argues that Will is asking for the ability to believe; it seems to me that Will already makes acts of faith in his references to God (58, 82), 'the heiȝe name' (73), and 'þe blissed barn þat bouȝte vs on þe Rode' (II.3). We agree that faith is intuitive (245–6) and that Will does want 'present, existing' experience of the person of God (248), which I would call divine wisdom. See his helpful comment on 'in my cors' (249).

[25] Bennett speaks of Will's lack of theology, (ed. 112). Kane makes a connection between study of Latin and understanding of English ('Music' 44). See also Carruthers, *Search* passim, and Schmidt, *Clerkly* 83. At VII.108, linguistic study is mentioned as an important means of understanding when the priest offers to 'construe eche clause' of the pardon; see Schmidt, *Clerkly* 85–87.

This I trowe be truþe; who kan teche þee bettre,
Loke þow suffre hym to seye and siþen lere it after.   (142–146)

The difficulty of lines 142–145 lies again in Holy Church's trick of using 'it' (142) and 'this' (145) with unclear antecedents. It is just possible that the sentence in 142–143 is in inverted order, with 'For to louen' as the antecedent for 'it.' Then the sentence would mean, 'It – loving – is a "kynde knowyng" that is truth, and that teaches [you] in your heart to love your Lord ...' Probably, however, the lines mean that a 'kynde knowyng' teaches you to love, that is, to be true. In either case or both, the point is that 'kynde knowyng' partakes of the nature of both knowledge and love (Murtaugh 8). The very ambiguities of the passage suggest the inextricable closeness, perhaps even identity, of realities for which we have different concepts and different names, as 'truþe' is equated with 'to louen' and perhaps also with 'kynde knowyng.' Moreover, the infinitive phrases in 143–144 seem to be parallel and synonymous, although they are in separate clauses; theologically, to love the Lord more than yourself *is* to avoid deadly sin whatever the cost. 'This I trowe be truþe' may mean 'I trust that what I have told you is truth (the fact)' or 'I believe that such heroic avoidance of sin is truth (fidelity)', or 'I believe that love, which is the avoidance of deadly sin, is truth (fidelity)' This ambiguity, too, is meaningful, suggesting that on a transcendental level, love, heroic faithfulness, truth, and wisdom may be equated.[26]

Although love is one of the chief subjects of Holy Church's discourse and *'Deus caritas'* is her touchstone, the English word 'loue' comes very gradually into her speech, most uses occurring in this sixth and last part of the passus (140–209). As a verb, 'louen' is used three times in the passus: 'To louen me' (78), 'to louen þi lord' (143), and 'louen leelly and lene þe pouere' (181). Thus it is clear that by 'louen' she means the act of 'charite' (188, 190, 193, 194); for other attachments and attractions she has other verbs, e.g., 'lay by hem' (30), 'yerne' (35), 'askeþ' (36), 'desireþ' (184). The noun 'loue' is used only twice in the early part of the passus, once in the proverb[27] where knights are not to leave those who need them, for love or money (103): this is Holy Church's only unequivocally earthly use of the word. All the others are analogous, like the uses of 'truþe' in 85–87 and 131, and with the same effects. Thus wrong, as 'lettere of loue,' hinders both good will and God (69). So, too, in 148–151, 'loue' means both the virtue and the divine person:

---

[26] 'Truth and love have by now become identical' (Bennett ed. 112).
[27] Blickl. Hom. 43 (O), 971 A.D.: Apperson, 'Love,' #36, 386.

For truþe telleþ þat loue is triacle of heuene:
May no synne be on hym seene þat vseþ þat spice,
And alle hise werkes he wrou3te with loue as hym liste;
And lered it Moyses for þe leueste þyng and moost lik to heuene

(148–151)

Line 151 has the same paradox that 87 has: 'truþe' is as 'dereworþe' as God, 'loue' the 'leueste þyng' and this can be so because 'truþe' and 'loue' are also names for God. The word 'leueste' means 'dearest,' a pun on 'most beloved' and 'most valuable,' continuing the 'tresor' imagery connected with 'truþe.' It may also suggest the meaning, 'the most [like] Love,' ('leueste'), a connotation emphasized by the phrase that follows, 'and moost like to heuene.' This redundancy is perhaps a way of insisting on the double meaning of 'loue' as virtue and person throughout the metaphorical passage which follows (152–162). It has been so well explicated by others that I omit it here.[28] But lines 163–165, which continue the meditation on love,[29] are among the most puzzling in the whole poem because of puns, repetition, and ambiguous antecedents. This is Holy Church's 'full' style, like that in 85–87, and it demands the same kind of unraveling:

And for to knowen it kyndely, it comseþ by myght,
And in þe herte þere is þe heed and þe hei3e welle.
For in kynde knowynge in herte þer [comseþ a my3t] (163–165)

In the first half-line, 'it' must refer to 'loue' (161), but the second half-line may be read in at least three ways. If the second 'it' also refers to 'loue,' the line says that in order for people to know love 'kyndely,' love must come to them by the power of God (cf. Bennett ed. 115). But there may be an ellipsis in the line. If there is, then it means that in order for Will to know love 'kyndely,' [Holy Church must explain that] love comes through the power of God (Pearsall ed. 51). The third possibility is that the second 'it' refers not to 'loue' but to the infinitive 'to knowen' (163); in that case, the line says that if anyone is to know love 'kyndely,' such *knowledge* must come into being through the power of God.[30] The odd thing about these ambiguities – an oddness entirely characteristic of all Holy Church's ambiguities – is that all the options make sense and are congruent with one another. The

---

[28] Both Ben Smith (21–40) and Kean ('Langland' 349–363) note the commonplace use of 'loue' to mean both God and charity, the action of the will. They point out scriptural, liturgical, and patrological sources and analogues to the images for love in lines 148–161; Heffernan adds others, and notes the ambiguity of 'it' in 153. See also Wittig, 'Dramatic' 56–67, Robertson and Huppé 46, Bennett ed. 113–114, Mills 201, and Mann 43 for some of the explication which has made this passage progressively clearer.
[29] Lines 163–165 are a gloss, I believe, on I John iv 7, 10–11, as I have tried to show in 'Kynde Knowyng as a ME Equivalent' (12).
[30] Murtaugh suggests another possibility, that 'it' refers to 'truth' as a 'kynde knowyng,' 9–10. Salter and Pearsall suggest 'love ... begins as a powerful impulse' (ed. 74).

line seems to me to resist being forced into a single reading and to exemplify the multiplication of meaning through coincidence of readings. Both love and the 'kynde knowyng' of love – the ability to know love (both person and virtue) thoroughly, experientially, affectively, as if by second nature – are gifts. They begin by the 'myght' of God acting on and in the heart, where his power dwells both personally and in grace (Vasta, *Spiritual* 44) as 'the heed ... the heiȝe welle.' Line 163, I believe, describes the reception of these gifts in the human heart, and 165, which looks so similar, describes their *results* (Murtaugh 9). Having received 'kynde knowynge,' one has from 'the fader' (166) a new power to have 'ruþe on þe pouere' (175), to be 'meke' (176), to 'louen leelly' (181).

Lines 173–174 take word play further. Jesus 'mercy gan graunte / To hem þat hengen hym heiȝ and his herte þirled'; the repetition of 'heiȝ' and 'herte' suggests further meaning for line 164: 'And in þe herte þere is þe heed and þe heiȝe welle.' The deep spring of love is 'in þe herte' (164) – in every loving heart, but particularly in the heart of Christ lifted 'heiȝ and ... þirled' (174). Line 174 also echoes 157, which says that love is

> ... portatif and persaunt as þe point of a nedle
> That myȝte noon Armure it lette ne none heiȝe walles.   (157–158)

The image of love 'persaunt as þe point of a nedle' suggests that when 'his herte' is 'þirled' in 174, it is pierced not only by the action of his enemies, but also by love. Paradoxically, then, love which can pierce 'heiȝe walles' (158) pierces the divine heart (and is thus itself pierced in the heart) opening the 'heed and the heiȝe welle' (164) from which he 'mercy gan graunte.'(173) Here, 'love is both a weapon and a person.'[31]

Puns in lines 172–173 further explain 163–165:

> Here myȝtow sen ensamples in hymself oone
> That he was myȝtful and meke ...   (172–173)

Because of syntactic ambiguity, line 172 may be translated either, 'You would be able to see examples [of God's might and meekness] in Christ alone (i.e., by looking at Christ)' and also 'Only in Christ (i.e., by dwelling in Christ) would you be able to see examples [of God's might and meekness].' In the primary reading, Christ is the object of knowledge, in the secondary, its source. For Holy Church, both are true, and so the pun works, saying that in Christ (in two senses) one has the power to see God. Such seeing can be regarded as a 'kynde knowyng' in the sense that it is natural ('kynde') for like to recognize like, for divine power which enables

---

[31] The phrase is Sister Jeremy Finnegan's. On the word play of this section, see also Anderson 19 and Norton-Smith 74.

human sight to recognize divine power in Christ. It is 'kynde' also because it (or the might associated with it) 'falleþ to þe fader þat formed vs alle,' (166), i.e., to 'Kynde ... fader and formour' (IX.26–27).[32]

In the next twenty lines, (179–199),[33] Holy Church returns to 'truþe' in order to distinguish true from false truth, the reality from the counterfeit, and she shows how she tests the treasure of truth for *'Deus caritas,'* distinguishing what belongs only to Caesar from what belongs to God. The passage is filled with negatives, privative words, and images of restriction (179–199), and Holy Church employs a series of verbal jokes, broad, obvious puns and plays on homonyms. Ridiculing that which is 'no truþe,' these complement earthy, sometimes humorous images, like that of the undesirable Malkyn and the chaste but absurdly encumbered curates (cf. Schmidt, *Clerkly* 139). Most notably, Holy Church plays upon misleading words, employing verbal irony to show that what appears to be truth (by various names) may be 'no truþe of þe Trinite but tricherie of helle' (198).

First, there is a common pun on the denotations of 'good,' with play on the ambiguous grammatical function of 'goodliche': '[Of] swich good as god sent goodliche parteþ' (182). As Schmidt points out, goods will be good for people only if givers 'goodliche parteþ' in the same way that God 'sent goodliche' (*Clerkly* 134–5). Then, in what may be a sort of word game with puns, Holy Church seems to demonstrate that 'Feiþ withouten feet is [feblere þan nouȝt]' (186) by punning on 'Feiþ,' 'feet,' and 'nouȝt,' each meaning a word as well as what the word represents. The line is a reference to James 2. 26, which she quotes in Latin at 187a: 'Faith without works is dead,' though in 186, Faith, instead of being quite dead, is personified like Good Deeds in *Everyman* as too weak to stand or walk. But if 'Feiþ,' 'feet,' and 'nouȝt' are read also as words which denote words, the line also says that if the word 'feet' is taken out of the word 'feiþ,' nothing is left but 'ih' or, more likely, 'h,' a breath. This is feebler than anything, 'feblere þan nouȝt.' As a sound, 'h' is even feebler than the word 'nouȝt,' which contains it in the aspirate 'ȝ' but surrounds it with stronger sounds.[34]

As she goes on to say that Faith is also 'deed' without works, she plays by *adnominatio* upon near-homonyms, 'deed' and 'dede':

---

[32] Various aspects of word play and play of thought on 'mercy' and 'mercyment' have already been pointed out by Pearsall (ed. 51) and Bennett (ed. 115), Stokes (91), Norton-Smith (73), Simpson ('Transformation' 164), and Schmidt (*Clerkly* 130–132).

[33] On a source for lines 188–189, see Schmidt, 'Langland, Chrysostom.'

[34] Ong ('Wit') and Alford ('Grammatical') give examples of Latin puns on 'word' as person and as verbal articulation, which may express a similar play of mind. Ryan, *Wm. Langland* 131, lists 'Feith ... feet' but does not discuss the pun. Since his list is so extensive, I do not always note the fact that he lists a pun.

> ... Feiþ withouten feet is [feblere þan nouȝt],
> And as deed as a dorenail but if þe dede folwe   (186–187)

Faith is 'deed' without any 'dede.' Although there is no ambiguity or verbal irony in the use of either word, their juxtaposition is ironic because almost the same sound represents antithetical conditions, that of death and that of lively works. The irony expresses neatly the point of this whole passage, that a word may mean opposite things, even life and death.

In the repeated phrase 'chastite wiþouten charite' (188, 194), 'wiþouten' means not only 'without' but also 'outside of,' and so the phrase refers not only to 'chastity lacking (not containing) charity' but also to 'chastity which is not dwelling within charity.' The pun makes this spatial image convertible, like the image of indwelling in the *'Deus caritas'* text.

In lines 192–193, Holy Church plays on sound and etymology with other puns:

> Manye Chapeleyns arn chaste ac charite is aweye;
> Are [none hardere] þan hij whan þei ben auaunced,
> Vnkynde to hire kyn and to alle cristene,
> Chewen hire charite and chiden after moore.   (190–193)

The phrase 'vnkynde to hire kyn' plays with what might be called an ironic violation of language. The history of the word 'vnkynde' alone makes a double meaning possible, and the context makes it inevitable. To be un-kind is not only unloving but also unnatural because against *Kynde*, nature. This double meaning is much more forcible here because 'vn-kynde' is used with 'kyn.' 'Kyn' repeats the center and etymological root of 'vnkynde,' drawing attention to the fact that in the word 'vnkynde' this root is cancelled out by the negative prefix. This suggests that being un-kind to kin is a negation of one's own kinship, a self-alienation. Perhaps it is even a self-negation, since the word 'vnkynde' has its own center and meaning negated. This word play makes the message of the line visible in a vivid way: the unkind chaplains negate and thus violate kinship, kind-ness, and nature (*kynde*) with their lack of love. 'Chewen hire charite' in 193 includes an ironic pun on 'charite.' When the chaplains 'chewen hire charite' they not only eat what people give them and what they ought to give others, but also destroy their own ability to love. To the chaplains, 'charite' might mean alms received or what they should give but have not given to the poor; there is the irony of an anti-pun in the gap between these meanings and the root-meaning, 'love,' which ridicules and condemns the chaplains. There is in the phrase also an ironic hint of Holy Com-munion, where the communicant 'chews' *'Deus caritas,'* a hint which em-phasizes the incongruity of curates communicating and thus taking *'cari-tas'* within them physically while 'charite is aweye.' The sacramental rite for them is as distorted as the words 'charite' and 'chewen' are, without their full meaning. To 'chewen' ought to imply gaining nourishment from, and to 'chewen ... charite' ought to mean drawing life from love. But to the chaplains, 'charite' means free (or misappropriated) food, and 'chewen' means to gobble up like a glutton 'and chiden after moore.'

In a rising intensity of anger and scorn, all these images and plays on words demonstrate negation or destruction linguistically and lead to the culminating clause, 'That is no truþe.' For although Holy Church does not actually pun on 'truþe' anywhere in these lines (179–199), 'truþe' is her central concern, and she plays on it in what might be called a riddle and a paradox in the lines which begin and end the passage, saying that if you are without love, 'þouȝ ye be trewe of youre tonge and treweliche wynne ... That is no truþe of þe Trinite but tricherie of helle' (179, 198). To be 'trewe' only in the limited sense of 'veracious,' to act 'treweliche' only in a financially scrupulous way, or to be merely 'clene of youre body' (195), is paradoxically 'no truþe of þe Trinite' (and therefore ultimately not truth at all) since, as she explained earlier, 'truþe' implies good will and therefore godlike love (89–90). It is supremely ironic that one can in some sense be true without possessing true truth. Her statement gives these forms of loveless activity no proper name. They are in a way nameless and unreal though utterly destructive. And therefore, while the phrase 'no truþe' (198) condemns unfaithful *actions* of avarice and lovelessness described throughout this passage, it also draws language itself into question, echoing and negating 'trewe ... treweliche' (179) and implying an ironic riddle: 'How can what is true be no truth?'

This irony – the use of 'trewe,' 'treweliche,' 'chastite,' and 'Feiþ' in lines 179–199 in relationship to 'no truþe of þe Trinite but tricherie of helle' – is a test of language, for Holy Church tests language as she tests truth, for the presence of '*Deus caritas*.' This passage shows that for her, the sign of corruption is not ambiguity, but emptiness or restriction – hence the images of emptiness and restriction in this passage (Stokes 88).[35] For Holy Church, words ought to express an expanding fullness of meaning, as if one meaning were inside another by analogy, etymology, sound, or logical implication. For her, words should swing free with their fullness of meaning present, active, and unhampered. The word 'trewe,' for example, should mean everything it implies – being like Truth, living in truth and hence in love, being like Christ, being a god and being in God. Having only a single denotation because of the context obviously does not falsify a word for her. Nor does punning ambiguity (e.g., 'dereworþe'). But if a context would allow all of a word's meanings, ('thouȝ ye be trewe of youre

---

[35] For other views on the nature and signs of linguistic corruption in *Piers*, see Carruthers (*Search* 52 and passim), and P. Martin (*Field* 61). Shoaf sees Dante and Chaucer as similarly concerned with the possibility of 'falsification ... no less falsification for going by the name of – one of several names – technological accuracy' (*Dante* 239).

tonge and treweliche wynne') and if, in spite of that, the word expresses only a surface meaning while all the normal implications of that meaning are 'yhasped' or 'lette,' then that word (like the action it denotes) is 'no truþe,' and is 'tricherie of helle.' Thus when she warns Will in the next passus against being 'enchaunted' through 'faire speche' (II.42), I believe she means that such enchantment takes place through words that carry only the barest obvious denotations while giving the lie to the resonating implications that should abide there.

At last (200–209), she turns from ironic exposure of false truth to her final praise of true love, true truth:

> For þise [ben wordes] writen in þe [euaungelie]:
> '*Date & dabitur vobis*, for I deele yow alle.'
> That is þe lok of loue [þat] leteþ out my grace
> To conforten þe carefulle acombred wiþ synne.
> Loue is leche of lif and next oure lord selue
> And also þe graiþe gate þat goþ into heuene. (200–205)

When she begins here to reconsider love itself, there are no more negatives. What would normally seem an image of restriction ('þe lok of loue' 202)[36] paradoxically becomes an image of liberation, since it does not keep anyone imprisoned but 'leteþ out my grace.' Moreover, exclusion is changed to access. The letting 'out' of grace is not exile like Lucifer's fall or the dismal state of chastity 'wiþouten' charity; instead it is a mission of power, mercy and liberation: 'To conforten þe carefulle, acombred wiþ synne' (203). This leads to Holy Church's conclusion about 'truþe,' with its double repetition of line 85 and its benediction:

> Forþi I seye as I seide er by [siȝte of þise] textes:
> Whan alle tresors ben tried treuþe is þe beste.
> Now haue I told þee what truþe is, þat no tresor is bettre,
> I may no lenger lenge; now loke þee oure lord.' (206–209)

The language of Holy Church is 'trewe.' She comes to Will and teaches him out of pure love, and everything she says is proved to be true as the poem advances. She seems to exemplify a particular mode of knowing which has its own techniques and difficulties of communication. She is the possessor of an accumulated wisdom which sees the whole in every part and which can perhaps be verbally expressed only in allusive, symbolic language, in which 'semantic coincidence penetrates to startling relations in the real

---

[36] The *MED* glosses 'lok' (lock) here as 'securing force of human love; also, the key of divine love' (n. (1) c). Though pronounced differently, 'lok' appears the same visually as 'lok' meaning 'sacrifice, gift' (*MED* 'lōk' n. (3)) and also as 'lok' meaning 'the act of looking ... presence' (*MED* 'lǫk' n. (4)). Play on all of these meanings is possible here.

order of things [and] ... the criss-cross of sound represents a genuine complexity of real relations' (Ong, 'Wit' 315, 319). Such language can be understood by an intuitive, active, receptive listener who will meditate on what she says, puzzle over it, and gradually hear implicit connections and allusions between apparently fragmentary parts. The problem is not so much with the language, but with interpretation. What Holy Church says is true, though cryptic. One has to work at interpretation, but the meanings are all available in her words.[37] Will misunderstands because he lacks the linguistic skill and the awareness of the probability of word play to enable him to interpret correctly. He is obviously not ready or patient enough to listen in the necessary way, nor does he know how. As he complains, he does not yet have a 'kynde knowyng.'[38]

His inability to understand Holy Church creates an irony which is partly comic, and the poet has made both characters plain enough to participate in comedy.[39] Their failure to communicate, which sends Will off on his search for a 'kynde knowyng,' also has about it the 'sort of pathos' which, as Charles Muscatine has shown, the style of the poem often creates (*Poetry* 107). The pathos allows for our identification with the narrator and our participation in his search; the comedy distances us from both characters, preparing us to see the whole journey, ours as well as Will's, with some wry and loving irony, and to read almost every character's words as the partly comic expression of a very particular, one-sided point of view. Of course, this very particularity is also an expression of what Elizabeth Kirk calls 'the limitations of the human consciousness, and the terrible obstinacy of its yearning' (*Dream* 40), which in turn creates more pathos. By the relationship between Holy Church and Will, the poet introduces us to this peculiar mix of tones, which helps us read the poem – play the game.

---

[37] I think Holy Church's words to Will are like the words of Yeats to a student with reading problems: there is nothing wrong with the language; the hearer needs to learn to understand it. For that reason, I differ with Mary Carruthers' view: 'The language used by Lady Holy Church ... has become a barrier to him. Such words as *tresore, kynde knowyng* ... do not inform – they merely confuse – because the words no longer have a stable referent' (*Search* 36), although I agree with her later judgement that in Holy Church's speech, 'meaning is conceived in an altogether ultimate fashion' ('Time' 186).

[38] On one level, such active, intuitive, receptive listening is what Langland means by 'kynde knowyng.' It is like the method of reading Scripture recommended in the medieval monastic life, *lectio divina*. See Chapter I. As M. T. Tavormina points out to me, 'Will's linguistic ignorance and dullness ... like his resistance to change of heart/ *affectus* and action, ... enables the poem to go forward since he keeps needing more instruction. ... So both cognition and affect are unready in him; he needs ... Wit/ Study/Clergy/Imaginatif and Patience/poverty of spirit/charity to "knowe kyndely" Dowel.'

[39] 'While her tone is not comic in the sense of "incongruous because unjustified," her high-handed and brisk disposition of explosive material and her snappy style of exegesis induce high delight in the reader' (Kirk, *Dream* 31).

Passus I prepares us in other ways as well. For one thing, we know that we are dealing with a puzzle. Then, the range of possibilities of meaning has been made available by this first teacher, even to the irony of a false truth, and the method of playing the game of heaven is at least familiar: attending to words, mining them for meanings, slipping from one meaning to another and sometimes holding several in tension at once. Holy Church's conclusion, 'Now haue I told þee what truþe is' (208) is both understatement and overstatement, sober truth and comic irony. She has spoken so that many meanings of 'truþe' resonate in the word in coherent relationship with one another. But in all its meanings, the very nature of 'Treuþe ... tresor þe trieste on erþe' (137) is experiential. It has to be *tried*. And Will, with 'To litel latyn' to understand words or word play very well, must try one approach after another as he seeks to experience Truth in a 'kynde knowyng' of love.

Chapter Three

Passus IX

Having been directed by Holy Church to the vision of Mede in his first dream, and then in his second dream having witnessed the conversion and abortive pilgrimage of the folk, Will awakens during the wrangling over Piers' pardon, and halfway through Passus VIII (68) he enters his third dream, in search of Do Well.[1] At the end of VIII, Will asks Thought to approach a long, lean personification named Wit[2] and challenge him '[To]

---

[1] I am using the usual numbering system, counting eight dreams, with the inner dreams falling within dreams 3 and 5. See Pearsall ed. 17; Schmidt ed. xxi and 'Inner' 33–37; Hussey 17–18. On the third dream, see Frank, *Piers* 49, Wittig, '*Piers*'; Harwood, 'Clergye'; and Longo.

[2] *OED* 'wit': '1. The seat of consciousness or thought, the mind: sometimes connoting one of its functions, as memory or attention. 2. faculty of thinking and reasoning in general: mental capacity, understanding, intellect, reason. 3. Any one of certain particular faculties of perception, classified as outer ... or bodily, and inner ... or ghostly.' Wittig speaks of 'the Wit of 9' as 'the soul under its cognitive aspects, the spokesman for knowledge and the knowable' ('*Piers*' 225, n. 59); other definitions include 'the *spiritus intelligentiae* or wisdom' (Bloomfield, *Apocalypse* 119); 'intelligence' (Lawlor *Piers* 91); 'the speculative intellect' (Robertson and Huppé 107 and Kirk, *Dream* 108); 'rational understanding' (Salter and Pearsall ed. 114); 'common sense' (Kaulbach '*Piers*'); 'some more active process of "understanding" [with] an ethical bias' (Norton-Smith 107); 'knowledge, the content of the mind that knows.... *scientia*' (Hort 89; Crane 9). Frank (*Piers* 50) defines 'wit' as 'the senses' (i.e., '*sensus*' as described by Anima at XV.29–39); so does Kean ('Justice' 85); Frank quotes Bartolomeus Anglicus 'Bk. III, ch. vi, where "wytte" is defined as "the vertue of the soule, wherby she knoweth thynges sensible and corporall, whan they ben present"' (*Piers* 50, n. 2). Jones identifies 'kynde wit' in *Piers* with '*sensus*' and adds, 'in Chaucer's Boethius, *wit* regularly translates the Latin *sensus*' (583). He and Wimsatt (111) and Quirk (182) identify 'wit' partially with 'kynde wit.' Wittig ('*Piers*' 225 n. 59) and Wimsatt (106–111), however, define it in Passus IX as containing the whole range of meanings. I find this explanation most in accord with Wit's words and style, though the mind's powers as '*sensus*' and 'kynde wit' seem to be emphasized in the passus. The *MED* defines *kynde wit* as 'natural reason' (capable of discriminating useful from harmful, good from evil, of guiding conduct and constructing a natural philosophy) 'kinde', adj. Harwood defines 'kynde wit' as '*vis cogitativa*, ... the capacity ... to perceive which objects *as a whole* are good for him ... through the power of comparison' ('Langland's Kynde Wit' 331). Some of my discussion of Wit's style formed part of my paper, 'Style as Identity: Passus IX of *Piers Plowman* B,' delivered at the MLA meeting New York, December 1984.

47

pute forþ som purpos to preuen hise wittes' (125). Passus IX is Wit's response.

The shape of Wit's discourse is hard to discern, for like Holy Church, he
switches from one subject to another without giving any explicit indication of the line of argument he is pursuing. Like her, he seems to go off on
tangents and he sometimes seems carried away by fancy. While he begins
and ends with definitions of Dowel (and offers three more in between, five
times as many as any other character offers),[3] the definitions neither cast
much light upon one another nor satisfy Will, and in between he talks
about creation and marriage, so the unity of the passus is problematic.
Unlike Passus I, this passus has no external shaping structure since it is an
almost uninterrupted free-flowing monologue rather than a catechism or
dialogue. Although Thought initially prompts Wit to speak by proposing
a question to him at Will's request, this question – 'Wher dowel [and]
dobet and dobest ben in londe' – is so broad that it covers all human action,
and it does little to form the passus. Will himself, who asked six questions
in Passus I and thus had a hand in shaping it, interrupts only once in this
passus, with a question that responds to Wit's words rather than directing
them (25). Wit's speech, therefore, appears to be a scattered, almost shape-
less collection of thoughts and feelings given whatever coherence it has by
its themes.

Wit plays on words less obviously and constantly than Holy Church,
though he is more jocose than she. It is significant that it is he who speaks
of speech as music (104–105), for he plays with coincidences of sound –
homonyms and examples of *adnominatio* and *antisthecon* that at first appear meaningless, seeming at once too far-fetched and too obvious to be a
vehicle for meaning. Yet attention to the passages where these aural coincidences occur will show that the playful, witty creation of likenesses in
names may suggest likeness between referents. What appears to be too
obvious or foolish a similarity to deserve notice proves to be full of meaning, and therefore a sly and ironic joke as well as a form of word play.

There are several peculiar things about the passus. One is its 'rambling'
quality (Frank, *Piers* 51), which presents a problem of unity. Another is
that it is one long chain of comparisons, which may tell us something

---

[3] The definitions occur at lines 11–15, 97–100, 110, 202–206, 207–208. Macklin Smith
notes that '*don* is clustered where the value of action is deliberated.' Although he finds
that in general in *Piers*, 'most "doing" is "evildoing",' I find rather that 'do' is almost
always a 'good' word in Wit's monologue. Although Wit once speaks of someone
doing evil ('þei doon yuel' 199), more characteristically he sees evil as undoing ('Allas
þat drynke shal fordo þat god deere bouȝte' 66) or as not doing ('He dooþ noȝt wel þat
dooþ þus' 95) or as destroying what has been well done ('Wandren [as wolues] and
wasten [if þei] mowe' 198). On Dowel, see also Frank (*Piers* 12), Middleton 'Two,'
O'Driscoll, and Norton-Smith: 'marriage and work are the clearest images to emerge
of Dowel' (108, 42–43).

about the nature of 'wit' (Lotto). But the strangest is its unstable tone, its sudden, sharp reversals of feeling.[4] While such reversals are to some extent typical of the poem as a whole, here they have an unusual regularity which shapes this passus. For the first sixty lines, where the theme is the creation of the body, Wit's tone is one of admiration. Suddenly, at 61, the theme shifts to sin and suffering and the tone to horror and dread. At line 110, Wit regains his optimism. With no preface, he begins with a new definition of Do Wel as 'trewe wedded libbynge folk' and for ten lines presents marriage as a blessed creation of God and human society, summing it up 'In erþe þe heuene is' (120). Then, as suddenly and extremely as before, his diction and tone become negative at 121 and remain so to the end (210). These extremes of tone are puzzling: to the degree that Wit, a personification, has characteristic qualities, his speech suggests a mercurial temperament and an ambivalence toward his subjects. Wit's initial optimism seems dangerously naive, especially in a guide (O'Driscoll 25); perhaps it leads inevitably to his disillusionment. Tone thus provides a dialectical structure for the passus which eventually leads Wit from a simplistic understanding of the abstract ethic revealed in the Pardon (VII) (Quilligan, *Language* 71) to a more complex and compassionate understanding of Do wel and Do yuel.

Passus VIII ends with the question which generates Passus IX. Will is speaking:

> ... I bad þoȝt þoo be mene bitwene,
> [To] pute forþ som purpos to preuen hise wittes,
> What was Dowel fro dobet and dobest from hem boþe.
> Thanne þoȝt in þat tyme seide þise wordes:
> 'Wher dowel [and] dobet and dobest ben in londe
> Here is wil wolde wite if wit koude [hym teche];   (VIII.124–129)

Will's request, of course, arises out of his vision of Piers' pardon with its terrifying simplicities: *'qui bona egerunt ibunt in vitam eternam;/ qui vero mala in ignem eternum'* (VII.113–114), and Wit responds with an equally simple allegory of Kynde's castle, which also presents pure good and evil, followed by a thunderous denunciation of sin. Though the effect of the whole passus and specifically of its use of language will be to complicate the abstractions of the Pardon-pattern, it begins with that pattern: good with its rewards, followed by evil and its punishments. Perhaps it would

---

[4] Edward Lotto pointed out Wit's use of comparisons in a paper at the International Medieval Conference, Kalamazoo, 1982. Crane notes that the 'wit' described by classical rhetoricians, including Aristotle (Rhet. III, x.5–xi.6) 'depends largely upon comparison' (14). The sudden reversals of feeling in IX may reflect Biblical antitheses like those in Ps. 1 or Wis. 3 and 4.

be more accurate to say that it begins with Wit's effort to domesticate that pattern.

Wit's first line is ironic and playful:

'SIreDoweldwelleþ', quodWit,'no3t a day hennes   (IX.1)

Priscilla Martin has noted the irony of Wit's suggestion 'that the wander-ings of the Dreamer constitute a too-physical search for Dowel which should be found within himself' (*Field* 117, 89), 'no3t a day hennes.'[5] An echoing play on sound supports this irony (Chamberlin).[6] 'Dowel' sounds like 'dwell,' and 'dwelleþ' sounds like a contraction of 'do-welleth,' which could be a comic verbalization meaning 'acts out do-well' or 'does well.'[7] In an aural joke, 'dwelleþ' is thus an echo and a trick, meaning both 'dwells' and 'does well'; it suggests that to do well is to dwell, i.e., that the power to do well dwells within us (Tavormina), and also perhaps that to do well is to dwell in God. Its teasing form plays with Thought's question and perhaps gently mocks Will's propensity to miss the obvious.

At the end of the passus, Wit repeats almost the same 'trick,' again emphasizing the connection between doing and dwelling with another play on sound. He says that:

> ... fals folk, fondlynges, faitours and lieres,
> ...
> Wandren [as wolues] and wasten [if þei] mowe;
> Ayeins dowel þei doon yuel and þe deuel [plese],
> And after hir deeþ day shul dwelle wiþ the same...   (196, 198–200)

Line 200 is ironic even aurally and visually; 'dwelle,' though still poten-tially a contraction of 'dowel,' here also echoes both 'doon yuel' and 'deuel' (199). Paradoxically, doing is against doing: 'Ayeins dowel þei doon yuel' (199). 'Doon yuel,' being parallel to both 'wandren,' (the opposite of 'dwelle' 200), and 'wasten,' (the opposite of 'doon' 199), is thus opposed both to 'do [well]' and to 'dwell,' and this recalls and plays upon the 'Dowel dwelleþ' play in line 1. Thus both at the beginning and end of his passus, Wit plays with sound, and through it, with meaning.

The allegory of Kynde's castle (1–24), with which Passus IX opens, starts simply, but quickly generates multiple personifications; all except the

---

[5] Several scholars comment adversely on the use of 'Do wel' as a noun: see Mills 194–195, P. Martin, *Field* 46–47; Quilligan, 'Langland's' 102; Carruthers, *Search* 81–83; cf. also Middleton, 'Two' 170–171 and passim. Dillon gives an interesting analysis of word play on 'wil' and '[do]wel' in VIII.128–131 and IX.202–210 (40–42).

[6] Ryan, (*Wm. Langland*) lists 'Dowel dwelleþ' as a pun (134), though he does not discuss it.

[7] Cf. Gerard Manley Hopkins, 'the just man justices' 'As Kingfishers' #57 (95).

suspicious 'proud prikere of Fraunce, *Princeps huius mundi*,' are flawless, as befits the form (cf. Kirk, *Dream* 108). It might be a charming story for children:

> 'SIre Dowel dwelleþ', quod Wit, 'noȝt a day hennes
> In a Castel þat kynde made of foure kynnes þynges.
> Of erþe and Eyr [it is] maad, medled togideres,
> Wiþ wynd and wiþ water wittily enioyned.
> Kynde haþ closed þerInne, craftily wiþalle,
> A lemman þat he loueþ lik to hymselue.
> *Anima* she hatte   (1–7)

In this context, the name 'kynde' at first represents a personification,[8] his name a translation of '*Natura*,' 'source of all living things ... a regulative force operating in the material world.' (*MED*, 'kinde' 8a). As such, the name has a great number of conventional connotations well known in classical and medieval tradition. One of these is that *Natura* is always concerned with the creation of the human body and the protection of the human soul, and another is her responsibility for generation and all aspects of sexuality. Thus the use of the personification Kynde is sufficient explanation for the otherwise odd fact that in ostensibly explaining Do Wel, Wit tells about the creation of the body; it also explains why he goes on to talk about marriage, though it does not explain an apparent ambivalence about both subjects. The rather intricate artificiality of Wit's style may derive from the style of typical *Natura* poems, as well.[9]

There are, however, several new elements in Wit's use of the *Natura* tradition. One is the suggestion of death in line 24: 'Til kynde come or sende.' *Natura* is traditionally associated exclusively with generation or creation, not death, but Wit introduces death, though by euphemism, making Nature slightly more ominous and more natural.[10] Another and more important change in the tradition is made when Will asks what Kynde is. Wit first affirms the convention by saying that Kynde is 'creatour of alle kynnes beestes,' and then alters it significantly:

> 'What kynnes þyng is kynde?' quod I; 'kanstow me telle?'
> 'Kynde', quod [he], 'is creatour of alle kynnes [beestes],
> Fader and formour, [þe first of alle þynges].

---

[8] Bennett points out that 'Chaucer was probably the first English poet to use "Nature" in a clearly personified sense, following the example of Alain and the Roman de la Rose,' and that Chaucer called Nature 'Kind' ('Appendix' 205, 207).

[9] On the Natura convention see Economou, *Goddess*; Bennett, 'Appendix'; C. S. Lewis, *Discarded* 34–39. Texts include Bernardus Silvestris, *Cosmographia*; Alanus de Insulis, *De Planctu Naturae [Complaint of Nature]*; Chaucer, *Parlement of Foules*.

[10] Schmidt notes the oddity of associating death with Kynde ('Inner' 39, n. 27). See also P. Tristram 156, 177–179, who notes that 'The alliance of Death with Kind is for the moment only' (179). See Kirk, *Dream* 111.

And þat is þe grete god þat gynnyng hadde neuere,
Lord of lif and of liȝt, of lisse and of peyne.   (25–29)

In identifying Kynde (*Natura*) with the Biblical God, the poet does something which, so far as I know, was entirely new in literature. In effect, he makes 'Kynde' a pun for 'God' and the personification '*Natura*,' thus synthesizing the ancient Biblical and classical traditions in a unique way.[11] The pun represents a shift in language as well as thought, attributing or at least making available for explicit attribution to 'þe grete god' all that was conventionally attributed to *Natura*.[12] The pun on Kynde is central to the passus, its subject matter, and its strange conflict of tones.[13]

In support of the pun, Wit inserts into his allegory of the 'Castel þat kynde made' (2) a paraphrase of Biblical accounts of creation, especially ps. 148: 5 (Vul.):

For þoruȝ þe word þat he [warp] woxen forþ beestes.
[And al at his wil was wrouȝt wiþ a speche],
Dixit & facta sunt,
[Saue man þat he made ymage] to hymself,
And Eue of his ryb bon wiþouten any mene.
For he was synguler hymself and seide *faciamus*
As who seiþ, 'moore moot herto þan my word oone;
My myȝt moot helpe forþ wiþ my speche'.
Right as a lord sholde make lettres; [if] hym lakked parchemyn,
Thouȝ he [wiste to] write neuer so wel, [and] he hadde [a] penne,
The lettre, for al þe lordshipe, I leue, were neuere ymaked.
And so it semeþ by hym [þere he seide in þe bible
Faciamus hominem ad imaginem nostram];
He moste werche wiþ his word and his wit shewe.   (32–44)

---

[11] In 2, there was play on the sound and etymology of the words 'kynde' and 'kynnes,' kind and kind, and this is repeated in 25–26. Martin points out that in 25–26, 'The play on the two meanings of "kynde" ("sort" and "God") highlights Will's misunderstanding: he is trying to limit the creator ("kynde") source of nature ("kynde") to being one sort ("kynne") of creature ... Wit instructs him both by explaining what "kynde" is and by using the word in its different senses correctly' (*Field* 89).

[12] See Tierney 317, and my '*Kynde Knowyng* as a Major Theme' 5–17. Since God is ordinarily, though not always, portrayed as masculine in *Piers*, the identification of God with Kynde is, as Bennett says, 'reason enough for his treating Kynde as masculine' ('Appendix' 209). Or perhaps Langland has fused the feminine *Natura* with the masculine Genius, since the word 'kynde' is etymologically related to the name 'Genius.' See C. S. Lewis, 'Kind,' *Studies*, 24–74, and my 'A Genius-Kynde Illustration.' Murtaugh comments, 'To call God "Kynde" as Wit had done was to speak of Him as intelligible through the order of nature which He had created' (88). Wittig shows that Langland is also using the tradition of '"monastic" moral psychology' in this section ('*Piers*' 212, 216–217). Cf. also Tavormina, 'Bothe' 330.

[13] Even some of the vocabulary seems to be generated by the centrality of Kynde; Wit has probably the largest kinship vocabulary in the poem, over 20 terms: 'douȝter ... sones ... Fader ... wodewes ... godfader ... godmoder ... godchildren ... trewe wedded libbynge folk ... hir kynde ... wyf ... issue ... belsires ... forefadres ... *pater* ... *filii* ... barn ... sire ... couple ... paire ... children ... wideweres ... wrecches out of wedlok.'

In line 32, Wit begins to play with words for making and words for speaking or writing, in a way which again joins the Biblical and *Natura* tradition as the 'Kynde' pun did. First, Wit uses the usual double meaning of 'word' (32, 37, 46), extended by Wit to its synonym, 'speche' (33, 38), for the spoken word (*'Dixit et facta sunt'* 33a) and the Word of God, the Son, who in John 1: 1–3 is described as Creator: 'In the beginning was the Word and the Word was with God and the Word was God ... all things were made by him.' Thus the beasts come forth 'þoruȝ the word þat he [warp] ...' (32–3); 'man' was made 'Wiþ his word and werkmanshipe' (46). Everything 'was wrouȝt wiþ a speche' (33). In the pun on 'word' (and 'speche') the Creator– 'the Word'–creates by speaking. For him, to speak is usually to make ('... al at his wil was wrouȝt with a speche': 33; cf. 32, 33a), and to 'make' is always to speak or write (e.g., 'to make lettres' 39; cf. 37, 38, 43–45, 52). John Alford shows that 'This fusion ... is encouraged, above all, by the Bible. For example, the Hebrew word *dabhar*, which occurs frequently in the Old Testament, can mean both "word" and "deed," and this is translated in the Latin Vulgate as *verbum*. ... On one level *verbum* represents the fusion of deed and word, and on another the fusion of Christ and his gospel' ('Grammatical' 744; cf. 754). In this verbal context, the conventional Biblical term for the human creature, 'ymage' of God (34), *'imaginem'* (43), also suggests a written image, and the poet insists on its root-meaning by the comparison of 'man' to a 'lettre' (39, 41). Moreover, Wit uses the verb 'to make' with the meanings 'to compose' a poem or write (Skeat II: 99). Thus, Wit says that without parchment 'The lettre ... were neuere ymaked' (41), and later, 'I myȝte make a long tale' (74). Lines 39–41 are a rather fantastic conceit: as Skeat said, a 'curious illustration of the Trinity' (II: 140),[14] comparing God the creator[15] to a writer who needs pen (the 'word'?) and parchment (the 'myȝt'?) to write his 'lettre' (humankind)). Though it complicates the explanation of creation, the conceit supports Wit's play on Biblical words, with its insistence that making is like writing and writing like making. It also supports the pun on 'Kynde' as both *'Natura'* and 'þe grete god,' by applying to the latter a simile (creating as writing with a pen) conventionally used for the former.[16] This identification of language with

---

[14] Murtaugh disagrees with Skeat because 'There is no clear differentiation of function as there usually is in discussions of the Trinity' (17, n. 23), but see Szittya, 'Trinity' 215. See Tavormina 'Kindly Similitude' on the C-Text comparison of marriage to the Trinity (XVIII.211–239); see also Ames 82.

[15] On 'God as Maker,' see Curtius 544–545 and Stock '"Making It"' 177–80. Didron notes that 'Buffalmacco in the first half of the 14th century, when painting the walls of the campo, still depicted Jesus, and not the father, creating the world from a vacuum' (II: 239–40). In manuscript illuminations, too, the Creator is sometimes made to look like pictures of Christ, e.g., Bod. L. MS Douce 211, f. 3r; Bod. L. MS Ashmole 1511, ff. 4, 4v, 5, 5v; and BM MS Royal 19 Dii, f. 5.

[16] Mander shows that the pen analogy is from Alanus de Insulis. 'There may be a sexual implication in Alanus' image of the reed pen [as used by Langland], but this in

creation is, as Mander points out (502), an oblique defence of poetry and is surely a major reason for the importance placed on 'speche' later in the passus (99–106).

The centrality of 'making' is demonstrated playfully in line 45, which also shows Wit's propensity for playing with sounds: 'And in þis manere was man maad þoruȝ myȝt of god almyȝty.' The word 'maad' at the center of the line is bracketed by repeated sounds: 'man,' 'manere,' on one side; 'myȝt,' 'almyȝty,' on the other. This is as simple as the play on 'Dowel dwelleþ'; perhaps it is meant by the poet to hint at the superficiality of so optimistic a presentation as Wit's has been thus far.

For this first section is wholly optimistic, charming, and strong in its sense of God's power as 'fader and formour' (Fowler, *Bible* 257). The castle seems bright and courtly (1–10). As Wit describes it, his tone is admiring. He emphasizes the excellence of Kynde's craftsmanship ('maad, medled togideres . . . wittily enioyned . . . craftily wiþalle'). There is a hint of trouble in the fact that it is 'a border castle (as is "man with a soul") [and] . . . could go either way' (Tavormina) and in the fact that '*Princeps huius mundi*' would like to win *Anima*; one is aware that this is another name for him who 'wrong is yhote' (I.63). But Kynde and his host of attendants seem to Wit to give *Anima* sufficient protection. If Kynde only lived there himself, we would think we were in the tower of truth. Style, too, expresses optimism, being curiously involuted and fanciful, abstracted from the real world and from the simplicities of the Biblical texts which it elaborates. It seems like a children's story or an escape. That is the nature of an ' "algebraic" analogy,' as Kirk suggests (*Dream* 107); there is very little *experience* in it (108), only the authority of classical and Biblical literature, which are intelligently, originally joined. Wit seems to be elaborating them in a deliberately witty way, working with words, weaving them through the passage. This elaboration perhaps imitates the process of creation as Wit understands it, for the passage is a creation, a making of something new by working with words in order to show wit, as Wit says God did in the first creation: 'He moste werche wiþ his word and his wit shewe' (44).

Perhaps Wit's extreme optimism is ironic. Both of the traditions which he has invoked – the Biblical tradition and the *Natura* tradition – explain and deplore human sin and suffering, i.e., the disobedience of Adam in Genesis and the misuse of sexuality in the *Natura* tradition, and Wit will deplore each of these in turn, later. But in lines 1–60, as Philippa Tristram says, 'Wit skates over the dilemmas' (53) in his optimism.

He certainly 'skates over' common connotations of the name for the castle, '*caro*':

> That is þe Castel þat kynde made; *caro* it hatte,
> As muche to mene as man wiþ a Soule. (50–51)

Wit translates '*caro*' as 'man wiþ a Soule,' but it can also mean the body or flesh, family or genus, or everyman or woman (DuCange 3, 6, 2). In some medieval works, it has negative connotations; Isidore, for example, defining it as '*ossa et sanguis*,' continues gloomily, '*Dictum autem ... caro a carendo vel a cadendo*' (*PL* 83: 22–23) (said, however [of] flesh as being needy or falling). The liturgy might have provided at least two powerful connotations. One, from psalm 64, sung at every Requiem Mass, suggests death – '*ad te omnis caro veniet*': 'to you all flesh shall come.'[17] The other promises hope; it is a quotation from John 1 said every day at Mass and used in *Piers* at V.500a: '*Verbum caro factum est*,' 'the Word was made flesh.' '*Caro*' contains 'care' within it aurally – the word which Wit will use later (157) to sum up all suffering.[18] Indeed, it is just possible that the poet means us to remember that there are only two structures in the poem called 'castel' and only two lines that begin, 'That is þe Castel ...' The one describes '*caro*'; the other, Wrong's 'castel of care' (I.61). Whether or not we remember, we can hear the ominous, sad sound of 'care' within '*caro*.' But Wit seems to use the word without connotation; for him, '*caro*' is only 'man wiþ a Soule.'

Wit seems unable at this point to integrate his knowledge of good with his knowledge of evil. As Quilligan suggests, perhaps his attitude is intended by the poet 'as a wrong-headed commentary on the text of the pardon' (*Language* 71). Having described a perfect world, Wit suddenly begins to describe a woefully miserable one at line 61, where the phrase, 'Much wo,' signals a sharp change of tone from admiration to condemnation:

> Muche wo worþ þat man þat mysruleþ his Inwit,
> And þat ben glotons, glubberes; hir god is hir wombe;
> ...
> Allas þat drynke shal fordo þat god deere bou3te,
> And dooþ god forsaken hem þat he shoop to his liknesse;
> *Amen dico vobis, nescio vos; Et alibi, Et dimisi eos secundum desideria*
> *eorum.*
>
> (61–62, 66–67)

---

no way detracts from its relation to the art of writing,' 503. On making and writing, see Aers, *Piers* 65–66.

[17] Sarum Missal 860. Alanus de Insulis sees the use of '*caro*' in ps. 64 as a reference to 'a just person': 'Dicitur etiam homo justus, unde in Psalmo: *Ad te omnis caro veniet*' ('Liber' 733). He gives nineteen meanings for '*caro*' used in Scripture; over half have connotations of fragility, danger, or evil, but the word is clearly ambivalent. Meanings include: '*reprobus*,' '*poena carnis*,' '*infirmus*,' '*homo justus*,' '*frater*,' '*mulier*' (732–733). Hugh of St Victor, in his work on marriage, quotes Genesis, where '*caro*' is used by Adam for Eve: '*caro de carne mea*' (Gen. 2) (481).

[18] Uses of 'care' include I.61, IX.157, XVIII.268, XX.201; uses of 'carefulle' include IX.161, X.59, XI.192, XIII.265, XIV.179. It seems likely to me that, as Hala says, 'The "castle of care" is also the "castle of *caro*," or the flesh' ('For She' n. 12).

Though the passage begins as invective,[19] its tone quickly changes to dread, sadness and pathos. These are especially strong in 66, 'Allas! þat drynke shal fordo þat god deere bouȝte,' because of Wit's introductory interjection and the punning adjective/adverb 'deere.' 'Deere' is an adverb modifying 'bouȝte,' so that the clause means 'whom God redeemed at such a cost' (Schmidt ed. 93); it may also be an adjective modifying 'god,' and the clause may also mean 'whom dear God bought.'[20] The two meanings work together, since God's dearness is the more apparent because of the terrible cost of the redemption which reveals, as Aquinas said, 'how much God loves' humans (*S.T.* IIIa 46.3). As an adjective, 'deere' adds tenderness to the line; as an adverb, it increases the sense of ironic and pitiful loss.

Wit here begins to make use of quietly violent verbal devices which demonstrate the identification he made earlier between creation and language. To describe the effect of sin as the undoing of creation, he 'undoes' or nullifies particular words by a variety of negating prefixes and suffixes, negative particles, and sometimes by denotation itself or grammatical mood. 'Fordo,' for example (66), is a verbal nullification – an undoing – of creation. As Schmidt says, it means that sin 'uncreates the creator's work' (ed. 328). 'Dooþ' is used in 67 as a modal auxiliary which makes God an object, almost a victim: 'And dooþ god forsaken hem,' so that causality, so fully in God's hands in creation, seems now to be held by sin. Both words, 'fordo' (66) and 'dooþ' (67) ironically negate (one by prefix and one by denotation) what 'do' means in the first lines of the passus (in 'Dowel' (1, 11) 'Dobet' (12), 'Dobest' (14) and the divine command, (15).) Wit also uses privative suffixes in 'faderlese' (70), 'helplese' (72); negative prefixes in 'mysruleþ' (61), '*nescio*' (67a), 'myseise' (78); and negative particles in 'noȝt wherwith to wynnen hem hir foode' (71) and 'He dooþ noȝt wel that dooþ þus ... Ne loueþ noȝt' (94–95). Nullifying of words as a demonstration of 'unmaking' and loss is a peculiar form of word play, like Holy Church's 'no truþe.'

Also throughout this section, when Wit speaks of people, he stresses their neediness. This emphasis is unexpected because of his previous optimism. In the first sixty lines of the passus, his words for human beings, made 'Thorgh myȝt of þe mageste' (53), were almost entirely abstract or

---

[19] It is possible that 'mysruleþ his Inwit' is based upon the common theological understanding that Adam's sin was an intellectual or spiritual sin of 'misrule,' disobedience or pride. Since Inwit is an aspect of Wit, the affront by sin to Inwit might be one reason for Wit's angry language here. See Mann 33.

[20] It is rather unusual for an adjective to follow its noun, but line 177 (IX) has an example: 'For coueitise of catel ne of kynrede riche' and K-D give another example in line 192, 'That dede derne,' so it is not impossible to read 'god deere' as noun and adjective, though the first reading is surely noun and adverb.

typical ('man' 31, 'Eue' 35) or, if concrete, then in Latin ('*caro*' 50). Now, as his English words for people suddenly become concrete, they also become privative. It is intensely ironic that 'Fauntes and fooles' (68), the one suggesting weakness and the other, incapacity, are the first concrete nouns to specify or illustrate 'man' and '*caro*.' This is perhaps an example of the principle that Priscilla Martin elucidates, the correction of the allegorical by the literal (*Field* passim). Wit's privative language not only names and explicitly shows the 'uncreation' of those valuable things needed for life (e.g., 'eise,' negated in 'myseise,' and 'help,' in 'helplese'), but also creates a tone of pathos sustained by the phrases, 'the litel barn' (80) and 'cryen at the yate' (82).

Wit's discussion of 'vnkyndenesse' is a further example of verbal nullification:

> Sholde no cristene creature cryen at þe yate
> Ne faille payn ne potage and prelates dide as þei sholden.
> A Iew wolde noȝt se a Iew go Ianglyng for defaute
> For alle þe mebles on þis moolde and he amende it myȝte.
> Allas þat a cristene creature shal be vnkynde til anoþer!
> Syn Iewes, þat we Iugge Iudas felawes,
> Eyþer of hem helpeþ ooþer of þat þat hym nedeþ,
> Whi [ne wol] we cristene of cristes good be as kynde?
> [So] Iewes [shul] ben oure loresmen, shame to vs alle!
> The commune for hir vnkyndenesse, I drede me, shul abye;
> Bisshopes shul be blamed for beggeres sake.
> He is [Iugged wiþ] Iudas þat ȝyueþ a Iaper siluer
> And biddeþ þe beggere go for his broke cloþes.   (82–94)

Wit uses the prefix 'vn' here as he used 'for' in 'fordo,' to suggest total negation of what is creative and loving. 'Vnkynde' in line 86 means, of course, 'unkind,' but it also means 'unnatural, unloving, unattached to kin' (*MED* 'kynde' 10c). The Christians at 86 are 'vnkynde til anoþer' and therefore unnatural, whereas the Jews are 'kynde' (89) – kind, natural in behaving rightly to kin, since 'Eyþer of hem helpeþ ooþer.' Wit has earlier used the noun 'kynde' for God (26, 50), and so the adjective 'kynde' in 89 has at least potentially the additional connotation 'like Kynde.' Because of ambiguous syntax, the phrase 'be as kynde' not only means 'be as kind/ as natural [as the Jews are]' in 89, but also suggests 'be as Kynde [is].'[21] There is another possible ambiguity in the line. The phrase 'of cristes good' is usually taken as an adverbial phrase modifying the adjective 'kynde' and meaning 'with Christ's goods' (Skeat II: 141, Schmidt ed. 94), and that is certainly its primary meaning, a gloss on the Latin text below: '*res pau-*

---

[21] In passages of brilliant word play, the Samaritan will make a similar point, XVII.251–280, 344–349.

perum christi,' 'the property of the poor of Christ.' But the phrase may also be an adjectival prepositional phrase modifying 'we' and meaning [who are] a possession of Christ's, or [part] of Christ's property or treasure' (*MED* 'of' 18a; 'good' n.2 12 (a)) or an adverbial prepositional phrase modifying the verb 'be' and meaning 'because of Christ's goodness (through its power)' (*MED* 'of' 20a; 'good' n.2 1). 'We,' therefore, not only dispense 'cristes good' in charity; 'we' *are* 'cristes good,' a powerful reason for being 'kynde.' Moreover, (and this recalls I.165), 'we,' who are Christians 'of cristes good' (by the goodness of Christ) have the power to be 'kynde' and 'as kynde' (in the sense of 'like Kynde') by drawing from Christ's goodness, i.e., 'of cristes good.' This multiple pun on 'of' and 'good' implies that the central phrase of 89, 'of cristes good,' is practical means, source, and motive of kindness and likeness to God.

Verbal repetition supports puns in this 'kynde'-passage (82–94) to make it clear that the helpless should not be outside or on the fringes of the human family, since it is 'a cristene creature' or 'a Iewe' who cries at the gates, and 'a cristene creature' and 'a Iewe' called to help. Kindness, when 'Eyþer of hem helpeþ ooþer,' is 'natural' in recognizing that they are all in one body, *'caro.'* The doom with which Wit threatens the commune explicitly is already implicit in word play, since 'vnkyndenesse,' the undoing of the bonds of 'kynde,' of nature and love, not only causes misery to others, but also cuts off the unkind from their kind. Denying their own flesh, *'caro,'* they find themselves already, by that fact, 'Iugged with Iudas.'

This whole section about the frailty of human nature, which presents 'vnkyndenesse' as an undoing of 'kynde,' comes to a climax with Wit's rather astonishing denunciation of wasting 'speche' and 'tyme':

> [Tynynge] of tyme, truþe woot þe soþe,
> Is moost yhated vpon erþe of hem þat ben in heuene;
> And siþþe to spille speche þat [spire] is of grace
> And goddes gleman and a game of heuene.
> Wolde neuere þe feiþful fader his fiþele were vntempred
> Ne his gleman a gedelyng, a goere to tauernes.
> To alle trewe tidy men þat trauaille desiren,
> Oure lord loueþ hem ...   (101–108)

'Spille' can mean 'kill,' 'destroy,' as well as 'spill, waste,' or 'spoil' (Skeat II: 440; cf. Schmidt, *Clerkly* 11), and 'tynynge' refers to irrevocable loss of what is natural, as in 'To tyne the corone' (C. 12. 167 Skeat), i.e., 'to become wholly bald' (Skeat II: 158). Thus this passage is about some important kind of destruction of language and time. 'To spille speche' may mean to use language deceptively to make what is evil look good, and thus to destroy language itself by unmaking communication and truth. Since 'speche' was earlier a synonym for the Word of God (33, 38), it is possible that the phrase is a pun referring also to the death of Christ who as the Word is 'a spire of grace,' 'a tender plant' (Is. 53. 2) in whom 'the grace of God our savior hath appeared' (2 Tim. 2), and who could also be called 'goddes gleman and a game [joy] of heuene.' And since to speak is to make, 'to spille speche' may also mean to undo creation and creativity, 'to fordo,' to be 'vnkynde.'[22]

Within this denunciation of destruction, Wit praises 'speche,' by metonymy the speaker, and perhaps the Word of God or God's breath (Shoaf, 'Speche'130), in three quite different metaphors, with puns. The first, in 103, ('speche þat [spire] is of grace') has a well-known pun on 'spire ... of grace' as 'shoot of grace' and 'blade of grass' (*OED* 'spire'). By alliteration and consonance, it also suggests (though it does not mean) 'spear of Grace' (*OED* 'spear' sb 1, 2), since in XIX, Grace, the Holy Spirit, will give each person 'wepne to fighte wiþ ... a grace to gide wiþ hymseluen' (XIX.226–227), and the first of the weapons Grace gives is 'wit with wordes to shewe / To wynne wiþ truþe' (229–230). With these denotations and connotations, the phrase suggests the commonness of words, their source in nature and grace, their power and inestimable value.

The third metaphor, 'game of heuene,' is ambiguous in several ways, since 'game' is certainly a pun and 'of heuene' may refer either to the place where the game is enjoyed or to its heavenly quality or source. Some of the possible readings of 'game' are 'joy' (*MED* 1), 'festivity' (2 (a)), 'sport' (2 (c)), 'game, contest, tournament, debate, battle,' (3 (a)), 'victory' (3 (b)), or 'joke' (4). Schmidt glosses 'game' as 'delight' (ed. 95), and if 'of heuene' is read as 'heaven's,' 'game of heuene' supplements 'goddes gleman' to indicate God's joy in human speech, and perhaps in his Son.[23] The translation 'festivity' would have the same effect, and if 'of heuene' is read as 'heavenly,' the effect is simply to attribute a divine kind of joy and revelry to human writing and speech. The reading 'heavenly game, contest, sport' fits well with Langland's practice of word play and with Will's belief in XII that writing poetry is a form of play (as 'holy men ... pleyden' 24) (cf. Kolve

[22] As Professor Tavormina suggests to me, 'tidy men might also be those who conserve the right times of things.' On 'spire of grace' see also Quilligan, *Language* 162 and Szittya, *Antifraternal* 253. The C Text (X.185, Pearsall ed.) is no more explicit about exactly what 'spille' means, but less extreme in denouncing it. Huppé sees it as falsehood, 183. Murtaugh explains the denunciation: 'Misuse of either [speech or time] is something like a sacrilege' 22. See the excellent treatment of 'spilling speech' in P. Martin *Field* 62–70, and in Aers, *Piers* 67. Vance summarizes a medieval tradition in which words are compared to seeds, including human semen (239–240). Thus, it is perhaps possible that Wit's horror of spilling speech may also be related to the Biblical denunciation of Onan, who 'spilled his seed' (Gen. 38: 9–10). See Shoaf, 'Speche' 131.

[23] In *Clerkly*, Schmidt suggests another possibility: 'if the *game of hevene* ... is, as Wit says, to avoid "spilling speech" ...' (16). The word 'game' seems to me to refer to 'speche' itself, and so to encompass not only this avoidance but also the positive artistry of speech. See Arthur 95–103.

13). In Passus XVIII, speech becomes a debate which is a continuation of a tournament, and possibly for that reason those meanings, too, may be here at least potentially, so that speech is not only God's pleasure and the writer's contest, game, and sometimes joke, but also a joust with which 'To wynne ... truþe' (XIX.230).

The musical 'Wolde neuere þe feiþful fader his fiþele were vntempred' (105) is notable not only for its metaphor[24] but also for a play on sound similar to 'Dowel dwelleþ.' Consonance between 'feiþful,' (the adjective for God) and 'fiþele,' (the metaphor for the human speaker or speech)[25] suggests not only that creature is like Creator, but also that this likeness lies in the quality of faithfulness (as 'truþe/trewe' already imply).

Wit's sudden statement, '[Dowel in þis world is trewe wedded libbynge folk]' (110), is startling.[26] Yet it is natural enough for a speaker who begins with the creation of the human body and family to move on to a discussion of sexuality and marriage, especially since he identifies the creator with Kynde, source of all fertility. The first half of the passus implies that to do well is to act or be like God, and this new definition initiates an argument that marriage is like God, a trinity and a 'heuene' (Huppé 183). Language itself subtly asserts a continuity between the two parts of the passus. The words repeated in the creation narrative, e.g., 'make,' 'werk,' 'wrouȝt,' occur again in the second half of the passus with more specific and human denotations and connotations, sometimes with the effect of puns (Wittig, '*Piers*' 222–223).

> [Dowel in þis world is trewe wedded libbynge folk];
> For þei mote werche and wynne and þe world sustene;
> For of hir kynde þei come þat Confessours ben nempned,
> Kynges and knyȝtes, kaysers and [clerkes];
> Maidenes and martires out of o man come.
> The wif was maad þe wye for to helpe werche,
> And þus was wedlok ywroȝt wiþ a mene persone
> First by þe fadres wille and þe frendes conseille,
> And siþenes by assent of hemself as þei two myȝte acorde;
> And þus was wedlok ywroȝt and god hymself it made.
> In erþe [þe] heuene [is] ... (110–120)[27]

---

[24] Turville-Petre notes traditional use of this metaphor: 'Poets are God's instruments, and it is only God who can give them the grace to write in his honor and to the edification of the people' (27).

[25] A 'metaplasmus' (Quinn 22). Huppé notes 'consonance and vowel harmony' ('*Petrus*' 165).

[26] Pearsall notes that 'The abruptness with which the discussion is introduced is due to the omission in B C of a fine passage in A ...' (ed. 189). Knight sees the transition as done 'clumsily,' but done so that 'the real can subsist in the poem along with the theoretical' (297).

[27] The six laudable types of descendants listed here contrast with the six types listed at 121–122, 'conceyued ... in [cursed] tyme.' Lines 112–114 suggest designs of trees of

For example, the verb 'werche,' used earlier in the passus for divine creation (44), in line 111 means 'labor' at some job to support the family,
paralleling 'wynne' ('earn') and 'sustene' ('support'). But it also serves as a
pivot, a pun, since it also has the meaning 'love sexually'; it is a transition
word between praise for honest labor and praise for good marriages. The
couple 'werche' together in both senses: they labor together in order to
earn, and together they have a family, 'hir kynde' (112). 'Kynde,' a word
which earlier was the name for Nature and God and the adjective for
kindness, in 112 means 'stock, progeny.' In line 115, 'werche' is probably a
pun again, since the wife is 'þe wye for to helpe werche'[28] both in the sense
that she helps support the family and care for it and in the sense that she
helps create it through sexual love. The very fact that both 'kynde' and
'werk' are used so prominently for divine being and action earlier in the
passus and for human family and work here suggests that labor and love
are like the divine creation, fulfillments of the plan of Kynde.

Although Wit's references to 'werche' and 'trauaille' suggest that he sees
the life of Dowel – marriage – as demanding, he gives in this passage
(110–120) as ideal a picture of marriage as he earlier gave of 'caro' (1–60). For
Wit, marriage is meant to be intelligent ('by assent'), harmonious ('acorde'), loving ('assent... acorde ... to helpe'), and generative ('For of hir
kynde þei come'). Lines 119–120, '... And þus was wedlok ywroʒt and god
hymself it made./ In erþe [þe] heuene [is],' thus are not simply a tag narrative summation, but a moral exhortation based on what has gone before,
with emphasis on the word 'þus': 'And þus' – with father and friends
having been consulted and the two partners, images of God, reaching
accord and assent – 'was wedlok ywroʒt and god hymself it made.' Then,
implying again that Dowel is likeness to God, he concludes: 'In erþe [þe]
heuene [is] ...' (120).

But the very next line begins with 'Ac' ('but'), and a series of pejorative
words like those in 61–109 express a kind of revulsion as Wit describes the
effects of sin upon marriage and sexual love:

Jesse and some trees of consanguinity where descendants grow on a vine or tree rooted
in a recumbent father-figure, or where a spreading tree with medallions depicting a
variety of persons illustrates the fact that confessors, i.e., kings, knights, emperors,
clerics; and virgins and martyrs 'out of o man come' so that they are all of the same
'kynde,' nature, genus, kin, or people. There are examples in Bodl. MS Bodley Rolls 3,
and BM MS Royal 15 E. vi, f.3.

[28] Many manuscripts (see K-D 399, n. 115) make the wife the 'weye' (the way) to help
work, an 'agent' (Goodridge 108), or 'means' (Margaret Williams 162). In the K-D
edition, however, the wife is a person, the 'wye,' an equal partner; this harmonizes
with line 118.

Ac fals folk, feiþlees, þeues and lyeres,
Wastours and wrecches out of wedlok, I trowe,
Conceyued ben in [cursed] tyme as Caym was on Eue   (121–123)

Even the creative words 'werkes,' 'makede,' and *'fecisse'* become negative:

[For] god sente to Seþ and seide by an Aungel,
'Thyn issue in þyn issue, I wol þat þei be wedded,
And noȝt þi kynde wiþ Caymes ycoupled [ne] espoused'.
Yet [seþ], ayein þe sonde of oure Saueour of heuene,
Caymes kynde and his kynde coupled togideres,
Til god wraþed [wiþ] hir werkes and swich a word seide,
'That I [man makede now] it me forþhynkeþ':
Penitet me fecisse hominem.   (127–133)

The word 'werkes,' earlier a word for creation, labor, and sexual love,
becomes (132) a word for disobedient acts. 'Makede' and *'fecisse'* are re-
pented of, as if God would 'undo' what he had made: 'That I [man makede
now] it me forþynkeþ / *Penitet me fecisse hominem.*' Other generative words
fall under negation: 'noȝt ...ycoupled ne espoused' (129). Words for
'word,' which are normally creative, become negative, too. What God
'seide' in line 127 is a negative prohibition; Seth acts 'ayein the sonde' of
God; and God's second word is a repenting of the word of creation: 'and
swich a word seide, / That I [man makede now] it me forþynkeþ' (*MED*
'forthinken' v. 1c). Thirty lines later, human words, too, are shown as
negative in unhappy marriages, where 'ianglynge' (169) and '[manye]
foule wordes' (171) are uttered and sometimes 'boþe be forswore' (175).

Wit's description of unhappy marriages (160–171) is practical, ironic,
plainspoken, and unusually concrete. It contains a set of uncharacteristically obvious, superficial puns, two of them on homonyms, a little like
Holy Church's passage of broad jokes (I.181–198):

[A] careful concepcion comeþ of [swich weddynge]
As bifel of þe folk þat I bifore [shewed].
[For] goode sholde wedde goode, þouȝ þei no good hadde;
'I am *via & veritas*', seiþ crist, 'I may auaunce alle.'
It is an vncomly couple, by crist! as me þynkeþ,
To yeuen a yong wenche to [a yolde] feble,
Or wedden any wodewe for [wele] of hir goodes
That neuere shal barn bere but it be in armes.
In Ielousie, ioyelees, and ianglynge on bedde,
Many peire siþen þe pestilence han pliȝt hem togideres.
The fruyt þat [þei] brynge forþ arn [manye] foule wordes;   (161–171)

Line 163 has the usual ironic play on 'goode' as 'possession' and 'virtuous
[person]' (*MED* 'good,' n. 2, 1a, 12a), and Schmidt points out a resultant
'anti-pun ... suggesting (and simultaneously rejecting the position) that
"wealth should wed wealth even in the absence of virtue"' (*Clerkly* 136).

The musical line 168 has a famous pun on 'bere' as 'give birth' and 'carry.' Line 170, besides its possible pun on 'pair' and 'pear' (related to 'fruyt' 171), may have a pun on 'pliȝt' as 'pledge,' as 'embrace,' and as 'endanger or compromise' (*MED* 'Plight' v. 1, 2), meaning that if they do not love one another, couples compromise themselves and endanger their happiness by embracing and pledging themselves to one another in marriage. Each of these plays on words makes a mocking juxtaposition of something precious with something disappointing: goodness with goods, parenthood with carrying a weight, a natural fruit with an unhappy couple whose insincere vows and embraces compromise and endanger them. In their mocking tone, therefore, these plays on words fit well with the literal, concrete, sometimes cacaphonous description of quarreling couples that follows (172–175).

A few lines later (179–194), Wit narrows the meanings of the creation-words to their most specifically sexual denotations as he presents his most balanced view of marriage, neither an idealization nor a denunciation:

> [Wideweres and wodewes] wercheþ [riȝt also];
> ...
> Wreke þee wiþ wyuyng if þow wolt ben excused:
> *Dum sis vir fortis ne des tua robora scortis;*
> *Scribitur in portis, meretrix est ianua mortis.*
> Whan ye han wyued beþ war and wercheþ in tyme,
> Noȝt as Adam and Eue whan Caym was engendred;
> For in vntyme, trewely, bitwene man and womman
> Sholde no [bedbourde] be; but þei boþe were clene
> Of lif and of [loue] and [of lawe also]
> That [dede derne] do no man ne sholde.
> Ac if þei leden þus hir lif it likeþ god almyȝty,
> For he made wedlok first...   (179, 186–194)

'Wercheþ' (179, 187), 'dede' (192), and 'do' (192) have changed their denotations; they no longer mean 'create' or 'labor,' but now mean 'make love, love sexually,' as fits the context. But although they are not puns, they carry with them the connotations of former uses, at least potentially, suggesting that sexual love, like labor, is like divine creation, a suggestion that fits with the speaker's conclusion: 'Ac if þei leden þus hir lif it likeþ god almyȝty, / For he made wedlok first' (193–194).

Wit ends his passus with several more puns. Dobest, he says, brings down the

> ... wikked wille þat many werk shendeþ
> And dryueþ awey dowel þoruȝ dedliche synnes.   (209–210)

John Lawlor points out comic, pointed 'wordplay upon *Wille* with which Thought had originally introduced the eager questioner. ... [Now], "Wille" is the last enemy to be overcome' (*Piers* 94). 'Werk' in line 209 has regained its broad denotation: any kind of human work, action, creation, or labor. The line therefore says that pride or wicked will/Will destroys many actions or good works, i.e., Dowel in its broad sense. In the context of this section, however, one should probably read 'werk' as a pun, meaning also sexual activity, so that the line also says that pride, the wicked will, destroys the sexual lives of married couples and drives away Dowel in the sense of 'trewe wedded libbynge folk.'

The change brought about in Passus IX is reflected most dramatically in the contrast between Wit's first and last lines, the first so optimistic: '"Sire Dowel dwelleþ ... noȝt a day hennes,' the last so ominous in its articulation of the possibility of disaster: '"And dryueþ awey dowel þoruȝ dedliche synnes."' Between beginning and end, even the best, most figural words and acts have become tainted (e.g., 'werkes,' 132) or have fallen under restriction ('but þei boþe were clene / Of lif and of [loue] and [of lawe also] / That [dede derne] do no man ne sholde' 190–192). Yet the change is not a simple reversal. Rather, the initial simplicity of Wit's ethical view has become complicated. He teaches Will that while doing evil leads to hell, evildoers may learn to do better through 'loresmen' (90) and receive grace to amend (201), and that while it is possible to do well, even to do best, it is impossible to be perfect. Wit's language, which was naive early in the passus, has become compassionate. His last two definitions of Dowel (202–210), more sober than the first (1–14), a trifle less severe than the second (97–100), more complete than the third (110), imply the presence in the community of those who need others 'To ȝyuen and to yemen ... To helen and to helpen' (205–206):

> Dowel, my [deere], is to doon as lawe techeþ:
> To loue [and to lowe þee and no lif to greue;
> Ac to loue and to lene], leue me, þat is dobet;
> To ȝyuen and to yemen boþe yonge and olde,
> To helen and to helpen, is dobest of alle.
> [Thanne is dowel] to drede, and dobet to suffre,
> And so comeþ dobest [aboute] and bryngeþ adoun mody,
> And þat is wikked wille þat many werk shendeþ,
> And dryueþ awey dowel þoruȝ dedliche synnes.'   (202–210)

These last two definitions also imply the need for humility. Wit says that Will needs to 'lowe þee' (203), 'drede' (207) and 'suffre' in the process of having his own 'wikked wille' brought down (208) by love. It is clear that everyone is a sinner; even Will is at least potentially 'wikked wille' (209).

But at the same time, Wit calls 'wikked' Will 'my [deere]' (202) ('my freende' in Skeat) as he warns the dreamer and gently, humorously, but implacably focuses on him, Will, not on the simple, clear abstraction about which Will wanted to learn. Will, of course, misses the point and begins the next passus by telling us of the by-play between Wit and his wife; he will not feel his own frailty until the end of Passus XI.[29] Not until X.148, after Dame Studye furiously attacks the humorous and long-suffering Wit, does Will speak again, and then in the flattering polite style (X.148–151) which reveals the detached, superficial attitude which will carry him through his conversations with Studye, Clergye, and Scripture, and cause Scripture to 'scorne' him at the beginning of Passus XI (1).

Yet Wit's teaching about creation and creativity, though limited,[30] partial, sometimes extreme, and evidently unclear to Will, is sound and challenging as far as it goes. Its implications reach forward as well as backward through the poem. Wit's ambivalence about the body and sex, in his awareness of their potential for good and evil use, foreshadows Will's vision and shame in Passus XI. Kynde, whom Wit introduces as creator of the body, will re-appear as teacher of sexuality in Passus XI and as bringer of death and teacher of love in XX, and will act out implications of his identity that Wit 'skated over.' Wit's valuation of work and of language will be confirmed by Grace in XIX, where some of his phrases recur (229–233). Wit's language suggests that divine creation, sexual love and marriage and all human labor and art are figures of one another, each 'werk' a new creation demanding effort, wit, artistry, and the revelation of one's mind, and that any such 'werk' or 'speche' is part of Dowel, of building, creating, 'making' with Kynde. This gradual development of the implications of puns on 'kynde,' 'werk,' and 'speche' suggests that the 'game of heuene' can be played not only with the puzzle of language but also with the figural puzzle of creation, God's poetry of wit.

---

[29] Kaulbach points out that finally, at XI, Will 'realizes that he is a man and that a man has sin ("*Nemo sine crimine vivit*")' ('The "Vis Imaginativa"' 23, n. 14).

[30] Pearsall notes that Wit 'reveals the limitations of his understanding' (ed. 190). Kirk, (*Dream* 107, 112) and Carruthers (*Search* 88–89) point out particular limitations.

Chapter Four

Passus XI (with XII.280–294)

Passus XI is a long (441 line), fragmented passus near the center of the poem, beginning and ending in 'wo' (4, 406). It introduces numerous speakers who appear and disappear, carrying on apparently unrelated discussions from contradictory points of view. The text itself is confusing: there are sections where we do not even know who is speaking,[1] and although the passus has been the subject of long and fruitful analysis, there is still very little agreement about the meaning of certain obscure lines and about the outcome of some of the interchanges. In it, as Judith Anderson writes, 'Langland positively lists toward chaos' (81).

Yet there is some thematic unity in the passus and in the third dream of which it forms a part. The ruling theme of this dream is the relationship between poverty and riches, if one takes those words in their widest senses.[2] The third and fourth dreams, Passus VIII–XII and XIII–XIV (which make up the 'Vita de Dowel'), are pervaded by those descriptions of poverty which caused Christopher Dawson to call *Piers Plowman* 'the cry of the poor' (250), as well as descriptions of the experience of human spiritual

---

[1] Skeat (II: 176, n. 128) and Wittig ('*Piers*' 260) take the unnamed 'oon' who speaks in this passus to be Lewte; Frank (*Piers* 60, n. 1) and Schmidt (ed. 334, n. 140) take him to be Trajan; Kaulbach understands him to be Imaginative ('*Vis*' 18), and Kirk, Scripture (*Dream* 136, n. 9); Chambers (*Man's* 136) and Donaldson (*Piers* 173) take him to be the dreamer; cf. Peverett 125–126. Some of the ideas in this chapter developed from a paper I gave at the Ninth International Medieval Conference, Kalamazoo, 1974.

[2] '. . . in Passus XI, Langland has used the dichotomy of rich and poor to hammer home a point about faith and works' (Wittig, '*Piers*' 261). Guy Bourquin speaks of the 'Exaltation de la pauvreté absolue' in XIV–XV (book 5), and Bloomfield says 'patient poverty is Do-Wel' (*Apocalypse* 5). William Ryan notes the vocabulary of poverty-wealth words and the 'endless thematic exploration' of poverty and riches in XIV–XV (*Wm. Langland* 56–60). Almost certainly, the choice of 'poverty' as symbol of all human need in Dowel is related to the importance of 'the right use of temporal goods' which Dunning sees as the theme of the Visio (*Piers* 6), and 'the problem of supplying the needs of the body,' which Howard sees as 'the poet's central concern' (166, 198–203). See Frank, *Piers* 63, n. 2. Godden equates poverty with 'hardship and suffering' and '*penaunce*' (145–149).

poverty – sinfulness, ineptitude, folly, the need for mercy and grace – and of the complementary experience of the richness of human gifts.[3] Passus XI is a good locus for examining how this theme is developed: not by explicit argument alone but also by figurative language and word play in which words themselves become a sign of wealth to be found within poverty. Since the Trajan argument begins in this passus and continues in the next, I shall discuss the Trajan passage from XII (280–294) in this chapter.

The action of Passus XI begins and ends with its focus on Will. At the beginning he enters an enchanted state where he enjoys the illusion of comfort and importance until removed from it by material poverty and the fear of damnation; at the end he has lost some of this fear but is more genuinely aware of his spiritual poverty and need, and he is willing to talk with Imaginative about them. Between these two points of concentration on himself, Will hears and speaks about human needs and achievements, access to divine comfort and richness, and the mystery of divine poverty.

To say that Passus XI has thematic unity in the theme of poverty and riches is not to say that it moves placidly in a single direction. On the contrary, the narrative is busy, jagged, even violent, with interruptions, interventions, conflicting voices, movement from one plane of dream to another, an extreme turn of fortune, and emotional upheavals – not just a simple swing between opposites, like Wit's, but a turbulence of swift changes in Will and a variety of strong emotions in others. The passus first moves from Scripture's scorn to Will's tears of woe and wrath; these tears are dried in the inner dream by the three concupiscences, to the distress of Elde and Holiness; Will then feels disillusionment and extreme anxiety, which are met by Trajan's exuberance and an unnamed speaker's tenderness; at the end, Will's wonder at Nature is lost in sarcasm, anger, and shame. This is a bruising, exhausting passus, full of cries, interjections, and unguided feelings, with several passages of quiet harmony at the center of its noisy swirl of themes and emotions.

Throughout the first episode of the passus, in the Land of Longing (1–62), Will[4] is totally passive, his most self-directed action being the docile 'By wissing of þis wenche I dide' (59). All other verbs which describe Will's activity are either grammatically passive: 'I was rauysshed' (7), or

---

[3] As Wittig says, 'this is not to suggest that Langland is using "poverty" only as a symbol. ... It is precisely because there are materially rich and poor, because the Gospel concerns their relationship to each other, and because spiritual wealth and poverty are determined to a large extent through their impact upon material wealth and poverty, that the physical can serve as a vehicle for the spiritual' ('*Piers*' 261). '... the material world is not merely a vehicle for expressing the immaterial, but on the contrary contains the heart of its meaning and its mystery' (Mann 27).
[4] I think Wittig is right in distinguishing 'the Will of the pilgrimage' from 'the Will of the inner dream,' ('*Piers*' 243). It is the latter to whom I refer here.

passive in meaning. Sometimes these latter are negative, describing what he did not do: 'of dowel ne dobet no deyntee me þouȝte' (48), 'I hadde no likyng' (49). Sometimes they express actions over which he seems to have no control: 'wepte I' (4), 'I weex aslepe' (5), 'a merueillous metels mette me' (6), 'I foryede youþe and yarn into Elde' (60). His passivity is further indicated by the fact that (applied to Will) the nominative 'I' appears only six times in 62 lines (1–62), and the objective 'me' eighteen times. For a good part of this section (17–49), Will does not act or speak at all – he is simply shouted at, exhorted, and ordered around by conflicting voices, eight of them, which create a sense of confusion and of the persona as dumb victim of his own 'likyng'. This is an extraordinary use of language. Will's passivity suggests the hypnotic death-like quality of life in the Land of Longing, a quality described by a speaker later in the passus: 'Whoso loueþ noȝt, leue me, he lyueþ in deeþ deyinge' (177).

This death-in-life quality of illusion, of a world which is thin and unreal, is further sustained by a pattern of word play like that in the Lady Mede episode, an ironic, illusory use of words as anti-puns.[5] Words are used in a narrow, disappointing way while the irony of a potentially fuller use echoes in them. For example, at the beginning of Will's 'merueillous metels,' Fortune promises him 'wondres':

> A merueillous metels mette me þanne,
> [For] I was rauysshed riȝt þere; Fortune me fette
> And into þe lond of longynge [and] loue she me brouȝte
> And in a Mirour þat hiȝte middelerþe she made me biholde.
> [Siþen] she seide to me, 'here myȝtow se wondres
> And knowe þat þow coueitest and come þerto paraunter'.   (XI.6–11)

There proves to be an ironic distance between the 'wondres' Fortune promises here and the 'wondres' that Will originally 'Went wide in þis world ... to here' (Pro. 4). This ironic gap is emphasized at the end of the Land of Longing episode by Will's use of the word 'merueille' when he angrily says to the friars who have turned against him:

> Ich haue muche merueille of yow, and so haþ many anoþer,
> Whi youre Couent coueiteþ to confesse and to burye
> Raþer þan to baptiȝe ...   (XI.75–77)

Will is not using verbal irony; he is genuinely amazed at the friars' avaricious foolishness (wryly suggested by the aural coincidence of 'Couent

---

[5] George Kane notes another interesting stylistic feature, hyper-alliteration in the speeches of the temptresses at XI.19, 20, 22 ('Music' 57). Murtaugh shows that lines 34–41 express and satirize 'fourteenth-century voluntarism at its most extreme ... [the] nadir of skepticism. [In line 39] ... The very term "truth," whose dual referent had symbolized a pact of love and intelligibility between God and man, is here used to dissolve the pact.' (84).

coueites'). But there is situational and dramatic irony in the fact that the only recorded 'merueille' in or near the 'merueillous metels' (6) is a disillusioning one – the disenchanting fact of the friars' avarice.[6]

The phrase 'parfit lyuynge,' in 'Pride of parfit lyuynge pursued hem boþe' (15), is an inherently ironic anti-pun, since as a form of pride, 'pride of parfit lyuynge' is opposed to the really perfect living of charity. Again in line 30 when Elde warns Will that he will find '*Concupiscentia carnis* clene þee forsake,' the primary meaning is that she will 'entirely forsake you,' but since 'clene' may also mean 'pure, chaste,' (*MED* 'clene' adj., adv.), it can also be read to mean that she will 'leave you chaste, i.e., abandon you to a life of chastity.' From Elde's point of view, both meanings are equally true, and the pun is ironic, surprising, and funny in its reversal of value. It also is perhaps a foretaste of XX.195–198, where Elde causes Will to become impotent (Tavormina).

As we have already seen, line 53 has a similar ironic pun on the word 'goode': '"Haue no conscience", quod she, how þow come to goode.' Coueitise, the speaker, is concerned with 'goode' in the sense of 'goods' and is without scruple as to the means of acquiring them. But it is possible to read her words as meaning not only, 'Have no scruple as to how you acquire goods,' but also, 'Take no thought about how you come to goodness' (*MED* 'good' n.2, 1; 6a; 12a). Coueitise does not mean to speak of 'goodness,' of course, but her words are capable of that meaning, and this capability is a latent ironic commentary on the moral implications of what she does mean to say, especially in the light of Will's self confessed state:

> ... of dowel ne dobet no deyntee me þouȝte;
> I hadde no likyng, leue me, [þe leste] of hem to knowe.
> Coueitise of eiȝes com ofter in mynde
> Than dowel or dobet among my dedes alle.   (48–51)

Here, 'likyng' means primarily 'desire' or 'pleasure' but also 'likeness, resemblance' (*MED* 'liking,' ger.2).[7] Line 49 must be read, 'I had no desire, believe me, to know the least thing about them,' but since there is a persistent theme in the poem that the ability to recognize something depends on one's own likeness to it, it can also be read, 'I had no likeness [to them],

---

[6] Will uses 'merueille' in the same ironic tone at IX.153 and the synonymous noun ('wonder') in his sarcastic comment to Reason at XI.374.
[7] All the play on likeness is related to the various mirrors in this dream. See Longo, 299; Wittig, 'Piers' 236–240; Murtaugh, 88; Carruthers, *Search* 96–97, 107, 128. Schmidt's gloss on XI.16 suggests also that in seeking his 'likynge,' Will looks after his 'looks' ('countenaunce') (ed. 118). Wittig argues that 'lond of longynge' also echoes the prodigal son's *terra longinqua*, 'land of being distant' from where Will ought to be: ('Piers' 234).

believe me, [to enable me] to know the least thing about them.' At line 20, also, Will looks in Fortune's mirror, and Fortune promises him his 'likynge':

> ... in þis Mirour þow myȝt se [myrþes] ful manye
> That leden þee wole to likynge al þi lif tyme'.   (20–21)

Although one would expect to see one's 'likeness' (one meaning of 'likynge') in a mirror, Fortune clearly means to promise him his 'pleasure.' The word 'likynge' in this context evokes both these meanings as well as a third, the 'likeness' of God in which Will is made. The fact that Fortune intends to promise Will pleasure, not likeness, is the more ironic since the reason he fell into the inner dream of the Land of Longing in 'wo and wrathe' was that Scripture accused him of not knowing himself, which would imply not being able to see his own likeness ('*seipsos nesciunt*' 5).

As Will emerges from the Land of Longing in the second section of this passus (62–170), patterns of verbal irony and passivity fall away. Will's last ironic word is 'merueille' at line 75: 'Ich haue muche merueille of yow.' Even before this, at line 64 the verbs predicated of Will become active as he takes a new resolution, albeit a negative one: 'I seide I nolde / Be buried at hire hous.' He takes over the direction of his own life again, and from this time on he speaks freely, with his usual interjections and arguments: 'By my feiþ! frere ... Riȝt so, by þe roode!' (71, 73)

In Will's sarcastic comments to the friars (70–83) there is relatively little verbal play, but Lewte, the next speaker,[8] plays on sound in 104: 'Thouȝ þow se yuel seye it noȝt first,' where 'se' and 'seye' are near-homonyms, and 'Thouȝ,' 'þow,' and 'noȝt' echo one another in assonance. Line 106 has half-rhyme, or what Schmidt calls 'pararhyme' (*Clerkly* 67) in 'loue' and 'looue': 'Neiþer for loue looue it noȝt.' Perhaps these plays on sound are to add piquancy to the difference between seeing and saying (104) and between loving and praising (106), since for the honest and loyal person (one of 'lewte'), each pair should work in harmony.

After Will's traumatic encounter with Scripture (111–117) and the lyrical p..ssage of comfort (117–139) which follows it, Trajan bursts into the poem in the first of a series of passages characterized by analogous and other polysemous terms used in puns. Although the passages have long been debated,[9] their word play has received little attention, yet it is crucially

---

[8] On the meanings of 'lewte,' see Skeat II: 387 ('fidelity, loyalty,' etc.); Bloomfield, *Apocalypse* 166; Kean, 'Love' 255–256; Clutterbuck 140.

[9] See R. W. Chambers, 'Long'; Dunning, 'Langland'; Russell; Evans; Ames, 47, 76, 192, 196; Gradon '*Trajanus*'; Whately (three articles) who refers to word play; Minnis, *Chaucer* 54–5; Morse 28; Adams, 'Piers's' 390–93. Schmidt, 'A Covenant,' emphasizes the 'dense and pregnant' nature of the B-passage and elucidates it. I approach it from a slightly different direction (word play), but my arguments support his conclusions.

important, for whereas some speakers seem to attribute Trajan's salvation to his good works and others to grace, the puns in the text balance the two causes of salvation and resolve the controversy in a remarkable way.[10]

The lines in Passus XI which are explicitly ascribed to Trajan (140–153, 170) give a theologically balanced explanation of his salvation. According to him, the things that were able to 'me cracche fro helle' were: 'loue and leautee and my laweful domes' (145), 'sooþnesse ... in my werkes' (147), 'grace' (149), 'loue and ... my lyuynge in truþe' (152). These passages, however, yield their full sense only if one is aware of their puns. His 'lyuynge in truþe' – the opposite of living 'in deeþ deyinge' (177) – obviously means living in human righteousness, but given the free use of 'truþe' as a divine name, the poet is allowing readers to see the possibility that 'lyuynge in truþe' also means 'living in God.' The same kind of double meaning is available in the word 'loue,' making both God and virtue the sources of Trajan's salvation.[11] The most obvious and dramatic of these puns occurs in 164, after an unidentified speaker has declared that Trajan was saved 'for his pure truþe' (156):

> Yblissed be truþe þat so brak helle yates
> And saued þe sarsyn from sathanas power   (164–5)

Line 164 foreshadows XVIII.321, where Truth (Christ) literally breaks hell gates and saves not only 'the sarsyn' but all people 'from sathanas power.' As Schmidt says, 'Here God's power breaking through hell's gates (cf.

See also Donaldson, *Piers* 173; Riach, 17; Burrow, 'Words,' 123; Longo, 299; Mazzeo; Coleman, *Piers* 108–146; Paull; Vasta, *Spiritual* 59–60, 95.

[10] Recent scholarship, e. g., the work of Pamela Gradon (1980), Janet Coleman, and John Bowers (especially 1–60), makes it appear very likely that Langland was aware of the predestinarian controversy of his time and consciously responding to it. Gradon shows that the configuration of texts and examples in Passus XI–XII indicates knowledge of earlier 'Pelagian' ideas, and Coleman indicates that Langland also knew some of the ideas of the *Moderni* (*Piers*, 136, 146, and passim), though Courtenay concludes that nominalist influence on late 14th-century poets is unlikely (378–9); cf Boitani 83. Scholars disagree about the nature of Langland's response to the *Moderni* and to popular understandings of their work, and attention to word play is a crucial element in understanding it. On the controversy, see, e.g., Courtenay; Leff 162–163; Oberman; Knowles 330; Murtaugh 74–88; Hort 112–113; Kane, 'Perplexities' 84–85; Baker, 'From Plowing' passim; Coleman *Medieval* 235–249; and O'Driscoll 26–28. Norman Blake (92) notes Patience's hesitancy about how 'in englissh ... it is wel hard to expounen' a definition (XIV.278); this is important, as in XI–XII there is no attempt to 'expounen' or solve the controversy on its own philosophical-theological terms (Woolf 'Some' 121). Rather, the 'answer' is poetry, a pun.

[11] Britton Harwood suggests further meaning for 'lyuynge in truþe' (152): that Imaginative (listening silently) understands Trajan's words 'lyuynge in truþe' to mean 'living in belief' and the Dreamer understands them to mean 'living in benevolence' ('Clergye' 288). The 'loue' of lines 145 and 152 may refer to Will's love or to Gregory's love; see Kean, 'Justice' 103.

XVIII.322–3) is hard to distinguish from the man's *truthe* which enabled *him* to "break out of hell" (140 above)' (ed. 335, n. 163). The pun, rather than making such a distinction, allows both meanings full sway, human virtue and the Divine Person, and thus neatly expresses the mystery of grace and works, of divine and human causality which, like the two meanings of the pun, persist and act together without invalidating one another.[12] Ironically, the *speaker* may mean that, as R. W. Chambers put it, 'Trajan's salvation depend[s] solely upon his own virtues' ('Long' 66), but the *poet* has resolved the most involuted of theological arguments in this pun, which in its structure is an emblem of the treasure hidden within the life of 'an vncristene creature' (143).

Later, in Passus XII, Will shows that he is still interested in the question of the salvation of those outside of Christendom, those who have not been christened:

> 'Alle þise clerkes', quod I þo, 'þat on crist leuen
> Seyen in hir Sermons þat neiþer Sarsens ne Iewes
> Ne no creature of cristes liknesse withouten cristendom worþ saued.'
> (277–279)

There is dramatic irony in Will's very statement of the problem: whether any 'creature of cristes liknesse' will be saved 'withouten cristendom' (Ames 83). By Will's own word, the creatures in question are 'of Christ's likeness,' but despite all that Holy Church, Wit, and the unnamed speaker of Passus XI have said on the subject, Will fails to see any connection between being like Christ and being saved.

Imaginative[13] makes no comment on this irony, but bursts into an argument which, although it begins simply, ends in one of the poem's most difficult passages. What Imaginative *means* by his answer as a whole is quite clear, and there is no critical disagreement about it: good persons will not be lost. But the exact meaning and implications of many of Imaginative's lines and the reasoning behind his conclusion are complicated, obscure, and much debated. The key to a solution lies in his word play.

---

[12] Philomena O'Driscoll sees all of Dowel (IX–XII) structured on a 'reconciliation of opposites' (19) as the Trajan debate is structured. 'The principle constantly important in the Dowel debate (and an implicit comment on the teaching of Bradwardine and the modern Pelagians): the part must not be taken for the whole.' She also notes that 'the conflict with which the debate began is recognized to have been an illusion' (28).

[13] The attempt to define Imaginative in relation to a source goes on actively. On Imaginative, see Minnis, 'Langland's'; Kaulbach, 'The "Vis Imaginativa"' 18; Middleton, 'Narration' 113; Anderson 86; Frank, *Piers* 63; Longo; Carruthers, *Search* 103; Kirk, *Dream* 140; Wittig '*Piers*'; Harwood 'Imaginative'; Murtaugh 91–92; Wimsatt 111; for earlier contributions, see Bloomfield, *Apocalypse* 172–173; Coghill, 'Pardon'; Jones; both Murtaugh and Longo give useful summaries of interpretations. Longo interprets Imaginative as a feminine figure.

Imaginative's first, strongest argument for the salvation of a *'Iustus'* or true person is based upon word play as Donaldson has shown:

> *'Contra!'* quod Imaginatif þoo and comsed to loure,
> And seide, *'Saluabitur vix Iustus in die Iudicij;*
> *Ergo saluabitur'*, quod he and seide na moore latyn.
> 'Troianus was a trewe knyght and took neuere cristendom
> And he is saaf, seiþ þe book, and his soule in heuene.   (XII.280–284)

The argument is based upon the canonical authority of I Peter iv.18 and reaches its conclusion by 'a splendid abuse of a quasi-negative [*vix*] to achieve a triumphant affirmation, one that St Peter, who is being quoted, … might well have found surprising' (Donaldson, 'Langland' 68).

Next, arguing from analogy that it is fitting for a just person to be saved (287–290) Imaginative plays upon 'truþe'/'trewe' (Ames 84):

> Ac truþe þat trespased neuere ne trauersed ayeins his lawe,
> But lyueþ as his lawe techeþ and leueþ þer be no bettre,
> And if þer were he wolde amende, and in swich wille deieþ –
> Ne wolde neuere trewe god but [trewe] truþe were allowed.
> (XII.287–290)[14]

'Truþe' has already been shown to be the value of Trajan's life (XI.141; XII.210, 283), roughly synonymous with justice (XII.281) and 'sooþnesse' (XI.147), perhaps with 'loue and leautee' (XI.145, 167) and 'leel loue' (XI. 162). By metonymy, it also means a person who lives in this state (Skeat II: 188, n. 209). In 287, these meanings are lifted to an awesome purity: perfect good will and observance of the best law one knows. In 290, the adjective 'trewe' describes both this human truth and God: 'trewe truþe … trewe god.' The repetition of the adjective implies that a person possessing 'trewe truþe,' even 'withouten cristendom,' is like God in possessing a quality which reflects God's name and nature.

As Whately shows, 'allowed' in line 290 means 'taken into account, validated, rewarded' (*'Piers'* 2–4). In XV.4, 'allowed' seems to mean 'praised,' 'requited,' 'gave credit for' ('And some lakkede my lif – allowed it fewe'). Will said in Passus X that the works of humans are hidden in the hands of God, who alone knows how a person and his works will be 'allowed þere' (X.439, 441) ('esteemed,' Skeat n. B. 10. 433; 'judged,' Schmidt ed. 115). When Patience later says that the poor 'dar plede and preue by pure reson / To haue allowaunce of his lord; by þe law he it cleymeþ' (XIV.109–110), the word 'allowaunce' seems to mean 'reward,' for some of

---

[14] 'His lawe' (287) is ambiguous because the antecedent of 'his' is uncertain. I think its primary meaning is the law which the true person knows, but Ruth Ames' interpretation, 'God's law,' may also be present in a double meaning which implies that following the best law one knows is always in harmony with God's law at least subjectively (192).

the rich will be 'disalowed' (XIV.131), 'unrewarded.' ('Of' in XIV.110 and in XII.291 means 'by, from.') As Whately notes (*'Piers'* 3), 'allowed' also has a legal meaning, '2. Law: To recognize or admit (a privilege, an excuse, etc.) as valid or binding, validate, confirm' (*MED* 'allouen.') Thus the argument proceeds to its conclusion: it is unthinkable that 'trewe god' would not recognize 'trewe truþe,' take it into account and hence reward it.[15] 'Truþe' must recognize (i.e., give credit for, reward, recognize as valid) 'trewe truþe' by his very nature: 'Ne wolde neuere trewe god but trewe truþe were allowed.' The line is similar to Christ's words (XVIII.398) when he explains why he will save all humankind: 'For I were an vnkynde kyng but I my kynde helpe.' In both lines, God and humans are linked by repetition of heavily connotative words ('trewe,' 'kynde') which lay a claim on God. Both lines suggest the impossibility of such a claim not being taken into consideration, since it appeals to God's nature.

Imaginative's last argument is obscure not only because of textual problems, but also because he is saying a number of things at once. It is as intricate as Holy Church's fullest lines, and must be puzzled out through attention to elaborate word play:

> And wheiþer it worþ [of truþe] or noȝt, [þe] worþ [of] bileue is gret,
> And an hope hangynge þerInne to haue a mede for his truþe;
> For *Deus dicitur quasi dans [eternam vitam] suis, hoc est fidelibus;*
> *Et alibi, si ambulauero in medio vmbre mortis.*
> The glose graunteþ vpon þat vers a greet mede to truþe   (291–294)

Words with similar meanings overlap and play upon one another in these five lines, words in the semantic fields of belief ('bileue ... truþe ... *fidelibus*'), of faithfulness ('truþe ... *fidelibus*'), and of treasure ('worþ ... mede ... *dans* (giving) ... graunteþ ... tresor'), re-associating 'truþe' as faithfulness with 'truþe' as belief and also with the image of treasure.

The 'wheiþer ... or noȝt' clause in 291 indicates uncertainty, but not uncertainty about the true person's salvation. Imaginative is certain about that: '*Ergo saluabitur.*' It refers rather to the unsatisfying nature of the argument he has just made, since reason or learning alone cannot prove with certainty the salvation of anyone, though an imaginative argument may show that the salvation of the just is fitting and something to be expected from 'trewe god.' This clause as K-D give it, literally 'whether it

---

[15] Cf. 'he is always faithful, for he cannot disown his own self' (2 Tim. 2: 13). Minnis writes about Imaginative's words, 'This fideistic argument is persuasive, if not provable in a purely rational way. It is therefore appropriate that it is delivered by Imaginatif and not Reson. ... imaginative thinking produces not certainties but possibilities, often in areas of thought where a mere mortal cannot expect to reach absolute certainty' ('Langland's' 85; cf. *Chaucer* 54). See also Martin, *Field* 95, on analogical arguments. These arguments (also called arguments from fittingness), with, of course, only probable conclusions, are frequent and respectable in medieval theology; see, e.g., *Summa Theologica*, IIIa.1; 36.1; 50.1.

will be by truth or not,' is ambiguous both because of the uncertainty about the antecedent of 'it' (Whately, *'Piers'* 5) and because of the uncertainty about how the expressed auxiliary verb is meant to be completed. The clause may refer to the works-grace controversy, the theology of the absolute freedom of God. If, that is, in the spirit of 14th-century theological dispute about merit (Minnis, *Chaucer* 55), 'allowed' in 290 is given its legal meaning, 'recognized as binding,' line 291 means 'whether or not the truth of truth will be recognized by God as binding [upon God],' (i.e., whether or not such a person can claim salvation by merit on the basis of works). The clause may also mean something like, 'Whether my argument is convincing or not ...'

There are many possible readings for the second half of the line, 'þe worþ of bileue is gret.' The simplest is, 'the value of faith is great,' with 'bileue' referring to the belief of the speaker and the church. This completes the line by contrasting the uncertainty of theology, especially of analogical arguments, with the certainty of faith. By doing so, it says that whether or not we can argue to the salvation of the just by logic, we know by faith (which is therefore our valuable source of certainty) that they are saved. It also says that whether or not the righteousness of the just will be recognized as binding upon God's justice – i.e., whether their salvation is won by merit or not – we can still be certain that they will be saved in some way, because our faith tells us so.[16] The first reading contrasts two sources of knowledge about the salvation of the just; the second contrasts two reasons for their salvation.

Other readings are possible if 'bileue' is taken to be the faith not of the speaker but of the true person whose salvation is in question (Whately, *'Piers'* 5–6), though a reader may be bewildered or outraged by the sudden ascription of faith where presumably there was no faith, i.e., in a 'creature ... withouten cristendom.' But by making a visual and aural parallel between verb and noun in 'worþ of truþe' and 'worþ of bileue,' the line suggests some meaningful connection between 'bileue' and 'truþe,' perhaps an inchoate faith within faithfulness. Indeed such a hint was available within current usage of the word 'truþe' itself, since *Cursor Mundi* used 'treuþe' to mean religious belief:

> Putyfar ... held ioseph in mensk and lare
> Al þou þair treuthes sundri ware.   (4246 Gött.) (*OED* 'truth' sb I.3b)

---

[16] K-D gloss this clause: 'freely "And the intrinsic value of faith is great, whether it actually comes to be faith in the true religion ... or not"' (209). As K-D explain, the 'common archetypal reading was *And wheiþer it worþ or noȝt worþ þe bileue is gret of treuþe*. The sense of this line is to say the least obscure' (209). A possible reading might be, 'And whether it [the validity of my argument / the fidelity of a true person] will or will not be "allowed," the faith of the true person is great.'

and in a contemporary translation of the gospel, 'great is thy faith' is rendered, 'Mikel is thi treuth.'[17] The likelihood that 'truþe' in line 291 of *Piers* is a pun meaning 'faith' as well as 'fidelity'[18] is increased by a Latin pun on *'fidelibus'* which follows (293). The simplest paraphrase of this puzzling line 291, then, is 'Whether my argument [that God, being true, will certainly reward human truth] is convincing or not – and whether or not the merits of the just are binding upon God – the value of faith is great [our faith which tells us that the just are saved, and their faith, which saves them].' Playing within and against this simplest reading are the other possible readings given above.

Even line 292, simple as it seems, has several possible meanings playing upon one another: 'And an hope hangynge þerInne to haue a mede for his truþe.' This is first of all a statement that hope, a certain expectation of reward for faithfulness, is contained within living faith – 'an hope hangynge þerInne' (Schmidt, 'A Covenant' 153). Imaginative's words can also perhaps be read as a statement that faith holds within it the person of Christ as well as the abstract virtue of hope, since the liturgy calls him *'Christus spes mea'*[19] and Paul prays in Eph. iii. 17, 'That Christ may dwell in your heart through faith.' The phrase 'to haue a mede for his truþe' may also be taken two ways. Those who have faith have hope of a reward (a 'mede') for their faithfulness.[20] If one also reads 'hope' to mean 'Christ,' then it is possible also (in addition to the first reading) to read that Christ our hope [is] hanging therein in order to win a reward (the whole human race) for *his* faithfulness. The suggestion, though audacious, is syntactically possible and in harmony with Christ's speech in XVIII, where he is fighting for what might be called a reward as well as a cause: 'mannes soule sake':

---

[17] *MED* files, Ann Arbor. I am grateful to Professor Sherman Kuhn and the staff for access to the files.

[18] 'Imaginative stresses ... the miracle that Trajan, invincibly ignorant of the Trinity and Incarnation, nevertheless was saved by his faith. ... Trajan's perseverance in the highest belief of which he was capable issued in further belief' (Harwood, 'Clergye' 288). He continues, 'truth itself can yield belief, from which hope always proceeds.' See Romans i. 16–18 and Heb. x. 38: *'Justus autem ex fide vivit'*; *'Justus autem in fide sua vivet.'* See also Schmidt: 'What I think Langland is saying is that "right action constitutes a sort of faith, an implicit assent to the (unknown) truth of revelation" ...' ('A Covenant' 153).

[19] *'Victimae Paschali,'* the 11th century Easter Sequence, part of which is paraphrased at XVIII.65 (*Sarum Missal*, Friday after Easter, 377); see also Rousseau. The indwelling of Christ is most explicitly stated at V.606–608. In a similar passage, Julian of Norwich says, 'owre lorde ... schewyd me my saule in myddys of my herte ... me thought it was a wirschipfulle cite. In myddys of this cite sittes oure lorde Jhesu ... for in vs is his haymelyeste hame' (Short Text xxii, 1–14).

[20] See Whately's discussion of the ways in which this echoes Scripture and theology ('*Piers*' 8–10).

> I fauȝt so me þursteþ ȝit for mannes soule sake;
> May no drynke me moiste, ne my þurst slake,
> Til þe vendage falle in þe vale of Iosaphat. (367–369)

There is continued word play in lines 293–294, where Imaginative quotes not only a line of psalm 22, but also a Latin text about God giving eternal life to his own, the *'fidelibus'* or faithful; he also refers without quoting it to a gloss on the psalm:[21]

> For *Deus dicitur quasi dans [eternam vitam] suis, hoc est fidelibus*
> *Et alibi, si ambulauero in medio vmbre mortis.*
> The glose graunteþ vpon þat vers a greet mede to truþe. (293–4)

That is, 'God is said as it were to be granting eternal life to his very own, that is, to the faithful, and elsewhere, "Though I walk through the valley of the shadow of death [I will fear no evil, for thou art with me.]" The gloss on that verse grants a great reward to truth.' Augustine's gloss, quoted in the *Glossa Ordinaria*, seems likely to be the one referred to here: 'Thou art with me, in the heart, through faith, so that after the darkness of death, I may be with you' (Skeat II: 188, n. 12. 290).[22] Thus ' "being with God" is the "great mede" that Ymaginatif points to' (Whately, *'Piers'* 10).

Who are the *'fidelibus,'* the 'faithful' to whom God is said to be giving eternal life, the people who are 'his own,' *'suis'*? The text suggests a double answer, since *'fidelibus'* is a pun meaning both those who are faithful in the sense of loyal or true, and those who believe. Both meanings are common in Latin literature.[23] The ordinary interpretation of *'fidelibus'* in line 293

---

21 Judson Allen ('Langland's') shows that in the pardon episode, the gloss Langland used for psalm 22 is that of Hugh of St.-Cher, which Allen gives (352); he also stresses the centrality of this psalm (353, n. 22); some of his comments are also pertinent to this passus (357–8).

22 Langland refers to the gloss without quoting it, but as Alford observes, 'The whole point of some quotations resides in the "etc." ' ('Role' 82). Augustine's gloss (most of which is quoted in the *Glossa Ordinaria* 876) is: *'non timebo mala, quoniam tu habitas in corde meo per fidem; et nunc mecum es, ut post umbram mortis etiam ego sim tecum.'* (*'Enarrationes in Psalmos,'* Ps. 22: 4, *PL* 36, 182); see Schmidt on play with the initial letters of *'dans eternam uitam suis* to spell *"deus"* ' (ed. 304).

23 *'Fides*: trust, confidence, reliance, credence, belief, faith. I. lit. ... *alicui or alicui rei fidem habere*, to place confidence in, ... Cic.; *fidem facere*, to awake confidence, Cic. ... II. Meton., A. that which produces confidence, faithfulness, fidelity, conscientiousness, honesty, credibility, truthfulness ... *exemplum antiquae probitatis ac fidei*, Cic.; *fidem praestare*, to be loyal, Cic.' *Cassell's Latin Dictionary*, 223–224. Both meanings were operative in the middle ages. *'I fidelis. Christiani dicti Fideles post susceptum baptismum, quia fidem susceperunt ... 2. fidelis, Subditus, vassallus, qui fidem suam domine obstrinxit'* (DuCange, 283). See such prayers as the offertory, *'Domine Jesu Christe, rex gloriae, libera animas omnium fidelium defunctorum de manu inferni ...'* (Requiem Mass, *Sarum Missal* 867) and the following from Du Cange: *'In Christiano viro prima est fides. Ideo recte Fidelis dicuntur, qui baptizati sunt.* lib. I *de Sacram.*, cap. l' (283). Skeat's C-text equates *'fidelitas'* with 'Treuthe' in Passus VIII, as Piers' directions, 'wher that Treuthe wonyeth' (197) have the rubric, *'ALTA UIA AD FIDELITATEM ...'* (203a). See Arthur 87–9, 103–5. Harwood notes that Trajan had faith and was ' *"super pauca fidelis"* and it is to the *"fidelibus"* that eternal life is given' ('Clergye' 288).

and of *'per fidem'* in the gloss would emphasize 'bileue.' God is giving eternal life to those with faith; he is with them in the heart through faith, as he is said to be in Eph. iii. 17. Traditionally, those who profess faith in Christ and make up the church define themselves as 'the people of God' (I Peter 2: 9–10) and 'the faithful,' i.e., *'suis,' 'fidelibus.'*

However, the words also bear a second interpretation because of the heavy emphasis throughout the passage on 'truþe' as 'fidelity.' In this reading, God gives eternal life to those who are faithful, i.e., true; he is with them in the heart through faithfulness, both through his faithfulness to them as 'trewe god' and their faithfulness ('trewe truþe') to their 'lawe' and his (287–88). And those who are 'trewe' (*'fidelibus'*) are his own, *'suis,'* just as those with faith are. The word *'suis,'* 'his very own,' parallels Christ's words in XVIII when he says to Sathan, 'Myne thei ben, and of me ... my kynde' (329, 398); in both passages, to belong to him, to be his, is the basis of salvation.

Both readings of *'fidelibus'* and *'fidem'* are linguistically possible. Tradition demands the first; the context demands that the second be added to it. And the pun which results from the double meaning of *'fidem'* and *'fidelibus'* increases the probability of a hidden pun on 'truþe' throughout this passage (287–294). True 'truþe' is faithfulness which, perhaps unknown to itself, contains faith within it (Schmidt, 'A Covenant' 153).[24]

Thus, in a set of overlapping puns whose variety of possible meanings makes them as difficult as a puzzle, Imaginative suggests what was already asserted in the puns of XI: that even though the 'trewe' may be 'withouten cristendom' as they walk through the valley of the shadow of death, *'in medio vmbre mortis,'* they are, without knowing it, God's own, his people, his kin. They share his life, which is grace. Their virtues – 'trewe truþe' – are the external evidence of this kinship and of the gift they carry within them. The obscurity of language perhaps suggests the difficulty of the theological problem of grace and works which preoccupied many 14th-century thinkers, and the many possible interpretations of these lines suggest the variety of points of view from which theologians needed to look at the question if they hoped to reach a valid conclusion. Yet the fact that puns enable one to see both 'virtue' and 'God' as causing salvation calls into question the question itself (O'Driscoll 28), showing (once one

[24] Wittig, *'Piers'* 279; Schmidt ed. 339, n. 292. 'Apparently, grace is given to such ... as Trajan who are filled with love and justice' (Longo 299). In his discussion of B. XV.381ff., Russell raises the same question that arises here: 'in what sense, we may ask, do these unbaptized have a faith that ... may produce salvation?' (110). On implicit faith in 'pagans' see *Summa Theologica* IIa IIae 1. 7 and 2. 7 ad 3; also Ia IIae 89. 6 and *'De Veritate'* (*Quaestiones Disputatae*) 14.10, 28.3. For other citations, see note 18 above, and Whately's notes (*'Piers'* 31–37).

sees the pun) that both 'solutions' *together* are true, and not in conflict.[25] This passage turns on what might therefore be called 'existential' or 'experiential' puns, since 'truþe' as used in 287 and *'fidelis'* (as *'fidelibus'* 293) denote referents which *as concepts* are separate, with separate names, but which existentially – in human experience – are related, even inextricable (Schmidt, 'A Covenant' 153). Like Holy Church's puns, these puns are revelations of unexpected treasure within 'truþe.'

In Passus XI, after the first Trajan episode, another aspect of unexpected treasure is revealed gradually:

> [For] oure Ioye and oure [Iuel], Iesu crist of heuene,
> In a pouere mannes apparaille pursueþ vs euere, (185–186)

In the many manuscripts which read 'For oure Ioye and oure hele' in line 185,[26] the first phrase is a pun, being both an adverbial prepositional phrase which gives the motive for the incarnation (for our joy and healing) and a compound subject in apposition with 'Iesu crist' (our joy and our salvation) (*MED* 'hele' 1 (b), 3). Kane-Donaldson's choice of 'Iuel' over 'hele' introduces wealth – the image of treasure – into this passage about poverty, echoing Holy Church's words about truth as treasure and linking the richness of heaven with its joy. The first few words are still temporarily ambiguous; until one comes to 'Iuel' it seems that 'oure Ioye' is being given as a motive, and this enriches further the connotations of the noun phrase 'oure Ioye': he is our joy and he came for our joy. 'Iuel' is also a common metaphor meaning 'beloved person' (*MED* 2 c). The pairing of 'Ioye' and 'Iuel' involves a lovely play with etymology, as 'Ioye' is Middle English for the Old French *'joie, joye,'* joy or jewel (*OED* 'joy').[27] Remarkably, this Joy who is a Jewel, 'Iesu crist of heuene,' is *'oure* Ioye and

---

[25] Thomas Merton wrote of the same question in our century: 'Once the question of grace and free will is reduced to a juridical matter . . . we are inevitably tempted to act as if everything that was given to free will was taken from grace, and everything conceded to grace was withdrawn from our own liberty. . . . Should such a division even be made at all? [It] . . . makes it almost impossible for me to grasp the paradox which is the only possible answer: that *everything is mine* precisely because *everything is His'* (36–37). See O'Driscoll 28. The conclusion to Whately's excellent explications seems to me to introduce the same illusory dichotomy in other forms, i.e., between the 'ethical' and 'sacramental' ('*Piers*' 11) and between 'the mediation of the Church' and 'works and love' ('Uses' 53). But the puns of this passage open a vision of fidelity and faith, works and grace as indissoluble gifts.

[26] K-D 448, n. 185. Skeat gives 'hele.' Schmidt gives 'juele' 124.

[27] Louise Mendillo notes also that 'Middle English *juel* comes to us from Old French *joiel* which meant both "jewel" and *jeu*' 'Word Play' 274. Cf. also Dembowski's discussion of *joie* as a 'polyvalent . . . term' in OF courtly lyrics (772), and Hatzfeld's treatment of English parallels to OF *joie* as 'joyful song' in the vocabulary of mystical writing. On Jesus as joy, see also Schmidt, 'Inner' 32; in *Clerkly* he notes kinds of 'ambiguity at the syntactic-rhythmical plane [that] can mirror a semantic ambiguity' (45), like that in line 185.

oure Iewel' as well as God's; the repeated 'oure' locates heavenly wealth and joy within humankind, even in its poverty. In the next line (186), the word 'pouere' in the phrase 'in a pouere mannes apparaille' may modify either 'mannes' or 'apparaille' or both, creating both a pun and a metaphor. Thus besides the literal reading, 'in the clothing of a pauper,' the line has the sense 'in poor–i.e., human–apparel,' and since metaphorically the most basic human apparel is flesh, it also means 'in human flesh.'

Word play then develops some of the implications of the incarnation for human kinship:

> For alle are we cristes creatures and of his cofres riche,
> And breþeren as of oo blood, as well beggeres as Erles.
> For [at] Caluarie of cristes blood cristendom gan sprynge,
> And blody breþeren we bicome þere of o body ywonne,
> As *quasi modo geniti* gentil men echone,
> No beggere ne boye amonges vs but if it synne made.   (199–204)

Ambiguous syntax in the last phrase of 198, 'and of his cofres riche,' suggests that everyone is rich and everyone is part of Christ's rich treasure.[28] 'Blody breþeren' (201) means both 'blood brothers' (*MED* 'blodi' adj. 4) and 'brethren through Christ's blood,' (Schmidt ed. 125), the pun expressing both fact and cause. Schmidt points out that in line 201, 'of o body ywonne,' means both 'redeemed by one body' and 'delivered/won from one body' (125). There seems also to be a third meaning – 'won out of one body' in the sense of 'born from one body.' This is suggested by the Latin phrase from 1 Peter 2, '*quasi modo geniti*,' 'As newborn babes, [desire the rational milk without guile]' familiar from the liturgy of the first Sunday after Easter, 'Quasimodo Sunday' (Attwater 416). By quoting this phrase, Langland introduces the idea of birth to a new life and a new 'kynde' or gentility for all people, who are 'of o body ywonne.'[29] Yet at the same time, there 'is noon wiþoute defaute' (215).

This paradox is explored a few lines later by the use of three words with the suffix '-lich':

> So bi hise werkes þei wisten þat he was Iesus,
> Ac by cloþyng þei knewe hym noȝt, [so caitifliche he yede].
> And al was ensample, [sooþliche], to vs synfulle here
> That we sholde be lowe and loueliche, [and lele ech man to oþer]
>   (238–241)

Jesus went about 'caitifliche,' a word which suggests not only misery but

---

[28] I am grateful to Professor Muscatine for this suggestion.
[29] See also XI.121 for an image of Jesus as mother. Many medieval writers speak of Jesus as mother, e.g., Anselm, Bernard, Julian of Norwich (Long Text, ch. 59, rev. 14, esp. 38–44). See Bynum, esp. 110–169, for bibliography and discussion. For word play on 'commune' (217–18) see Schmidt, '*Lele*.'

also criminality (*MED* 'caitif'); it has several possible meanings: 'wretch-edly, like a captive, like a wicked man' – and therefore like 'vs synful here' (240), i.e., like a human. 'Loueliche' (239) means 'lovely' and suggests 'like Love.' 'Sooþliche' (240) means 'truly' but also suggests 'like truth': all was an example that reveals the true nature of truth. Ambiguities in the last two lines of this passage continue to develop this paradox:

> Many tyme god haþ ben met among nedy peple,
> Ther neuere segge hym seiȝ in secte of þe riche. (244–245)

In the first line, 'nedy' in 'nedy peple' may be either restrictive or non-restrictive. As restrictive, it describes people who are poor, the opposite of 'þe riche' in 245 (*MED* 'riche' a. 7). As non-restrictive, it describes all people, and notes that all people are needy, so that the double meaning is like that in line 186, 'pouere mannes apparaille.' The phrase 'in secte of þe riche' can also have two meanings, with a pun on both 'secte' (Skeat II: 212) and 'riche': 'in the clothing of the kingdom' and 'in the clothing/ retinue/ sect of the rich.' So the two lines mean that God has more often been met among the very poor than among the very rich, and also that God has been met among humans in their poor flesh, whereas no living person has seen him in his divinity, the dress of his kingdom.

These themes are crystallized in the famous 'walnut simile,' 'the climac-tic figurative analysis of a picture which has haunted the preceding hundred-odd lines' (Kaske, 'Walnut' 653):

> As on a walnote wiþoute is a bitter barke,
> And after þat bitter bark, be þe shelle aweye,
> Is a kernel of confort kynde to restore.
> So after pouerte or penaunce paciently ytake:
> Makeþ a man to haue mynde in god and a gret wille
> To wepe and to wel bidde, wherof wexeþ Mercy
> Of which crist is a kernell to conforte þe soule. (260–266)

The simile is brief and, except for some difficult syntax, rather clear, and it is what it says: it has a kernel rich in meaning. As Kaske explains: 'Through its significance as the sweetness of internal devotion which consoles the just and patient, the *nucleus* is made to suggest also the sweetness of the indwelling Christ; while its related significance as the sweetness that follows tribulation suggests also the sweetness of the heavenly reward in Christ. This unifying principle in the figure also identifies the earlier

> ... kirnelle of conforte. kynde to restore (253)

as a probable allusion to the restoration of fallen human nature through Christ.' ('Walnut' 653)

'Kynde,' in the phrase 'Kynde to restore' which Kaske quotes (262), may be a triple pun, meaning not only human nature, but all of nature, and meaning also the word 'kynde.' That is, the word, stripped of the denotation 'God/*natura naturans*' which it acquired in IX, is diminished in meaning, just as nature and human nature in reality are diminished by sin. In the triple pun, Christ, who as God has been identified with Kynde, will restore 'Kynde' to 'kynde,' restoring the word to its fullest meaning, as he restores human 'kynde' by uniting it with God in his own person, and as he restores all of 'kynde' through the redemption. This pun on 'kynde' sharpens awareness of the 'restoration' of the word 'confort' also in this passage. In the Land of Longing, the shell of the verb 'to confort' describes the activity of Concupiscence of Eyes, with only a surface meaning: 'Coueitise of eiȝes conforted me anoon after' (XI.46). But here the kernel, the etymological meaning of 'confort,' 'strength,' is able to come to life and become operative, 'a kernel of confort kynde to restore.'

After the walnut simile, the speaker continues to 'dispute' with Will (320), until the personification Kynde comes into the poem for the second time (326), this time as a teacher of love and of new life 'þoruȝ þe wondres of þis world' (322). The name 'kynde' is restored to the fullness of meaning it had in Passus IX; this is made quite clear by a play based on ambiguous syntax, sometimes called *apo koinou*. Will is taken out to the mountain, 'Thorugh ech a creature kynde my creatour to louye.' (326) 'Kynde' can be in apposition with either 'ech a creature' in the sense of 'all creatures' or with 'my creatour' (Martin, *Field* 94–95).[30] The pun on 'kynde' implies what the action itself means: Will is to love 'Kynde' his 'creatour' in 'kynde,' 'ech a creature.'

Yet when Will gets into his argument with Reason, which follows, the word 'kynde' takes on a pejorative meaning. Will is shamed by Reason's statement that because Will is human, he will sometimes fall since he will be bound to 'folwen his kynde' (403), i.e., follow his fallen nature, not his creator. This pejorative use of 'kynde' clarifies further the use of the word in the walnut simile, for the 'kynde' which needs restoration and comfort is this 'kynde' which causes Will 'to ben ashamed.' The irony of this ambivalent repetition is central to the action, since Will, awakening from a vision of Kynde that might have been expected to give him a 'kynde knowyng,' feels not wisdom but a 'wo' (406) like that he felt at the beginning of the passus, four hundred lines earlier (4).

One reason for his 'wo' is that Reason berates him and causes him to feel shame. In doing so, Reason repeats and plays upon forms of the verb 'suffre' nine times in three languages, within just eleven lines (377–386).

---

[30] Skeat gives 'Thorugh ech a creature and Kynde – my creatoure to louye' (XI.317). 'Kynde' may be a pun in this version, also, summing up 'ech a creature' in 'nature,' and meaning also 'my creatoure'; he is still to love his creator (Kynde) through 'ech creature and kynde.' 'Kynde' can also mean 'type': hence, 'through each creature, through each type of creature, through the Creator.' See White, 'Langland's' 244–247.

At least two of these uses are puns: 'Who suffreþ moore þan god?' (380), and 'Ac he suffreþ for som mannes goode' (382). The primary meaning of 'suffreþ' is 'waits' or 'tolerates,' so that the first line means, 'Who tolerates more than God? Who is more patient?' and the second, 'He waits for the good of someone.' The references earlier in the passus to 'cristes blood' (201) and the emphasis upon Jesus' presence in 'his pouere apparaill and pilgrymes wedes' (236) suggest another interpretation as well: who suffers, endures pain and shame, more than God? He suffers for someone's (everyone's) good (P. Martin, *Field* 93; Kirk, 'Who' 101).

The general effect of Reason's diatribe is negative, stressing the inevitable follies and weaknesses of humanity and leading to a discussion with Imaginative on the usefulness of shame and need. The Reason episode and the inner dream end (at 406) thirty lines before the end of Passus XI, so the long passus ends raggedly, its narrative structure in tension with passus structure. The raggedness fits the style of the passus as a whole, even though its fragmentary episodes, tense, ironic, and uncomfortable, enfold central passages which are a 'kernel of confort.'

As Will awakens (406), he sees Imaginative looking at him. After brusquely comparing Will to 'a dronken daffe' (427) and implying a hope that Will may be chastened and corrected by the shame he is feeling (434), Imaginative betrays some humor by playing on sound as he describes the 'dronken daffe' getting out of a 'dyk':

> And shame shrapeþ hise cloþes and hise shynes wassheþ,
> Thanne woot þe dronken [wye] wherfore he is to blame.'   (433–434)

'Shynes' means 'shins' and is a metaphor for 'sins.' Some humor lies in the fact that a 'dronken wye' might pronounce 'sins' in just the way Imaginative does.[31] Surprisingly, Will takes no offence:

> Why ye wisse me þus', quod I, 'was for I rebuked Reson.'
> 'Certes', quod he, 'þat is sooþ.'   (438–439)

So off they go companionably.

The action of Passus XI seems to go in many directions, yet images of misery and fleeting glimpses of true and false comfort succeed one another so frequently that they do form a theme. Is there any pattern in the relationship of these images to one another? It seems to me that the answer is yes and no: not a stable nor a universal pattern, but a frequent and shifting

---

[31] I have found no parallel imitation of drunken speech, but Chaucer's characters allude to speech changes: 'I am dronke; I knowe it by my soun' (*CT* I.3138) and 'And thurgh thy dronke nose semeth the soun / As though thou seydest ay "Sampsoun, Sampsoun"' (VI.553–4). R. H. Robbins entitles lyric #117, characterized by apparently meaningless repetition, 'Monologue of a Drunkard' (106; see note, 265).

one, in which the images of comfort and treasure are usually discovered 'wiþInne' something or someone. Some are found where they might be expected, as a child finds a mother's milk within her breast (121), but more often in this passus, comfort or treasure is found within an unlikely person or condition: Trajan's 'truþe' in 'an vncristene creature,' 'confort' inside the walnut with its 'bitter barke,' 'oure Ioye and oure Iuel ... In a pouere mannes apparaille' (185–186). The marvels of nature (their wonder is insisted upon at 347, 350, 351, 360, 364, 367, 374) are external and visible, yet there is also a sense of even greater hidden wonder, since Will is invited to love his creator 'Thorugh ech a creature' (326). This theme is related to and accompanied by ordinary reversals of appearance and reality, so the 'conforte' and 'loue' of the Land of Longing are illusory, and later in the passus, the 'pouere' are also 'riche' (198–199) and treasured. These reversals, disappointments and discoveries lead to the extremes of surprise, wonder and shame which Will feels in the passus.

Words, too, occasion surprise. In the Land of Longing, the poet demonstrates how deceiving words like 'conforte' and 'loue' can be when they retain only a surface meaning. In the Trajan passage in XII, Imaginative plays with words as Holy Church does in Passus I, though in a more complicated way, until they give a glimpse of the reality and inner harmony of the causes which disputants perceive as contradictory. Imaginative's passage, like Passus I, is amazing in the coherence of insights which the combination of multiple readings affords, even though putting them together is difficult; Passus XI.185–266 is easier to read and offers comparable surprises through word play.

The effect of word play is certainly the familiar sense of shifting, which causes a sudden change in perspective. The shift may be semantic, or syntactic, or literally a shift in point of view, as when 'we' are suddenly seen to be the 'mede' of truth (XII.292) and the treasure in Christ's coffers (XI.199). In Passus XI, such shifts seem to create not so much a tone of insecurity as a sense of almost endless possibilities.[32] They are sometimes ironic, but their overall effect seems to me to be wonder.

It will be the work of Passus XIII–XIV to explore further the moral poverty of humankind and to deepen the realization of sin as the universal human lot. Sin, seen falsely as 'confort' in the Land of Longing, will be fully realized as 'care' by the end of Passus XIV, when Haukyn sobs, 'So hard it is

---

[32] Salter sees such sudden changes as the revelation of 'a universe blessed by metamorphoses' (*Fourteenth* 107). Muscatine describes Langland's penchant for 'the sharp transition ... the line or half line that suddenly turns the mood or thought around ...' (*Poetry* 104, 102). Cf. Wells 124. Murtaugh speaks of 'explosions of meaning' (8), and Chamberlin explores reasons for the reader's feeling of 'discontinuity ... [finding the] text choppy.'

... to lyue and to do synne' (325). As Kirk says, this image of 'Hawkin weeping in his dirty coat' is the master image of human 'finiteness' (*Dream* 158, 155). Even more than destitution, ignorance, pain, or lack of baptism, sin is poverty. 'Wit and wisdom ... murþe and manhod' (XII.295, 297) and above all, 'truþe' (293) in all its senses, are 'tresor' (295). In the punning line, 'Conforte þi carefulle, crist, in þi riche' (XIV.179), the word 'carefulle' will gather up all the poverty explored in Dowel (IX–XIV), material, intellectual, and spiritual, in the prayer of Patience. The juxtaposition of 'carefulle' with 'riche,' which means 'kingdom' but inevitably suggests 'riches,' brings the reader back again to the figures where Christ is within the bitter, hard walnut as he is within nature, at the center of Trajan's 'trewe truþe,' and somewhere within Haukyn's tears. For if, as Haukyn says, 'Synne seweþ vs euere,' and if as Will found, 'pouerte pursued me and putte me lowe,' it has also been made clear that 'Iesu crist of heuene, / In a pouere mannes apparaille pursueþ vs euere,' and is to be found in every 'tresor' as its cause, and within every kind of poverty as 'a kernel of confort kynde to restore.'[33] Words not only say this; they illustrate it, by their poverty in the Land of Longing and by their layers of meaning in other places, which gradually reveal truth within truth.

Yet simply to say (as I believe) that the walnut is an emblem[34] of the passus, the Vita, and perhaps the poem, its surprising 'confort' buried 'wiþInne' the poem near its center, or to point out the promise of 'a hope hangyng þerinne,' is also to oversimplify and thus belie the 'feel' of the poem. We meet 'wo' and 'confort' concurrently in Passus XI, as elsewhere in the poem; this helps to cause what Priscilla Martin calls 'conflict between "optimism' and ''pessimism', between the argument and the atmosphere of *Piers*' (*Field* 32). In Passus XI an atmosphere of 'wo' is created not only by insistence on poverty and sin, but also by the incidental figures of 'a commune womman' (217), 'the carefulle ... the croked' (192), and 'a goky' (307), and by the hapless turmoil of the dreamer who begins the passus in 'wo and wraþe' (4) and ends it saying ruefully, 'Ther smyt no

---

[33] This intense awareness of the immanence of God illustrates Langland's celebration of what Lawton calls 'the possibility, and the power, of direct access to the "supernatural",' which, as he suggests, may be a particular characteristic of 'Christian lay allegory.' He seems, however, to see this awareness as subversive of historical Christianity with its 'scheme of ecclesiastically mediated sacrifice.' (25) This dichotomy, too, seems to me to be foreign to Langland, who shows the 'direct access to the supernatural,' I think, as a complement and effect of historical institutional Christianity, though not limited to it. We can see this complementarity in the figures of Holy Church and Piers, and in such passages as I.152–174, XVIII, XIX.3.

[34] I am using the term 'emblem' as defined by Hanning: 'a symbolic artifact ... within a narrative that transcends its role as an element of the fiction ... and becomes a powerful comment on the artistic enterprise of its creator' (1).

þyng so smerte, ne smelleþ so foule / As shame' (436–437). This atmosphere is not wholly dispersed by the 'confort' which puns offer.

The form of the pun itself gives us a model for approaching this apparent discrepancy. Puns by their very nature keep two thoughts or feelings quite different from one another in a state of tension, inviting the reader to accept both extremes rather than to choose between them. The pun seems to be on a small scale what the symbolic shifts of Piers' identity and the shifts of time and level of consciousness are on a large scale: a way of being 'trewe' to experiences – feelings, thoughts, beliefs, sensory realities – which seem logically discrete and divergent but which in fact coexist, as 'wo' and 'confort' coexist in this passus.

Chapter Five

Passus XVIII

Passus XVIII is in every sense the climax of *Piers Plowman*; it is also, as Morton Bloomfield argues, 'in a profound sense ... the true end of the poem ... [since within it] the final victory ... is foreshadowed' (*Apocalypse* 125–126). Here, language is able 'to wynne ... truþe' by its freedom and fullness. For in style as well as content, Passus XVIII is about liberation. Its narrative tells of the redemption of the world through the confrontation of Death by Life and demonstrates the freeing of the mind from misconception by a process of correction and conversion. Its structure exemplifies freedom as a mean between rigidity and formlessness. Its speeches explain the freedom of the new law and the liberation of people from sin and death, and in both rhetoric and word play they exemplify a contrast between rigidity and freedom: the rigidity of falseness and literalism,[1] the freedom of wit and truth.

The structure of the passus is uncharacteristically symmetrical, with two short passages on each side of three central scenes. These central scenes, the joust (10–109), the debate of the four daughters of God (110–260),[2] and the harrowing of hell (261–406), are framed by a scene at the very beginning and a scene at the end of the passus about Will's waking life (1–6, 425–431) and, within that frame, by a pair of passages about music as Will goes to sleep and awakens (7–9, 407–425). In both these pairs of framing scenes, the second fulfils the first, showing that the events which

---

[1] By 'literalism,' I mean not the proper understanding of a literal text, but reading which ignores figurative or ambiguous meanings and connotation. In the same sense, I think, Martin notes that 'Throughout the poem he [Langland] pours scorn on literalism of belief' (*Field* 115. Cf. Quilligan, 'Langland's,' 106–7; Robertson and Huppé 94; Lawlor, *Piers* 168, 274; Burrow, 'Words' 114; Schleusener 43–48; and Mary Carruthers' important discussion of false and redeemed language in *Search*).

[2] On the 'Four Daughters of God' (a conception based, as Skeat pointed out, on ps. 84: 11 (Vul.), see Skeat II: 253–254 and Hope Traver; see also Bertz 322, Baldwin 64–65, and Schleusener 43–48. See Norton-Smith (83) for a different analysis of the structure of this passus.

have come between have caused a change. That is, as the passus begins, a weary, anxious Will attempts vainly to reach the Samaritan and finally 'leans toward Lent' and sleeps until Palm Sunday; at the end of the passus, a marvelling, purposeful Will awakens and worships at Easter. He has changed from a miserable, frustrated 'recchelees renk' (2) to a hopeful, effective leader of his family (426). The two musical passages move from the singing of the weak on Palm Sunday to the robust bell-ringing of 'men' on Easter, together with the harping and singing of angels. This is parallel structure but it is not evenly balanced; the second part is 'better' than the first. The structure itself tends towards change and resolution as the action moves from the passion to the resurrection. Each of the three central scenes, too, is basically symmetrical in structure, but each has within it some alteration of pattern that throws the balance off by pulling to the 'right,' toward the end, toward change and resolution, and this slight imbalance keeps the pattern from rigidity.

Not only structure, but also language demonstrates a movement toward freedom, contrasting rigid literalism with 'fulfilled' language. I take the term 'fulfilled' from a Latin pun used in Christ's speech: *Non veni soluere legem sed adimplere* (349a). Metaphorically, as it is usually translated, *'adimplere'* means 'fulfill, perform,' and thus the statement means 'I have come not to destroy the law but to fulfill it.' But literally, *'adimplere'* means 'fill full,' and the effect of the poetry of Christ and some of the other speakers in the passus is to fill language – even the language of law – full of so much meaning that it becomes a revelation.[3] Those who tell the truth in the passus speak in a free, playful, witty way which often surprises; those who make errors usually do so because of too restricted an understanding or use of words. This contrast is most vivid and most certainly deliberate in the debate of the four daughters and in Christ's rebuttal of Lucifer, where the freeing effect of word play is given definitive value. But there are also other examples of language restricted unreasonably in errors, lies, half-truths, and mockery.

As the passus begins, Will is

> Wolleward and weetshoed ...
> As a recchelees renk þat [reccheþ of no wo]   (1–2).

'Recchelees' means 'irresponsible' in the sense of not staying home, not wearing proper clothing, and being 'a lorel'; and echoing 'reccheþ of no

---

[3] Judith Anderson speaks of 'the verbal complexity which is inseparable from imaginative fullness in these Passus [XV–XX]' (129). Note also Shoaf's statement about Chaucer and Dante: 'suspicious of metaphor, they discovered in metaphor nevertheless liberation from the fear of definition and category and nomination' (*Dante* 13).

wo,' it also suggests that Will is unaware even of discomfort because driven by the need to find the Samaritan who looks like Piers. This is ironic, since in other contexts, 'recchelees' can mean 'carefree' (Donaldson, *Piers* 171); Will is full of a care so profound that it frees him from ordinary compulsions and conventions.

There is a more obvious play on words at 17, as Will begins to sleep:

> Olde Iewes of Ierusalem for ioye þei songen,
> *Benedictus qui venit in nomine domini.* (17–17a)

'Olde Iewes' means 'ancient Jews, Jews long ago,' but it also suggests 'elderly Jews,' since it echoes 'olde folk' in line 8: 'And how Osanna by Organye olde folk songen.' Both the 'olde folk' and the 'Olde Iewes' are singing the *'Sanctus'* of Will's Palm Sunday Mass, and the repetition of 'olde' provides a lovely linking echo which suggests the telescoping of centuries in Will's dream-liturgical experience. The ancient Jews of Jerusalem sing *'Benedictus'* 'for ioye,' i.e., out of their joy; but in the light of Passus XI, 'for ioye' may also suggest that as Christ enters the city, they are singing for him, 'oure Ioye and oure Iuel, Iesu crist of heuene' (XI.185). The line has added effectiveness from the possibility of both meanings at once: their song is sung as an expression of their joy and for him who is their joy.

As Christ rides in, Faith explains to Will:

> 'This Iesus of his gentries wol Iuste in Piers armes,
> In his helm and in his haubergeon, *humana natura;*
> That crist be noȝt yknowe here for *consummatus deus*
> In Piers paltok þe Plowman þis prikiere shal ryde,
> For no dynt shal hym dere as *in deitate patris.*' (22–26)

As has been pointed out, the overriding pun throughout the first scene is 'the figure of Christ's fulfilment of Law as a "joust" [which] links naturally with the "justice" thus satisfied' (Lawlor, *Piers* 272; cf. Huppé 178).[4] As Quilligan notes, 'Puns can be dangerous, as in Lady Meed's abuse of language; but puns can also provide the rationale for a subtly exfoliating pattern which extends over an immense stretch of narrative. The pun on "just," in fact, helps to correct the reader's tendency to misread. ... Christ ... has redeemed ... the language of the poem' (*Language* 79). Other puns create particular effects within this pattern. For example, the phrase 'of his gentries' in line 22 means 'of his nobility, in his nobility' (Schmidt ed. 220), modifying 'wol Iuste' and explaining how and why he will fight. This meaning continues the characterization of Jesus as a noble and gracious

---

[4] Both Baldwin and Quilligan ('Langland's') explain the joust and the debate in legal terms, in the framework of 'justice.' Baldwin sees them as 'duels, legal ordeals' (64).

knight (Bennett, *Poetry* 101; Lawlor, *Piers* 164). But 'gentries' is also fairly close in sound to French *'genitrice'* and Latin *'genetricis'* ('of [his] mother') and, in this passage so laced with Latin, it may be a play on one or the other, balancing the reference to the Father (*'in deitate patris'*). In this reading, the phrase would modify 'Piers armes,' giving the source (his mother) from whom Jesus obtained his vulnerability, i.e., his 'armes,' *'humana natura.'*

Will misunderstands the nature of the joust, perhaps through too narrow an understanding of the Good Friday liturgy.[5] The fact that Will's words are intended by the poet as a mistake is made immediately clear, as Will is corrected by Faith (28):

> 'Who shal Iuste wiþ Iesus', quod I, 'Iewes or Scrybes?'
> 'Nay', quod [feiþ, 'but] þe fend and fals doom [to deye].   (27–28)

Will's error, which is so quickly corrected,[6] is followed by other errors and falsehoods, which form a pattern throughout the passus. Some examples are in speeches by the 'pelour' (41–45), the 'rybaud' (50), Lucifer (277–285) and 'the deuel' (300–303). The 'rybaud,' ignoring the normal implications of the respectful title 'rabbi,' reverses its connotations, making a taunt of it ('Aue, raby!' 50); the 'pelour' repeats a metaphor as if it were literal, so that it becomes an accusation ('This Iesus of oure Iewes temple Iaped ... / To fordoon it on o day' 41–42), the devil tells a half-truth which implies a lie: 'I wolde haue lengþed his [Christ's] lif' (303), and Lucifer understands only part of the truth he quotes and so is beguiled by it:

> For hymself seide ...
> If Adam ete þe Appul alle sholde deye
> And dwelle wiþ vs deueles; þis þretynge [driȝten] made.   (280–282)

Those who make mistakes or tell lies are sometimes confronted immediately, as Will is, as Truth and Righteousness are later, and as Lucifer is when he is blamed by the other devils (286–294; cf. Alford, 'Literature' 944–945). Other abuses of language may be so ironic in context that they need no correction except the implicit one of Christ's victory. This is the case with the 'pelour,' the 'rybaud,' and 'the deuel.' The ironic pattern of

---

[5] I mean, for example, John 18–19, where John speaks of the particular group against Jesus as 'the Jews,' and the medieval Good Friday prayer, '*"Oremus et pro perfidis Judaeis"* ... non dicitur hic *Flectamus genua,*' made standing rather than kneeling, unlike the other prayers of the day (*Sarum Missal* 327). Obviously, John, being a Jew, did not mean that all Jews opposed Jesus, but a naive, literalist reading can give that impression. St-Jacques has shown happier influences of the liturgy on Passus XVIII–XX: 'Langland's Bells,' 'Langland's Christ-Knight,' and 'Conscience's'; see also his 'Middle English Literature and the Liturgy.'

[6] However, Quilligan points out that 'Jesus does indeed joust with scribes,' in the sense that he does battle with literalism ('Langland's' 106).

their errors suggests the possibility of interpreting two other speeches as ironic errors, those of Faith at 92–109 and Book at 257–260; they will be discussed below. Taken together, the lies, errors and sarcasm demonstrate ways in which language can be 'false'; truth in the passus, especially in Christ's speech and action, uncovers this falseness and makes freedom from it possible.

Major puns in the passion scene have been well analyzed,[7] but a few observations may be added on the Longeus episode. Having pierced Christ's side, he cries:

> 'Ayein my wille it was, lord, to wownde yow so soore.'
> He sighed and seide, "soore it me aþynkeþ!
> For þe dede þat I haue doon I do me in youre grace.
> Haue on me ruþe, riȝtful Iesu', and riȝt wiþ þat he wepte.　　(88–91)

The repetition of 'soore' in lines 88–89 emphasizes Longeus' grief; though the meanings of 'soore' are obviously somewhat different in the two uses: 'to wound you so severely ... it is a matter of painful distress to me,' still the use of the word 'soore' in both phrases suggests that he feels in himself the pain he inflicted (*OED* 'sore' adv. 1, 4b). Use of cognates in 'the dede that I haue doon' (90) emphasizes that the deed is irrevocable; yet it will be undone by an act for which the same root, 'do,' is used with another denotation, as he says, 'I do me in youre grace': 'I place myself in your grace' (*MED* 'do,' C. 21. 93 refl.). Thus 'a shift in the sense of *doon* accompanies Longeus' conversion' (Macklin Smith). A deed amends for a misdeed; a free act of repentance frees Longeus. This is dramatized through a pun on 'riȝt' in the next line. The second half of the line means 'and right then he wept,' but as Schmidt has shown (*Clerkly* 126), it can also be read, 'and justified with that, he wept,' i.e., justified either with that prayer or with that 'ruþe' (cf. *OED* 'right' II.5). The repetition of 'riȝt' suggests a movement of grace, of 'ruþe' and righteousness, from 'riȝtful Iesu' to Longeus, 'riȝt wiþ þat. ...' Christ is 'riȝtful' and therefore able to communicate righteousness, which flows to the knight, making him 'riȝt' in spite of the 'dede ... doon,' and enabling him to weep. Both meanings of 'riȝt' are operative at once in the pun, suggesting the immediacy of mercy: 'righteous, right as he spoke, he wept.'

Faith, who corrected Will for seeing the Jews as Christ's opponents, here 'gan ... felly þe false Iewes despise' (92). Faith's attitude is commonplace in

---

[7] Most recently by J. A. W. Bennett in *Poetry of the Passion* 108–109; see also Ames 125–126, Quilligan, *Language* 78, Schleusener 53–61, and Schmidt ed. 350. Baldwin (71) discusses the 'spere ... vnspered' pun of 86, as do Huppé (178), Quilligan ('Langland's' 109), and Norton-Smith (85).

medieval writings.[8] But this does not explain the gap within this poem between his tone and Christ's tone later, or Holy Church's tone in I: 'And yet wolde he hem no wo þat wrouȝte hym þat peyne' I.169. Nor does it explain the contrast between this speech and Faith's earlier speeches, i.e., his correction of Will and his initial identification of Jesus as a Jew, 'a fili dauid!' (15). Given these contradictions and the pattern of ironic errors and falsehoods in this passus, I suggest that Faith's speech is meant to be read as containing ironic error.[9]

The name 'Feiþ' can mean not only belief, but also fidelity to law or justice. As belief, Faith perhaps accurately represents the faith of Will (and some of Langland's contemporaries), but incorporates only imperfectly Lady Holy Church's loving belief as expressed in Passus I. As fidelity to justice or law, Faith suggests the English law which, as Anna Baldwin shows, prescribed just the penalties Faith mentions. Yet he does not represent the fullness of 'good feiþ' (347) which Christ will invoke as an argument against the devils for the salvation of 'al mankynde,' including the Jews (397). The name 'Feiþ' is thus being used in a restricted way, as the names 'Truþe' and 'Riȝtwisnesse' are used later in the passus. The distinction between the fullness of what a word can mean ('good feiþ' 347) and what it expresses when unnecessarily restricted ('Feiþ' 92) is another example of anti-pun; since the word is personified, the distinction between possible meanings becomes a new and subtler step in the 'game,' and it gives awareness of the possibility not only of lies or half-truths like Lucifer's, but also of errors made by superficial, relatively thoughtless reading or listening to authoritative texts: limitations, partial understandings, well-intentioned but destructive errors. The adverb 'felly' in line 92 is also a suggestive pun, since (if we are to approve Faith's words) it can mean 'angrily' and (if we are to disapprove them) it can mean 'cruelly, treacherously, sinfully' (*MED* 'felli(che, adv. 1,2).

There is no immediate correction of Faith, however, and because of his furious language, the first scene ends off-balance, in imperfect vision. Faith's ominous prediction of the Jews descending into slavery (103–109) causes Will to see them as monsters and to be afraid, and 'What for feere of

---

[8] Baldwin has shown the legal sources which explain why one who touched the body of a king with a weapon and 'cried craven' would be penalized in the way Faith describes (71). Ames explains the imagery of blindness and the spear from other medieval traditions about Jews (126).

[9] This is the first example but not the last in the passus of 'an argument... put into the mouth of one "good" abstraction only to be proved absolutely wrong' (Evans 275). If 'Truþe' can be wrong (Truth!), why not Faith? As Priscilla Jenkins [Martin] points out, 'in the course of the poem allegorical characters come to be seen as variously inadequate' ('Conscience' 127, cf. 133); see also Middleton, 'Two' 185.

þis ferly and of þe false Iewes,' he escapes to another plane of thought, descending to the twilight world of '*inferna*' toward some fuller vision and language.

The most formal contrast of inappropriately restricted and therefore erroneous language with truthful, figurative, playful language occurs, of course, in the debate of the four daughters of God. Constrained literalism, which, as Quilligan points out, makes one less sensitive to literal meaning ('Langland's 106–7), leads Truth and Righteousness into error, but Mercy and Peace achieve a marvelous fullness of knowledge through intuitive openness to the fullness of language, which is distinguished by various forms of wit.[10]

The first speech of Mercy (127–141) is mysterious, almost riddling, in its language, so much so that the literal-minded Truth judges it 'a tale of waltrot!' Not only its particulars but its whole form and tone are paradoxical. That is, her speech is serene and firm, with the structure of a cool, lucid exposition: 'it bitokneþ . . . And þat is cause . . . In menyng þat . . .' Yet within this almost scholastic framework her actual words are a series of apparent contradictions and ambiguities. She presents mystery as if it were quite clear:

> Haue no merueille', quod mercy; 'murþe it bitokneþ.
> A maiden þat highte Marie, and moder wiþouten felyng
> Of any kynnes creature, conceyued þoruȝ speche
> And grace of þe holy goost; weex greet wiþ childe;
> Wiþouten [wommene] wem into þis world broȝte hym.   (127–131)

Mercy begins with four paradoxes about Mary and the incarnation familiar from liturgical and theological writing. She may be punning in line 130, 'and weex greet with child,' on 'greet' as 'large' and 'spiritually great,' i.e., 'blessed among women.' Her language becomes more figurative as she plays on the identification of Jesus with light:

> And þat is cause of þis clips þat closeþ now þe sonne,
> In menynge þat man shal fro merknesse be drawe
> The while þis light and þis leme shal Lucifer ablende.   (135–137).

She uses the traditional pun on 'sonne' with metaphors of 'clips' and 'merknesse' and the paradox of the blinded light-bearer, Lucifer. At the

---

[10] Denise Baker points out that 'The argument of Truth, Righteousness, and Lucifer, is, of course, identical to the position expressed earlier in the *Visio's* so-called pardon: "*Qui vero mala ignem eternum*" (VII.114) . . . no pardon at all. . . .' ('The Pardons' 468). Bertz speaks of the 'myopic vision of Rightwisnesse and Truthe,' while 'Mercy and Pees can see the future' 323, 322. The pairs of sisters are also distinguished by representing 'the concept of equity as opposed to precedent' (Birnes 79), and perhaps by St Augustine's idea that God's truth demands punishment, but God's mercy demands mercy (*In Ps.* 50:11, *PL* 36: 592–3, in Donna 133).

same time she plays on 'closeþ'; the literal 'clips' closes off the sun and encloses the Son in darkness as it marks the closing of his life.

Paradoxes continue in Mercy's incantatory recital of prophecies that sound like riddles:

> For patriarkes and prophetes han preched herof ofte
> That man shal man saue þoruȝ a maydenes helpe,
> And þat was tynt þoruȝ tree, tree shal it wynne.
> And þat deeþ adown brouȝte, deeþ shal releue.' (138–141)

Her ambivalent repetitions and contrasts are familiar from many patristic and liturgical texts, such as the preface for the Mass in Holy Week:

> *Unde mors oriebatur, inde vita resurget,*
> *et qui in ligno vicerat, in ligno quoque vinceretur.*

In this pattern of word play,[11] opposite effects are associated with the same nouns. The paradox works, of course, because of the traditional ambiguity of these nouns. The 'man' who saves is Christ; the 'man' saved, all humankind (139); the 'tree' (*'ligno'*) (140) and 'deeþ' (141) of loss are those of Eden (and 'deeþ' perhaps also the antagonist of lines 29–30: 'Deeþ seiþ he shal fordo and adoun brynge / Al þat lyueþ ...'). The 'tree' (140) and 'deeþ' (141) that 'shal ... wynne' (140) and 'releue' (141) are those of Calvary.

Though her first line is 'Haue no merueille ... murþe it bitokneþ' (127), Mercy's speech is a 'merueille,' a cause of wonder, and when she bids Truth, 'Haue no merueille,' her assurance has some 'murþe' in its irony. Unfortunately, Truth has little sense of either 'merueille' or 'murþe,' and so the mysterious, puzzling character of her sister's speech, ringing though it is with warmth and hopefulness, seems to her the sheerest nonsense.

Truth's tone is petulant as she replies, 'It is trufle þat þow tellest; I, truþe, woot the soþe' (147). The only hint of word play in any of her lines, her use of 'truþe ... soþe' here, is probably unintentional on her part. Her speech is forthright and exasperated, a combination of declarative pronouncements and exclamatory objections to Mercy's words. Truth's name means 'faithfulness,' a reference to God's faithfulness to his promises and perhaps her own human faithfulness to his words as she understands them. Quite rightly, then, her first argument against Mercy is based on Scripture, an apparently plain statement from *Job*, which gives her an absolute certainty ('soþe') which she cannot find in Mercy's liturgical texts ('sawes'):

---

[11] *'Praefatio ... Dominica in Ramis Palmarum, et in Feriis usque ad diem Parasceves,'* (*Missale ad usum ... Herfordensis* 121–122); *'Praefatio dicitur in utroque festo Sanctae Crucis,'* (*Sarum Missal* 606). The play on words is called *permutatio*, as Salter and Pearsall point out (ed. 160). Pearsall notes similar uses in liturgical hymns (ed. 325).

> It is trufle þat þow tellest; I, truþe, woot þe soþe,
> For þat is ones in helle out comeþ [it] neuere.
> Iob þe [parfit] patriark repreueþ þi sawes:
> *Quia in inferno nulla est redempcio.'*   (147–149)

Truth takes the text from *Job* quite literally; ambiguities hidden in the text escape her. The medieval theologians recognized an ambiguity in the word *'infernus'* which might mean either 'hell,' from which there is no escape, or 'lower regions' like the *'inferna'* where the four daughters are standing, from which there is escape.[12] But unaware of the ambiguity, Truth thinks her authority is clear and solid. The human suffering implied in her reading fails to trouble her; her attention is on her sister's logic or illogic, and on what seems to her an attack on scripture. People *in inferno* are not her responsibility, and she speaks of them as if they were unreal or unimportant. Her juxtaposition of irritated slang with glib scriptural quotation creates a sense of unreality and detachment even from pain:

> That þow tellest', quod Truþe, 'is but a tale of waltrot!
> For Adam and Eue and Abraham wiþ oþere
> Patriarkes and prophetes þat in peyne liggen,
> Leue þow neuere þat yon light hem alofte brynge
> Ne haue hem out of helle; hold þi tonge, mercy!   (142–145)

Truth's language is simple and literal. Even her reference to 'yon light' (145) seems purely literal; she has no idea that the light is a person.

In her reply to Truth, Mercy continues to be serene: she speaks 'ful myldely,' yet she takes the plight of those in *'inferno'* personally – 'I hope þei shul be saued' (151). This time she argues 'Thoruȝ experience,' by which she seems to mean folk experience as preserved in hymns, proverbs, and traditional folk remedies. These lead her to paradoxical conclusions about the workings of God; she is absolutely committed to these conclusions ('I dar my lif legge'):

> 'Thoruȝ experience', quod [heo], 'I hope þei shul be saued;
> For venym fordooþ venym, [þer fecche I euydence
> That Adam and Eue haue shul bote].
> For of alle venymes foulest is þe scorpion;
> May no medicyne [amende] þe place þer he styngeþ
> Til he be deed and do þerto; þe yuel he destruyeþ,
> The first venymouste, þoruȝ [vertu] of hymselue.
> So shal þis deeþ fordo, I dar my lif legge,
> Al þat deeþ dide first þoruȝ þe deueles entisyng.   (151–159)

12 In the Mass for the Dead, the offertory prayer says, *'libera animas omnium fidelium defunctorum de manu inferni'* (*Sarum Missal* 867). It goes on to speak of *'Tartarus,'* evidence that one continuing use of the word *'inferni'* was the classical one. *'Inferna'* as a substantive, in Tacitus, for example, means 'the infernal regions' (Anthon). Skeat gives a patristic statement illustrating a similar use of *'inferna'* II: 261. The double meaning of 'helle' causes Sattan to make the same mistake in the York 'Harrowing of Hell' (stanzas 24–25, in Sisam 180–181).

Suitably, she expresses folk experience in language modeled on the conventional paradoxical public language of liturgy and the Fathers, with ambivalent repetitions of 'venym' (154–157) and 'deeþ' (158–159) which work like her earlier plays on 'man,' 'tree,' and 'deeþ' (138–140). All such verbal play expresses Mercy's sense of wonder and mystery.

As Righteousness and Peace approach, Truth and Mercy react characteristically. Instead of meeting Mercy's argument from experience on its own ground, Truth turns to a higher authority: 'Rightwisnesse ... woot moore þan we.'(165–166) While Mercy gravely accepts the seniority of Righteousness: 'That is sooþ,' this phrase, by which she accedes to factual truth, may be slightly ironic as it evokes also the absolute truth (the normal meaning of 'sooþ')[13] which contains and surpasses such facts:

> 'That is sooþ', seide Mercy, 'and I se here by Sowþe
> Where pees comeþ pleyinge in pacience yclopþed.   (167–168)

The dialogue of Peace and Righteousness, like that of Mercy and Truth, contrasts two attitudes, two ways of reading, thinking, and speaking. The participles applied to the two sisters seem related to their styles. Righteousness comes 'rennynge' (165); like Truth's speech, hers is direct, quick, impersonal, explosive, and literal in its reading of Scripture and its conclusions. Except for a metaphorical proverb (201) and a possible pun on her sister's name (199), her speech is entirely literal, as is her severe interpretation of *Genesis* (191–202). Through lack of imagination, her Biblical interpretation is as mistaken as Truth's, assuming that God's 'doom' (191) has to be eternal, though 'after' (193) need not be interpreted to mean 'forever':

> [At] þe bigynn[yng god] gaf þe doom hymselue
> That Adam and Eue and alle þat hem suwede
> Sholden deye downrighte and dwelle in pyne after   (191–193)

When Peace comes, she is not running, but 'pleyinge' (168). Consistently 'pleyinge' with language, she speaks in metaphors, understanding and interpreting the metaphorical meaning of the darkness which surrounds them and the light which they see approaching – 'merknesse of synne,' (177), 'Ioye bigynneþ dawe' (181). Perhaps in 'Ioye bigynneþ dawe' she also plays on the idea of Christ 'oure Ioye' as son/sun, who will rise from the dead. Like Mercy, who said 'murþe it bitokneþ' (127), Peace understands the coming of Christ as a matter for rejoicing: Adam, Eve, and Moses 'shul synge' and 'I shal daunce þerto,' (179,180), so she is already 'pleyinge.' Like Mercy, she is personally, lovingly involved in what she says. She understands the psalms to be letters from love (183–188):

---

[13] 'immer ist *sooth* das Wort für diese "absolute" Wahrheit,' Heraucourt 78. See also Ch. II, n. 18, above.

For Iesus Iustede wel Ioye bigynneþ dawe:
Ad vesperum demorabitur fletus & ad matutinum leticia.
Loue þat is my lemman swiche lettres me sente
That mercy, my suster, and I mankynde sholde saue,
And þat god haþ forgyuen and graunted me, pees, & mercy,
To be mannes meynpernour for eueremoore after.
Lo! here þe patente', quod Pees, '*In pace in idipsum,*
And þat þis dede shal dure *dormiam & requiescam.*'   (181–188)

Like Truth and Righteousness, therefore, Peace depends upon Scripture
for her knowledge, but she receives it in a more personal and active way
than they. She finds her own name written in Scripture (187) and her own
duties outlined there, and in joy she comes to take them up. Where Truth
and Righteousness see less than is actually written in the text, understanding the letter but not all of its meaning, Peace sees more in the letter than
they do. She speaks as she reads, playing with revelatory ambiguities in
the letter, not to avoid its implications but to discover them.

In the last section of her speech, for example, she plays with words and
with logic itself in several ways to suggest what cannot be expressed
literally:

Forþi god, of his goodnesse, þe firste gome Adam,
Sette hym in solace and in souereyn murþe,
And siþþe he suffred hym synne sorwe to feele,
To wite what wele was, kyndeliche [to] knowe it.   (218–221)

Line 220 can be read, 'And then he allowed him to sin, in order to feel
sorrow.' Since it is only under the aspect of sorrow that Peace (like Julian of
Norwich)[14] considers sin at all, it is especially suitable that the words be
juxtaposed. One wonders if it might also be read, 'And then he allowed
him to feel sin-sorrow,' like Shakespeare's 'heart-sorrow' (*Tempest* III.3.
81) and like the 12th-century expression, 'sin-bote' (*OED* 'sin' sb. 6). The
two readings would support one another, since the peculiar sorrow God
allowed Adam to feel was sin-sorrow.

In these lines, Peace also picks up the theme of 'kynde knowyng' which
the poet had developed to great potency by verbal play and then apparently abandoned in Passus XV. By word play, she uses it to explain the fall,
the incarnation and redemption, and to suggest her theology of grace:

And siþþe he suffred hym synne sorwe to feele,
To wite what wele was, kyndeliche [to] knowe it.
And after god Auntrede hymself and took Adames kynde
To [se] what he haþ suffred in þre sondry places,
Boþe in heuene and in erþe, and now til helle he þenkeþ
To wite what alle wo is [þat woot of] alle ioye.   (220–225)

---

[14] Julian of Norwich, Short Text, xvii–xviii, especially xviii 25–27.

The phrase 'kyndeliche to knowe it' (221) means, of course, 'to know it thoroughly,' but further meaning is suggested by the next lines: 'god ... took Adames kynde / To se ... /To wite' (222–225). God, took 'Adames kynde' in order to know suffering by nature, experientially, i.e., 'kynde-liche.' This suggests that 'kyndeliche' in 221 means that Adam will know 'what wele was' not only thoroughly but also naturally through sharing in the nature of God, who 'woot of alle ioye.' The two uses of 'kynde-' words imply the paradox that God's knowledge of 'wo' is the direct cause of Adam's knowing 'wele ... kyndeliche.'

Peace's words, like Mercy's, are so filled with paradoxes that they suggest a world of transformation or conversion, where opposites are not simply contradictories.[15] In her last line, 'Ne what is witterly wele til wey-lawey hym teche (229),' she plays on the sounds of 'wel ... weylawey': the promise of 'wel' and even of a 'wey' to it are echoed in the interjection 'weylawey' itself, fittingly since she believes that 'wo into wele mowe wenden at þe laste' (204).

Obviously, the daughters fail to agree, since their modes of argument, their two kinds of knowledge and language – pedantic literalism and playful wit or wisdom – are so different (Birnes 79, Kaske 'Speech' 123).

Book joins them at line 232. It is uncertain what he is meant to represent (Kaske, 'Speech' 120–121, 132–133). Book is usually interpreted as 'Scripture,' but Kaske suggests that he may represent 'primarily the *littera* of the New Testament' (121) or liturgical books, and shows that the conventional themes of Book's speech are drawn from a variety of sources (133). It is clear that part of his speech is in fact a paraphrase of Scriptural texts (232–249, 252, 255), and that other parts ('Symondes sones,' 'his moder gladie,' and the loss of the Jews) come from other sources. So it seems that he represents something that includes both Scripture and other texts. The word 'boke' itself would allow, for example, the meanings 'the law,' 'book-learning,' or simply 'books' (*MED* 5c, *OED* 6).

Whether Book represents Scripture, the letter of Scripture, books in general, the law, or book-learning, it is he about whom the daughters have been arguing, since all four have quoted the law from Scripture and other sources, interpreting their sources differently. Yet Book is unable to re-solve their conflict (Schleusener 48). The poet allegorizes that very fact in Book's language.

At times, his language is richly figurative, and Book uses several puns. He begins:

---

[15] In my view, Peace implies not that opposites are only 'apparent opposites' (Car-ruthers, *Search* 145) but that God has the power and love to share real suffering, to pardon real sin, and to share his joy with human beings, and thus to bring good out of evil, without making evil good. For further discussion of 'kynde knowyng' in Peace's and Christ's speech, see my *'Kynde Knowyng* as a Major Theme' 11–15.

'By goddes body', quod þis book, 'I wol bere witnesse
That þo þis barn was ybore þer blased a sterre... (232–233)

The popular expletive which he uses here, 'By goddes body,' is an example
of the figure called *'communicatio idiomatum,'* the attribution of Jesus'
human functions or properties to God. Book uses this figure quite consistently, e.g., 'god ... wente on [water]' (242), 'god þolede ... on roode'
(249–250), as other characters do in other parts of the poem. Book's first use
of it, in 'By goddes body,' is also a pun, since besides being an expletive, it
is also literally true as an adverbial phrase modifying 'bere witnesse': it is
by the body of God being born, walking on water, and dying on the cross,
that Book proves his points. Besides this initial pun, Book puns on 'heuynesse':

The Erþe for heuynesse þat he wolde suffre
Quaked as quyk þyng and al biquasshed þe roche. (247–248)

This pun balances its primary meaning, the sadness of the Earth as a
personification, with the essential quality of earth as an element, its density or heaviness.

Yet in a difficult passage,[16] Book seems to betray an insensitivity to
words by restricting the meaning of the word 'kyn' in a way that excludes
those who might be expected to be included in it:

And I, book, wole be brent but Iesus rise to lyue
In alle myꝫtes of man and his moder gladie,
And conforte al his kyn and out of care brynge,
And al þe Iewene Ioye vnjoynen and vnlouken; (255–258)

One of the current meanings of 'kyn' was 'a race, people, tribe; clan, family'
(*MED* 'kin' 1a). The *MED* cites its use in *King Horn* to denote 'people': 'of
saraꝫine kenne' (34/614, c.1300) and its use in the Wyclif Bible to translate
L. *genere*: 'I [Paul] of the kyn (L. *genere*) of Israel' (Phil. 3. 5, c.1384). Yet Book
restricts the meaning of 'kyn' in 257 to 'immediate family,' saying that
while Jesus will comfort 'al his kyn,' he will disperse all the joy of the Jews.
By setting 'al his kyn' (255) in an antithetical relationship to the Jews, he

---

[16] There are two contradictory readings current for lines 255–60. The more common
reading interprets 258, 'And disperse/un-join all the joy of the Jews,' and it is this
reading upon which I am commenting. It is possible that Book's words are meant to
imply that the Jews are not Christ's kin spiritually although they are by blood, but
Christ seems to condemn this view at 377. If, however, Richard L. Hoffman is right in
reading line 260 '... [I, Book, will] be lost,' (63) the last lines become a hopeful prophecy
of the salvation of the Jews, and 258 can be read 'And unyoke and unlock the joy of all
the Jews.' This reading is more natural for 'Ioye' and for 'vnlouke' which have consistently affirmative connotations throughout the poem. But it rests upon what Donaldson has shown to be a syntactically improbable reading of line 259 ('Grammar'). Wittig
('The ME "Absolute Infinitive"') does not discuss Hoffman's reading.

ignores or denies their kinship to Jesus. Langland is too sensitive to words to have overlooked the apparent contradiction; besides, the repetition of 'al' points up the likeness between the two phrases, objects of parallel verbs. Within the context of this scene where two daughters have shown in their speeches that limiting the denotations of words inappropriately and without compassion (e.g., *'Inferno'*, 'after', 149, 193) can lead to erroneous judgements, I think the most likely interpretation of 257–8 is that Book's conclusion is meant to be in error, too, because he fails to see the full meaning and implications of his word 'kyn.'

But how could Book make a mistake, especially if he represents or includes representation of Scripture? The use of Scriptural quotations by Truth and Righteousness to prove their errors has prepared us for the possibility. 'Bokes' are only books, not the fullness of truth, as Trajan suggested in XI: 'baw for bokes' (140); 'Lawe wiþouten loue ... ley þer a bene!' (171). Thus, I think Book personifies 'books,' which may either be interpreted carefully, with imagination and love, so that they tell their whole truth, or may be interpreted in a superficial, constricted way which ignores part of their meaning so that they occasion error.[17] Both possibilities have been exemplified in the debate of the daughters, and both are exemplified in Book's speech. The varied quality of Book's language seems to be the index to his perception. When his language is free and playful, Book speaks accurately of love, of the witness of the elements to Christ, and of Christ's divinity. When he misuses the word 'kyn' by arbitrarily limiting its denotation, he errs and misleads. Sometimes he speaks the language of Mercy and Peace, sometimes that of Truth and Righteousness, and thus he cannot resolve their argument. Ultimately, what will correct Book's error will not be words, but Christ's actual blood-relationship to the Jews and the implications which Christ draws from that relationship (394–398). In a sense, Book will finally be corrected in exactly the way his own first words suggest, 'By goddes body' (232).

In its use of language as well as its content, Christ's long speech (327–403) in the third scene is an exact fulfillment of the promise *'Non veni soluere*

---

[17] In another context, Elizabeth Salter has pointed out how Trajan's 'Ye? baw for bokes!' (XI.140) expresses 'disillusionment with allegorical authority which, as we have seen, is such a perplexing and original feature of the poem' (*Fourteenth* 111). 'Langland repeatedly calls attention to the heuristic shortcomings of personifications by exploding their narrative and dramatic consistency in mid-scene' (Middleton, 'Two' 185). Adams sees all of *Piers* as cast in a 'progressive ... and self-corrective mode' ('Nature' 291). Laura Brown, who sees Book as posing 'questions about the nature of faith and Biblical authority,' also suggests that he shares the 'lexical authority' of Truth and Righteousness, their 'dogmatism and literalism,' as well as the 'faith ... and experience' of Mercy and Peace.

legem sed adimplere' (XVIII.349a; Matt. 5. 17). That is, his words are 'trewe': they are used precisely and they fulfill promises and prophecies exactly. Yet they are at the same time truly astounding because 'filled full' of the whole range of their meanings and their hitherto unforeseen implications.

The repetition of 'I' makes Christ's speech a self-revelation and suggests the extent of his involvement in human destiny. Other striking verbal patterns are punning repetition in the first section (327–349), *contentio* or verbal antithesis in the second (350–370), and the exploitation of multiple connotations of particular words in puns and echoing patterns in the third (371–403).[18]

It is generally recognized that everything about the first section suggests the balance of the old law: the content of the argument, the apparent equality of the litigants (Birnes 84), and the verbal pattern of the old law by which Christ is arguing, *'Dentem pro dente et oculum pro oculo'* (339a):

> ... lo! here my soule to amendes
> For alle synfulle soules ...
>
> ...
>
> *Ergo* soule shal soule quyte and synne to synne wende,
> And al þat man haþ mysdo I man wole amende.
> Membre for membre [was amendes by þe olde lawe],
> And lif for lif also, and by þat lawe I clayme
> Adam and al his issue at my wille herafter;
> And þat deeþ in hem fordide my deeþ shal releue
> And boþe quykne and quyte þat queynt was þoruʒ synne;
> And þat grace gile destruye good feiþ it askeþ.   (327–328, 340–347)

Visually and aurally, repetition of words makes a balance which represents what the words signify. However, it becomes a balance of love as well as justice, since not the sinner's 'membre,' 'soule,' 'deeþ' or 'lif' but Christ's own, become 'amendes,' the innocent for the guilty. This is a fulfillment, a filling the old law full of love, as each repetition of a word with a new meaning has an effect similar to that of a pun.

Two conventional puns have the same effect. 'Amendes' means 'reparation' or 'satisfaction' in the legal sense, a kind of balance. It has only that

---

[18] Like the language of Peace, Christ's language incorporates intuition, reliance on experience, puns, and patterns of repetition and antithesis, especially antithesis which leads paradoxically to something new, like 'al þat man haþ mysdo I man wole amende' (341). But unlike hers, his language is also a model of clear, orderly legal form (Birnes 71). His language is also like that of Holy Church. Both have as their purpose the revelation of God, but whereas her speech is intuitive, her transitions hidden, her changes of subject unexpected, his speech is inferential, his transitions and modulations explicit and clear: 'Alþouʒ ... Thus ... *Ergo* ... So ...' etc. (See Carruthers, 'Time' 183–184). In every way, Holy Church is more implicit, Christ more explicit. Her speech seems utterly simple and his intricate, but his is clearer than hers. Hers reveals little of herself; his is a self-revelation both of his humanity and his divinity.

sense in 342: 'Membre for membre was amendes.' 'Quyt' (340, 346) means 'to pay back (for), to settle accounts (for).' Both words also have other meanings, however, more in keeping with the new law, and except in line 342 which describes the old law, these 'new' meanings are operative along with the 'old' ones. That is, 'to amend' is 'to change, to mend, to heal,' and 'to quyt' is 'to acquit, release or redeem' as well as to requite. (*MED* 'amenden,' 'amende(s)'; *OED* 'quit'). Thus in line 327, 'my soule to amendes,' the 'amendes' for which he offers himself means both 'just satisfaction' in a transaction of justice and 'relief' or 'well-being' in a transaction of mercy, the one transaction achieving the other. In line 341, 'al þat man haþ mysdo I man wole amende,' 'wole amende' is a promise not only to make legal restitution but also and at the same time to remedy, mend, comfort and restore to health all 'þat man haþ mysdo': to make the world new again. In the same way, in 'soule shal soule quyte' (340), the verb 'quyte' means both 'repay for' under the old law and also 'acquit, release and redeem' under the new. His death will 'both quykne and quyte þat queynt was þoruȝ synne' (346). To 'quyte' is to avenge Satan's guile, but 'quyt' is also a synonym of 'releue' (345) and means 'to release, deliver, redeem' what was 'queynt.' The three alliterative verbs play upon one another, 'quykne' and 'quyte' responding to three different senses of 'queynte'; that is, Christ will 'quykne' or restore to life what was 'destroyed,' will 'quykne' or rekindle what was 'quenched,'[19] and will 'quyte' or release what was 'suppressed, oppressed.' The effect is a greater degree of surprise than usual, because the unexpected 'new' meaning of each pun is qualitatively and emotionally different from the expected meaning, as love is different from justice. Yet the one meaning does not replace the other; justice is fulfilled, not destroyed, by love. 'Deeþ' does not *become* life, nor justice love.[20] A real death makes amends for the evil that death did, and this creates new life.

In the second part of Christ's speech (350–370), this balance of repeated words is joined and gradually superseded by balance of opposites in the figure of *contentio*. 'Grace' opposes 'gile,' Christ's true 'liknesse of a leode' contrasts with Lucifer's false 'liknesse of a luþer Addere.'[21] Whereas rep-

---

[19] Chaucer uses 'queynte / And quyked' for a fire *KT* I (A) 2334–2335.

[20] This seems to be Mary Carruthers' position in *Search* 145, 147, where she describes language as completely redefined by Christ. C. D. Benson sees 'logic and right ... superseded' 201. I see Christ's speech as fulfillment rather than rejection of language or logic.

[21] I think the 'gile' which turns against Lucifer is his own: 'go gile ayein gile!' (357). To fool a villain by telling the truth is not total resignification of words as Carruthers suggests (*Search* 146, 147), but a freeing of language from 'fals.' Lucifer is said to have 'Falsliche and felonliche' caused Adam to sin (351) 'þoruȝ gile' (353) by being 'in liknesse of a luþer Addere' (354) because in fact he was not an adder, whereas Christ demonstrated 'grace,' not 'gile' (353) 'in liknesse of a leode, þat lord am of heuene'

etition suggests balance and therefore equality between claimants, antithesis, working into the balance of repetitions, turns that balance. By using antithesis, Christ reveals the true nature of the 'doctour of deeþ' and himself as 'lord of lif' and begins to speak as a victor before the law:

> Now bigynneþ þi gile ageyn þee to turne
> And my grace to growe ay gretter and widder.
> [Þe bitternesse þat þow hast browe, now brouke it þiselue];
> That art doctour of deeþ drynk þat þow madest.
> For I þat am lord of lif, loue is my drynke   (361–365)

'Turne' (361) is therefore a key word here. Its primary meaning is 'recoil upon' (*OED* 'turn' v. 32). One wonders whether two other meanings, recorded only later, might already be in use here, together with the primary meaning; both fit the context. One is the sense 'to weigh down' a scale or balance (*OED* 49, from 1590): it is the devils' 'gile' here which turns the balance of justice, condemning them. The second later meaning which would fit well here is 'to become bitter, sour' (*OED* 46, from 1548); the drink which the doctor of death made is also beginning to turn.

The turn being made, the language leaps into the future indicative, as Christ looks to the last judgement and fully assumes his position as king and judge, using, as Birnes points out, 'His most powerful argument: His royal prerogative,' thus completing his legal case (85):

> And þanne shal I come as a kyng, crouned, wiþ Aungeles,
> And haue out of helle alle mennes soules.
> Fendes and fendekynes bifore me shul stande
> And be at my biddyng wherso [best] me likeþ
> Ac to be merciable to man þanne my kynde [it] askeþ.
> For we beþ breþeren of blood, [ac] noȝt in baptisme alle.
> Ac alle þat beþ myne hole breþeren, in blood and in baptisme,
> Shul noȝt be dampned to þe deeþ þat [dureþ] wiþouten ende:
> *Tibi soli peccaui &*   (371–378)

He 'fulfills' the language used earlier in the passus and the poem,[22] using it

---

(356), because in fact, besides being lord of heaven, he *is* 'a leode.' Both used disguises, but one was false and the other true. The ways in which words are true or false are very similar to the ways in which likenesses are true or false. Christ in XVIII uses words as he used his 'disguise,' to surprise, not by lying, but by telling amazing truth. See Schleusener, who also argues that the conventional 'divine trick' does not subvert justice (36); he divides Christ's speech at a slightly different point and includes elements I do not mention here, 53ff. Cf. Kaske on the incarnation as 'trick' ('*Gigas*' 182–185).

[22] Both A. C. Spearing (*Criticism* 129) and Elizabeth Salter *Introduction* 49–52) discuss the effects on this passage of what Salter calls 'verbal and conceptual reminiscences' from earlier parts of the poem. This is another very important form of verbal and mental play.

without any restrictions. There are no limits on his being 'merciable' (375); within human nature, all are his 'breþeren of blood' (376); none is excluded from his 'kynde,' 'al mankynde' (397). A new antithesis, the alliance of himself with 'al mankynde' against guile, bitterness and death, corrects the misleading antitheses proposed by others which have preceded it (e.g., justice vs mercy, the word of scripture vs the promptings of love, the Jews vs Jesus, those 'withouten cristendom' vs the saved, the 'lerned' vs the 'lewed'), first explicitly (371–378), then implicitly by continuing para-dox (389), proverb (394–395), and word play. He plays especially upon the word 'kynde,' which appears four times, twice as a noun, once as an adjective and once as the root of a compound noun:

> Ac to be merciable to man þanne my kynde [it] askeþ
> ...
> Ac my rightwisnesse and right shul rulen al helle,
> And mercy al mankynde bifore me in heuene.
> For I were an vnkynde kyng but I my kynde helpe,
> And nameliche at swich a nede þer nedes help bihoueþ: (375,396–399)

The noun phrase, 'my kynde' in 398 means 'my kin' (*MED* 'kinde' 10), which includes all his kin by blood, 'al mankynde' (377). In 375, 'my kynde' is a pun, perhaps a triple pun. Because of the incarnation, its primary meaning, 'my nature,' is double, since Christ has two natures or *kyndes*, and both meanings fit and enrich the line, since he responds to his people both as blood brother and as Love. 'My kynde' can mean 'my kin,' here, also, since people – his kin – ask mercy of Christ. His 'nature' responds to his 'kin,' as he explains by metonymy ('Ac blood may noȝt se blood blede but hym rewe' 395). In line 398 there is a triple meaning also in the adjective 'unkynde' (unkind, unnatural). He is not unkind, but kind; and it would be unnatural, against both his human and divine natures to be unkind: inhuman to reject his kin, and against his divine nature to be other than 'caritas' (cf. Fowler, *Bible* 293).

Lines 397–398 make it quite clear that Langland's Christ frees people and language not with the 'absolute freedom of God' as interpreted by the extreme *Moderni* (if that means that God could reward evil or punish good, arbitrarily), but with 'treuþe' to his own 'kynde,' which is paradoxically both freedom and, in some sense, need (Mann 43).[23] If he did not have this kind, natural 'nede' to be true to his own nature(s), he would be 'an vnkynde kyng.'

---

[23] See Mann's beautiful treatment of need: 'God is driven by a need which is as concrete, as impossible to paraphrase, as the need of hunger or thirst. ... The daring of Langland's imagination is nowhere more clearly seen than in the way he legitimates the redemption not by man's need, but God's' 43. 2 Tim. 2: 13 is relevant here, also: 'he is always faithful, for he cannot disown his own self.' Cf. also Schmidt, 'Langland and' 29. On the 'absolute freedom' of God, see Coleman, *'Piers'* 18, her *Medieval* 245; and Bowers 8–9, 17–18, but also Courtenay 299–303. (See also Ch. IV, n. 10, above).

Truth and Righteousness, who knew the 'doom' of God but not his forgiveness, are corrected, converted, and reconciled to their sisters by Christ's revelation of the meaning of their own names (Carruthers, *Search* 144), which are fulfilled – filled full – by Christ's play on them: 'I may do mercy þoru3 my rightwisnesse and alle my wordes trewe' (389). His righteousness has been shown to include taking Adam's 'kynde' and learning 'alle wo' in order to fulfil the law and free humans justly. His truth has been shown to include fidelity not only to his word but also to his kin and to his own nature, which is love. Early in the debate, it was only an irony that Truth had the same name as God. By the end, she reflects him.

Truth and Righteousness can finally dance because they have been freed from the limits on their meaning. Both of them recognize 'sooþ' in the words of their sisters (416, 420), and Truth learns to play, embracing and kissing her sisters, trumpeting, singing and dancing (417, 422, 424), quoting the Book of Scripture in its fullness of meaning (423a), and finally playing with words:

> 'Trewes', quod Truþe, 'þow tellest vs sooþ, by Iesus!   (416)

The expletive 'Trewes' ('Truce!') has 'trewe' in it, a play on Truth's own name and on the 'sooþ' she now finds in Peace's words. Her use of the word 'sooþ' acknowledges the ultimate truth of her sister's words and perhaps also acts as a name for God whom Peace proclaims ('tellest'). 'By Iesus' is a pun, both an expletive and an adverbial phrase expressing the source of the 'sooþ' she now has.

Christ's presence and speech have a simpler but pronounced effect on Will, who reacts at dawn on Easter Sunday by the symbolic action of returning to the community, calling his family to creep to the cross and kiss it 'for a Iuwel' (428).[24] Raymond St-Jacques has shown that a jewelled processional cross was actually used on Easter morning in the Sarum rite ('Langland's Bells' 131–132). Figuratively, the jewel-image echoes the images of the treasure of truth and 'oure Ioye and oure Iuel, Iesu crist of heuene,' and its conflation with the image of the cross creates a vivid metaphor of the redemption.

Passus XVIII demonstrates, in a more specific way than any previous passus, that language is 'a game of heuene.' It is a game of encoding and deciphering and of restricting or freeing words. Success in playing it by

---

[24] Professor Tavormina pointed out this return to community to me. Both Fowler (*Piers* 145) and Norton-Smith (44) discuss the meanings of 'crepeth,' and both Fowler and Salter ('Figural' 86) discuss what Fowler calls Will's 'spiritual regeneration' (*Piers* 146).

speaking (as, for example, Peace speaks) requires respect for experiential knowledge as well as truth to the etymology and various current meanings of a word insofar as they are appropriate to a context. Those who play the game successfully by interpreting as, for example, Mercy interprets, are those who treat language as precious and revelatory, playing with it until the fullness of every possible appropriate meaning becomes clear; in doing this, they are personally involved in the outcome and enlightened by love, as Mercy, Peace, and Christ are. It is therefore a game in which the interplay of love and truth in felt knowledge, intuition, and experience are crucial. The game also involves the recognition and correction of errors – misuses or misunderstandings of language, whether lies or innocent misinterpretations, ranging from what many fourteenth-century listeners or readers would have considered blasphemy to what they would probably have considered normal. Each error, in contrast to 'fulfilled' language, reveals a lack of freedom and fullness. The game is played most perfectly by Christ, whose 'grace' against 'gile' fulfills language and the law in ways which are faithful yet literally marvelous; he keeps promises scrupulously, yet he says something genuinely new which is motivated by fullness of love and revealed through word play. Freeing words to be all they can be, their 'kynde' restored, he wins the game of the debate as he wins the joust, for the prize of humankind.[25]

But the game of the poem is not over. Will and the reader will return again to a world where language is straitened by glib liars like the friar who penetrates the Church-fortress with his 'lettre' (XX.325), and misinterpreted by naive listeners who hear only the letter of what is said ('"Thow art welcome", quod Conscience ...' XX.356). 'Many a fals truþe' (XX.118) is used to make evil appear good. The force of falsehood in XIX–XX is awesome, and therefore it has been argued that language is finally rendered impotent at the end of the poem and that despair is its final tone.[26]

[25] Schmidt shows that Christ wins 'in mastery of *truth*' (*Clerkly* 133). Julian of Norwich uses the word 'game' for the redemption. She laughs 'myghttelye,' 'Ioyande in god for the feende ys ouer comyun,' and says, 'I see game, that the feende ys ouercomenn.' (Short Text viii 41, 46, 48–49).

[26] Christopher Dawson (244) for example, writes of the ending in terms of despair. In *Search*, Carruthers argues that the very fullness of Christ's language 'leads directly to the apocalyptic breakdown of the poem in Passus XX,' because by making words mean too much, he makes them 'meaningless in human terms' (147). She points out examples of 'the disintegration of meaning ... pure sophistry, the distortion and emptying of language' (157, 158) as proof that 'the search for a rhetoric in which human language can be redeemed and made truthful has proved futile' (169). However, in 'Time' she sees the end of the poem as a 'moment of conversion' (178), and 'Conscience's cry after Grace' as an echo of the 'cry of Saint John which ends Revelation': 'Come, Lord Jesus!' ('Time' 186). As I have tried to show, I agree with the latter, not the former view. I also agree with Boitani: '*Piers Plowman* ends a moment before the tragedy ... and two moments before the final jubilee' (73). On false language, see also Adams, 'Nature' 278–9 and Schmidt, *Clerkly* 133, 137.

Yet deceptiveness and misuse of language are nothing new in the poem; they formed part of Will's first lesson from Holy Church, and Wit denounced their hatefulness. False and foolish characters have demonstrated throughout the poem how meaningless and false words can be, and ironically their words mock them. The only thing that would really corrupt the language of the poem in these last passūs or make it powerless would be a lack of irony or pathos when language is misused. But neither is lacking. We have noted, for example, the brilliant irony of the pun on 'Noble' in XX.132, which mocks the emptiness of one meaning by the fullness of the other; there are many instances of such ironies throughout the last two passūs, each evoking and depending upon the reader's awareness that empty words *are* empty. The fact that evil or weak characters corrupt language or are corrupted through it is therefore an occasion for irony and a cause of sadness, but not a sign that the *poet's* language has failed; rather, it is a sign that he is telling the truth.

Painful as it is, the ending is 'trewe' and its language is still 'a wepne ... to wynne ... truþe.' Even Will learns something about the game of words. When, for example, Kynde tells him to 'Lerne to loue' (XX.208), he understands enough 'to rome / Thoruȝ Contricion and Confession til I cam to vnitee' (212–213). Conscience, too, learns at last, through his disastrous error of letting the friar in, to distrust the letter alone and to use words in the fullness of their meaning to cry for help:

> 'By crist!' quod Conscience þo, 'I wole bicome a pilgrym,
> And [wenden] as wide as þe world [renneþ]
> To seken Piers þe Plowman, þat pryde [myȝte] destruye,
> And þat freres hadde a fyndyng þat for nede flateren
> And countrepledeþ me, Conscience; now kynde me avenge,
> And sende me hap and heele til I haue Piers þe Plowman.'
> And siþþe he gradde after Grace til I gan awake.   (380–386)

Language still has meaning and power. Conscience *talks* here ('quod') and cries out ('gradde') in words which are a way of seeking ('gradde after Grace'), words which Will can hear and which change his state of consciousness ('til I gan awake'). Conscience uses the most specific, concrete, particularized and personal words that exist – proper names – precisely as 'wepne.' He begins with a punning expletive that explains the source of his strength, 'Bi cryste ... I wole bicome a pilgrym.' The other names he calls are also puns and are 'full,' since each has been the subject of extensive word play in the poem; he goes to seek Piers the Plowman, with the help of Kynde, crying out to Grace.[27] He may very well be calling on the 'þre louely persones' of God (XVII.46), who have never in the poem failed to respond,

[27] Although both Fowler (*Piers* 163) and Bloomfield ('Allegories' 35) identify Piers with Grace at the end, I think they remain two separate persons, as at XIX.225.

but have come when least expected: Kynde, associated in IX with the 'fader,' Piers in XV with *'christus,'* and Grace in XIX with *creator Spiritus* (Schmidt, 'Langland and' 19). Certainly Conscience is calling upon all that 'Kynde' means in its perpetual fertility, terrifying strength, powerful love; on Piers as companion, Samaritan, *christus*, Peter; on Grace as Spirit of creativity, 'goddes owene kynde,' source of Piers' power, as well as created share in the *kynde* of God. Part of the game for the reader is to hear the echoes and implications of the multivalent names which Conscience calls. They make his cry of anguish also a cry of hope and power.[28]

[28] As Skeat says, 'What other ending can there be? or rather, the end is not yet. We may be defeated, yet not cast down; we may be dying, and behold, we live. We are all still pilgrims upon earth. *This* is the truth which the author's mighty genius would impress upon us in his parting words' (II: 285).

Chapter Six

The 'Game of Heuene' and
the Meaning of Piers Plowman

As the foregoing chapters demonstrate, word play is one of the principal formal elements in *Piers Plowman*. It achieves a variety of poetic effects, packing the poem with meaning, linking ideas and images, cutting through arguments in a dazzling intuitive way, mocking both deceivers and deceived with irony, and offering a vision of the coinherence of divine and human. At the same time, especially when it is ironic, word play shows truth to be hard to come by, impossible to restrict or contain, and easy to betray or belittle.

Word play is an unsettling device. Knowledge that there may be verbal play anywhere throughout the text makes the language of the whole poem seem unstable and unfinished; one is always wondering whether there is more meaning than that already perceived. Even when a play on words offers a vision of coherent relationships, the vision it offers is at best sudden and evanescent. One can remember it or grasp it over and over, but in a sense the meaning is not permanent and solid or totally available like the meaning of a univocal word. This is perhaps part of the reason we enjoy word play: we are pleased at a surprise. But there is also something frustrating about word play. Being illogical it can neither prove nor be proven. One either sees it or one does not. Its meaning, like the entire structure of the poem, shifts before our eyes.

For word play is only one element, though the most common one, in a *mélange* of shifting formal devices which create the 'strange integrity and coherence' of *Piers Plowman* (Muscatine, *Poetry* 105). Various images of buildings, for example, 'melt into each other' (Kirk, *Dream* 199) and 'one scene reels ... into the next' (Muscatine, *Poetry* 88), just as one meaning of a word melts into another without warning. The figures of Piers, the Samaritan, and Christ, shifting, almost coalescing, separating, suggest a play of mind upon various aspects of a mystery, not unlike word play. Conversions, such as Piers' decision when he tears the Pardon (VII.119 ff), cause

111

reversals in action which are similar in their effects to shifts in the meanings of words. Re-focusing by correction of error is another narrative device which adds to the reader's sense of instability and expectation.[1] The dream, the symbol, the *figura*, too, all resemble the pun in having more than one meaning, in being non-inferential, unpredictable, decipherable only by a certain play of mind, and not susceptible of explanation by simple schemes.

Even the unorthodox narrative structure of *Piers Plowman* has a peculiar harmony with word play, and word play is a clue to its meaning.[2] The puzzling 'inconclusiveness' or 'endlessness'[3] of the poem is like the incompleteness of word play, which is by nature unfinished until a reader or listener finishes it by finding its unexpected meaning. *Piers Plowman* ends at a beginning, almost where it began (Barney, *Allegories* 87). It does not 'go anywhere' because the end (that is, the victory and the promise) is not at the end but in Passus XVIII (Bloomfield, 'Allegories' 32; cf. Woolf, 'Some' 121) and in utopian visions throughout the poem (e.g., III, XVII). In another sense, its end (its goal, that which the protagonist is seeking, 'treuþe') is potentially there all along, from Holy Church's explanation of Treuþe to Conscience's realization that Grace is there to cry to. Thus the narrative, like its word play, moves not so much toward meaning as with meaning. That is perhaps one reason why the psalm verse quoted at two moments of stress in the poem is 22:4: 'Though I walk through the valley of the shadow of death I will fear no evil, for you are with me' (VII.120–121; XII.293).[4] The meaning of the poem, like the meaning of its puns, is always within it, though accessible or perceptible only occasionally, partly, and briefly.

---

[1] The pattern of error and correction as necessary steps in the search for truth is also to be found in Dante's *Paradiso* (e.g., III.19–30, XXIII.70–72) and in *Pearl* (e.g., stanzas 24–5, 36, 40, 77), where the dreamers make mistakes and are (sometimes severely) corrected by their guides.

[2] The greatest problem in *Piers Plowman* studies is the structure of the poem; see Muscatine, *Poetry* 106–109. Kirk, for example, argues, 'The poem's continuity is not in the argument ... but in its unfolding from human image to human image' (*Dream* 200). Priscilla Martin sees a dichotomy between 'orthodox' and 'agnostic' readers, i.e., 'critics who see conflict in the poem and critics who deny it,' those who approach the poem moving 'from the formal qualities of *Piers* to a description of Langland's religious position, [and those who move] ... from accepted theology to a scheme of the poem' (*Field* 32). Earlier scholars sometimes saw the lack of a 'symmetrical, distinctly drawn picture' as a sign of artistic failure (Stubbs 75; cf. also S.B. James 40). On disruptions in the narrative, see Middleton, 'Narration' 101–111.

[3] John Burrow speaks of the 'endlessness' of the structure (*Ricardian* 66); cf. 97. See also Pearsall, 'The "Ilchester"' 192; Carruthers, 'Time' 178–188; Hamilton 29. See Muscatine, *Poetry* 72 and Martin, *Field* 54 on 'inconclusiveness.'

[4] Judson Boyce Allen pointed out the centrality of psalm 22:4 as the beginning of the A-text continuation; 'the pardon passus is not about pardon, but about Psalm 22, as understood by Hugh of St.-Cher' ('Langland's' 353, n. 22).

These unsettling qualities of structure and style[5] seem to many critics antithetical to, or subversive of, the beliefs expressed in the poem, and the contrast between its 'conservative Christian doctrine' and its 'sense of instability' (Muscatine, 'Locus' 122) is sometimes perceived as a dichotomy (cf. Martin, *Field* 32, 34).

However, a dichotomy, which poses a choice between alternatives, may not be the best model for understanding the relationship of style and meaning in *Piers Plowman*. The nature and prevalence of word play in the poem suggest that the pun, in which contrasting elements coexist meaningfully, is a more helpful model, since within *Piers Plowman*, the stability of coherent meaning, argument, or inner form interpenetrates, inheres within the instability of shifting outer forms. The paradox of *Piers Plowman* is that its inner form of coherent belief is not weakened by the apparent incoherence of outer form, nor does the inner form visibly organize and transform the outer form except in Passus XVIII.[6]

This pun-like relationship between inner and outer form, between secrets and sequence, supports and demonstrates the view of life which the narrative imaginatively asserts, i.e., the immanence of God within unstable creation. Style and structure express what explicit statement cannot fully contain: the faithful yet unexpected presence of God within the world. For although in *Piers Plowman* God is transcendent as well as immanent, ('The tour on þe toft, ... truþe is þerInne' I.12), the narrative never takes us to the 'tour' nor offers any heavenly vision 'Ther Treuþe is in Trinitee' (I.133). Rather, through symbol, figure and word play, it offers many experiences of the immanence of God. God is 'wiþInne' everything and everyone in the poem except sin: within Kynde (XI.326), 'trewe' persons (XII.287–292), 'þyn herte (V.606),' Piers (XV.200a, 212), 'In a pouere mannes apparaille' (XI.186), 'in hir liknesse' (XI.187). In *Piers Plowman*, God's presence does not nullify or even necessarily purify the creation in any obvious way, any more than the 'sentence' of the poem unifies its outer form in any obvious way. In the world of the poem, turbulent realism, even surrealism, testifies to the painful universal human experience of poverty, frailty, and confusion. 'Kynde' can cause shame (XI.403), one can exile oneself from one's own heart (V.613–15), and the poor remain

---

[5] I think the most precise description we have of Langland's style is Muscatine's: 'the periodic establishment and collapse of the dream frame, the alternation of allegory and literalism, the violent changes of tone and temper, the peculiar equivalence of concrete and abstract terms, and the indistinctness of the genre. Along with these, the shifting locus of action produces an effect that, for lack of a better term, I have called "surrealistic"' ('Locus' 121–122; cf. *Poetry* 107).

[6] I am using terms of Wellek and Warren: 'outer form (specifically metre or structure) and ... inner form (attitude, tone, purpose – more crudely, subject and audience)' (231).

hungry (XIV.160–163). The discovery of God 'wiþInne' is always a surprise, a wonder, a momentary, evanescent glimpse of 'oure Ioye' (XI.185) within ordinary, painful, confused experience. For Langland's vision of Treuþe is paradoxical; although the word 'treuþe' means absolute reliability and is used in the Bible to signify God's utter faithfulness, Treuþe in the poem is always beyond our full comprehension, and reveals itself only partially, in unexpected forms, people, places, and words. That is why the reader must play or shift in order to be 'trewe' to the text and to read it successfully.

The structural strangeness of *Piers Plowman* causes the reader to enter into a particular way of looking at experience, perceiving all forms of human poverty and, at the same time, the faithful presence of God *within* this poverty. From this point of view, ordinary experience and the experience of faith, rather than being antithetical, interpenetrate one another. The form of the poem and especially its word play point to this world view, as one glimpses the poem's certainties through such unstable forms as puns and symbols. The experience of discovering more and more meaning in word play is a model of the experience of discovering Christ in the poor, Kynde in nature, Treuþe in the 'trewe.' As R. W. Chambers suggested long ago, Langland, like Dante, must have hoped to bring his readers to happiness (*Man's* 171); perhaps he hoped to do this by teaching us to read experience as we have to read his poem – patiently, lovingly, playfully – as a 'game of heuene.'

If this is so, we still must ask why the poet felt it necessary for experience to be expressed in so unstable, so surrealistic a form. One reason, as Muscatine suggests, must be the poet's intense, painful awareness of 'the instability of the epoch' (*Poetry* 107) with its traumatic social and religious change. Langland was a conservative thinker, influenced, as Bloomfield has shown, by Benedictine monastic thought (*Apocalypse* 75–77). He drew from the deep, ancient sources of Scripture, liturgy, and doctrine, rather than from contemporary theological opinion. When he did write of theological disputes, as, for example, the works-grace controversy, he favored the mysterious and profound answer which a pun suggests, and thereby questioned the value of the theological argument. Directly or indirectly, he must have been aware of the concerns of the *Moderni*, for the questions which concerned them most were of passionate interest to him (cf. Bowers 10–14). His use of language, however, demonstrates a belief in words as vehicles of truth,[7] like that of the earlier *Modistae*, whose 'basic assumption ... [was] that language reflects reality and that grammar provides us with clues to the nature of being' (Bloomfield, Review 102), a theory opposed by

---

[7] 'Langland accepts implicitly the medieval identification of language and nature' (Alford, 'Grammatical' 754). See Ch. I, n. 25 above.

what we have traditionally called 'Nominalism.' In *Piers Plowman*, analogical word play and frequent play on words of 'likeness' express a firm conviction that the world is the image of God and that words are 'trewe' when they refer analogically to human and divine realities. Although no word or thing or person except Christ can reveal all of Treuþe, for Langland words, things, and persons do reveal Treuþe in a partial, limited, indispensable way. Then, too, everything in *Piers Plowman* depends on the belief that God can be known, even experienced in this world: that is the whole point of the poem. The very nature of God is the focus of Will's search – a 'knowyng' of the 'kynde' of God. It seems that to the extreme *Moderni*, God's nature was unknowable, arbitrary; to Langland, though it was ineffable, it was the most secure basis for all Holy Church teaches ('I do it on *Deus caritas*,' I.86) and the final argument for human salvation ('I were an vnkynde kyng ...' XVIII.398; 'Ne wolde neuere trewe god but [trewe] truþe were allowed,' XII.290). In all these areas, Langland may have felt himself to be an embattled thinker, defending ancient beliefs against a 'new scholasticism' which seemed to threaten the faith itself (Spearing, *Criticism* 133). As Muscatine says, 'For him, the road to the New Jerusalem has become newly devious, the structure of the moral world newly problematical' (*Poetry* 107).

In another and less troubling way, 'the instability of the epoch' may have made him comfortable with unbalanced, inconsistent structures. Fourteenth-century English churches were often as hybrid in structure as *Piers Plowman*. Leominster Priory, for instance, in the town where he may have been born, had in Langland's lifetime (and still has) a Norman aisle, a 13th-century Gothic aisle, and a 14th-century Perpendicular aisle. Such mixtures are common. Different styles seem to have been accepted as congenial, unified, perhaps, by their living purpose. One could hardly live and worship in such surroundings, which have a strong, generous beauty, without becoming acclimated to inconsistency.

But *Piers Plowman* shows more than an ability to tolerate inconsistency and reflects, I believe, more than the instability of the period. It seems to reveal that the poet *needed* puns and other shifting forms in order to be faithful to the truth as he saw it. He went out of his way to avoid the clarity of scholastic distinction, choosing instead word play, ambiguity, and a slippery double vocabulary with both false and true, ironic and non-ironic uses of the same words, and using, for example, an almost inscrutable pun to resolve the great theological controversy over works and grace.[8] His

---

[8] As Spearing wrote, 'The central effort of his poem ... is directed against the making of intellectual distinctions and towards the building up of large ... ideas' ('Verbal Repetition' 737); '... congruence and consonance are not its ultimate values' (Carruthers, 'Time' 187); cf. Barney, *Allegories* 93.

satire mocks oversimplification and purely theoretical distinctions wrongly applied in the existential order. This is related to his sensitivity to 'a universe blessed by metamorphoses' (Salter, *Fourteenth* 107), especially changes of heart and mind which recur so often in his poem.[9] Shifting structures, including verbal play, in *Piers Plowman* are means of suggesting more truth than univocal words, logical arguments, and stable structures could convey. Paradoxically, the poem's certainties are most compellingly expressed not in explicit statement, but in 'instabilities' like puns, symbols, and other shifting devices.

A final reason for the poet's choice of these unpredictable and slippery forms and structures in *Piers Plowman* is, of course, that *Piers* is a poem narrating not theology, but experience. Ann Middleton attributes to Langland the 'invention of experience as a literary category' ('Narration' 110), and she sees this invention with its concern for 'earthly experience' in the 'here and now' as 'perhaps the major literary invention of the 14th century' (121).[10] Bloomfield has argued that *Piers Plowman* is

> perhaps the first poem in English (and perhaps in any European language) that concentrates on the problem of the self and religious existence and that raises questions rather than answers them. It is a literary work which itself deals with the problem of interpretation rather than offering a text for interpretation. ... It is truly an existential poem because it wrestles with the paradoxes of existence ('Allegories' 37).

As a narrative of experience, wrestling 'with the paradoxes of existence,' *Piers Plowman* focuses on the experience of faith seeking wisdom. Within the narrative, 'treuþe' is hard to find or understand or win – or say – even with good will (and even when Will is good). It is seen or found (or finds Will) suddenly, momentarily. It must be 'won' over and over, and then can be seen only partially;[11] sometimes, as in Holy Church's discourse, it is stated so fully that an ordinary listener cannot grasp it all. This is especially

---

[9] Burrow ('Words' 119) and Carruthers ('Time' 178–179) have both brought out the structural importance of conversions in *Piers Plowman*.

[10] Anderson, too, sees his 'manipulation of allegory as an exploratory ... mode' (4) related to the 'shifting, cycling, echoing movements' of the narrative (5). Salter suggests the experiential nature of the poem when she describes it as 'a critical chart of human difficulties, ... a seismograph of universal pain' (*Fourteenth* 112), and Allen calls it 'an experiencing text' (*Ethical* 281). Cf. also Schmidt, 'Inner' 36. See Ch. II, n. 18, on Heraucourt's theory about the word 'treuthe' as a 14th-century expression of 'experience'; certainly Langland's term 'kynde knowyng' refers to experiential knowledge. As I have pointed out above, some of the puns in *Piers Plowman* are 'existential' in the sense that they show in relationship things which are related existentially rather than logically. Perhaps this existential, experiential quality is one reason scholars have found the writings of mystics so helpful in studying *Piers*.

[11] 'Langland is unique among medieval poets in his insistence on that partialness and inadequacy [of religious language] – it is the anguished premise of his poetry' (Carruthers, *Search* 173).

ironic, since the word 'treuþe' means stability, faithfulness, and cognitive penetrability or accessibility. In fact, the imagery of Passus V implies that it is the nature of 'treuþe' always to be faithfully present 'wiþInne,' and that all instability and uncertainty are the seeker's:

> Thow shalt see in þiselue truþe [sitte] in þyn herte
> In a cheyne of charite
> ...
> Ac be war þanne ...
> ...
> The boldnesse of þi bienfeet makeþ þee blynd þanne,
> And [so] worstow dryuen out as dew and þe dore closed
> (V.606–607, 609, 612–613)

Here, 'truþe' is evidently present and in some sense accessible, remaining 'in þyn herte'; but one may be 'blynd' to it or him or 'dryuen out as dew' from one's own heart by one's own ill will. Though truth is within, the seeker may be 'out.' Augustine wrote of this in the Confessions: 'Where then were You and how far from me? I had indeed straggled far from You ... Yet all the time You were more inward than the most inward place of my heart' (III. vi.48–49). The same pattern is seen in XI, where 'Iesu crist of heuene / In a pouere mannes apparaille pursueþ vs euere' (185–186). The key word is 'euere' – 'always,' which implies faithful presence and accessibility, yet a little later the text continues, 'Ac bi cloþyng þei knewe hym noȝt, [so caitifliche he yede]' (239). Even though truth is present, always pursuing, the one pursued may be unable to perceive it or him.

When truth is received or perceived, the vision is sometimes indirect and implicit; thus Will says that he sees charity 'neuere sooþly but as myself in a Mirour' (XV.162) (cf. Anderson 131–132). Even when it is full and explicit, as in Passus XVIII, Will's experience is that vision (a 'kynde knowyng') cannot be controlled, although it can and must be sought ('Wolleward and weetshoed wente I forþ after ...' XVIII.1), and it is only temporary. So Will has to learn in his search for 'kynde knowyng' both to pursue actively and to receive patiently, with love as motive. Thus, when his love for the Samaritan awakens a new alertness, he pursues the Samaritan: 'I soiourned noȝt but shoop me to renne / And suwed þat Samaritan þat was so ful of pite ...' (XVII.86–87), and this ultimately leads to the vision in XVIII. But such vision or loving communion is described in Piers as it is in the New Testament, not as an end, but as a driving force ('The love of Christ drives us,' 2 Cor. 5: 14), so that Piers must end not in stasis, but in a new pilgrimage or pursuit (cf. Hamilton 34). Yet Imaginative points out a need for patience, as well as activity: 'Haddestow suffred .../ Thow sholdest haue knowen ...' (XI.413–414). The patience Will needs is a form of surrender, like his surrender to the Church's celebration of Lent at the beginning of XVIII: 'And lened me to a lenten ... Reste me þere ... ' (5, 6).[12] Everything Will learns comes to him in the pure receptivity of dreaming. Since dreams themselves are an archetypal form of surrender, of listening, seeing, and playing,[13] the plurality of dreams in *Piers Plowman* emphasizes the importance of these receptive, playful elements in Will's search for 'treuþe.' The search is both active and receptive, stable and unstable, and its results cannot be fully controlled.

Thus, even the argument of the poem is not purely stable, though it may fairly be called conservative; the narrative of Will's experience reflects a paradoxical coexistence of certitude and tension, stability and instability, the one discoverable only 'wiþInne' the other.

The form of *Piers Plowman* is mimetic of this experience. The ragged, illogical, slippery structure and texture of the poem express the bewildering changes and confusions of Will's experience seeking God, being found by him, and needing still to seek.

At the same time, the form of the poem is also ludic, causing readers to *undergo* Will's experience in aesthetic form, involving them in the text as in a game which will recreate the experience for them in 'play.' Like Will within the fiction, the reader, too, needs to learn loving, patient yet active attention and surrender to meaning, in order to decipher even the word play of the poem, let alone its other puzzles. As Lawlor says, *Piers Plowman* is 'a poem which is concerned not with the exposition of doctrine as a contribution to the reader's knowledge, but with the individual reader's apprehension of truth, his growing into awareness, as the poem proceeds. ... [The poem communicates] the very pressure of experience itself' ('Imaginative' 124). Part of its truth lies in its painful circuitousness and inconclusiveness, which effect what a formally balanced structure could not. The poem *becomes* an experience, its unfinished, riddling character causing the reader to feel something of what Will feels, to play as Will plays, to learn something of what he learns.

It is precisely in this representation of the *experience* of a life of faith that Langland differs most sharply from Dante. And while the clarity of form which Dante has taught us to expect of a Christian poem is perfectly designed to express what Christians believe life is *sub specie aeternitatis*,

---

[12] With respect to patience, Burrow writes, 'virtues of quiet steadfastness and long-suffering [are] ... perhaps the only kind of heroism viable in Chaucer's latter-day world' (*Ricardian* 110), and Kirk notes that Will's questions can be 'answered only when he has learned to view them with patience, not rebelliousness' ('Who' 97). Cf. also Spearing, *Criticism* 134, and Schmidt, 'Inner' 35–6 on patience, receptivity and *suffraunce*.

[13] Howard notes that 'dreams and games have in common their removal from everyday practical affairs, their "unreality," and their element of unpredictability' (*Three* 285). See Constance Hieatt on the dream form, especially 90–97.

the unpredictable form of *Piers Plowman* is truer to the existential Christian *experience* of faith seeking wisdom in this life. Traditionally, this experience has been reported to be unpredictable and dark. As Walter Ong explains,

> ... Christian faith is in no sense reducible to a satisfying feeling of confident trust which solves one's uneasiness concerning the outcome of life, nor is it a satisfying culmination of intellectual life, an intellectual or volitional ultimate. Rather, it is an essentially unsatisfying state ... It leaves the mind in one way or another restless and tense. ... In its relation to poetic tension, the tension associated with supernatural faith has a particular relevance of its own because it is ... acute. ... The superlative acuteness of the intellectual stress or tension accompanying supernatural faith is not contravened by the absolute certitude... investing the same supernatural faith. Indeed, both the stress or tension and the certitude are traceable to the same conditions
> ('Wit' 333–334).

Ong's description of the experience of faith is not unusual or eccentric.[14] The Epistle to the Corinthians describes the faith-experience as a kind of darkness to be contrasted with vision: 'We see now in a dark manner as in a mirror, but then, face to face; now I have only glimpses of knowledge; then I shall know even as I am known' (I Cor. 13: 12). Will's image of seeing charity 'neuere sooþly but as myself in a Mirour' (XV.162) is partly taken from this description. Mystics and theologians testify that even when faith blazes into moments of the loving communion of *sapientia* (wisdom or 'kynde knowyng'), these moments are partial and passing, like the visions in *Piers* of the redemption and of 'treuþe' in the heart.[15]

---

[14] 'Faith itself ... [is] concerned with invisible things, that exceed human reason. ... we must not attempt to prove what is of faith, except by authority alone, to those who receive the authority, while as regards others it suffices to prove that what faith teaches is not impossible' (Aquinas, *Summa Theologica* Ia 32. 1; cf. also Ia 1. 5). Explaining the much earlier theology of St Gregory the Great (6th century), Leclercq says: 'It is not in seeing, then, that the vision of faith consists, but in looking with love and a great longing to see. It is not merely a knowledge of God, an act of the understanding, but an act of love by which we possess the divine truth though as yet only imperfectly and obscurely, whereas in heaven we shall lay hold of it fully and clearly' (*Spirituality* 26–27). See also Vincent McNabb's application of Aquinas' theology: 'the mind that looks merely at the object of faith and not on the guarantee of faith will experience a feeling of repulsion, of darkness, or ignorance which it will mistake for denial. This feeling will cause it great pain when it contrasts the feeling of satisfaction, light, knowledge, which it experiences when viewing the world presented to it by its external senses. But for its consolation it should remember that faith is certitude rather than knowledge. It is the calm reliance which a mind places on another higher mind. It is not an immediate contact with an object, but an intercommunion of mind with mind' (109–110). As Priscilla Martin observes: 'Langland raises questions in his poem about problems in Christian experience ... Possibly the paradoxes of Christianity ... must, when deeply felt, produce such tension' (*Field* 32, 31). On Will as 'restless and dissatisfied,' see Kane, *Middle English* 234.
[15] Sister Jeremy Finnegan points out to me St Bernard's description of mystical experience, often quoted in the middle ages, '*Rara hora, parva mora*' (Sermon XXIII on the Song of Songs: 15. 2).

Ong sees puns and other forms of word play, therefore, as 'simply a *normal* means of dealing with the mysteries of Christianity' ('Wit' 323). He shows, for example, that in certain medieval Latin hymns which seek to probe central Christian mysteries, the tension and stress of faith are reflected in and evoked by a paradoxical, punning style requiring a play of mind upon things which inference cannot grasp.

The language of Jesus as presented in the gospels has some of the same paradoxical, witty qualities which Ong notices in medieval hymns and which characterize the language of *Piers Plowman*. Some of his parables might be described as puzzles (e.g., 'that seeing, they may not see ...' Matt. 13: 13); so might his paradoxes (e.g., 'Unless you eat the flesh of the Son of Man and drink his blood, you will not have life in you' John 6: 53), his puns (e.g., John 4: 10 on 'living water'/ 'flowing water'), and many metaphors (e.g., 'I am the vine; you are the branches' John 15: 1). The mind must play with such words, images and ideas, if it is to begin to penetrate them.

The wisdom literature of the Hebrew Bible is characterized by a similar playful, riddling, punning style which causes the reader to 'wrestle with the text.' According to Reges, this style is intended to suggest that 'the search for salvation, for wisdom, is not experienced as simple.'[16] Thus Biblical wisdom books, especially *Proverbs, Qoheleth* (*Ecclesiastes*), *Job* and the apocryphal books of *Sirach* (*Ecclesiasticus*) and *Wisdom*, use riddles, paradoxes, dialogues and puns to tell of the surprising, unstable character of reality ('All is vanity' Eccl. 1.2). Such literature tends 'to tear asunder a coherent sense of time. ... It is especially apposite to those elements of experience that are felt to be unsuitable for the narrative coherence of story or the abstract coherence of a conceptual system' (James Williams 23–24). Other religious texts, too, like the visions of Daniel and Ezechiel in the Hebrew Scriptures, and the *koans* of Zen Buddhism, suggest that playful, figurative, enigmatic language may be necessary or at least appropriate in any religious text which seeks to evoke the genuinely transcendental as it is experienced in this life. Such religious texts are fundamentally different from theological texts, which are as clearly rational as possible. The reason seems again to be both mimetic and ludic, i.e., both in order to represent those elements of religious experience which are supra-rational and to evoke a play of mind in the reader which may lead to wisdom.[17]

---

16 From unpublished lectures on the Wisdom Literature of the Bible delivered at Rosary College, 1985, by Sister Marie Stephen Reges, O.P. Wisdom literature characteristically uses assonance, alliteration, proverb, many synonyms, parallelism, dialogue, fable, allegory, and other devices. Crenshaw mentions also the riddle. James Williams notes the importance of 'the *word* – language and conversation' and of the recurrence of events in scriptural narrative and wisdom writings (37, 40). See my '*Piers Plowman* and the Books of Wisdom.' Donaldson points out violations of time sequence, e.g., in Passus XX ('Apocalyptic' 76–77).

17 James Simpson suggests that there may be progressive development in *Piers Plowman* from 'The modes of argument ... restricted to the domain of human, rational

Thus, paradoxically, the pervasive sense of instability in *Piers Plowman*, rather than contradicting its argument, instead supports it. By incarnating the 'sentence' of divine mystery in an unstable style, Langland 'makes' the experience of a surrealistic world interpenetrated by Treuþe; he also enables readers to participate in this experience aesthetically as in a game whose verbal play may serve to prepare minds for the act of faith which is itself paradoxical, including as it does the experience of certainty within the experience of incomprehension.

The kind of unity we may expect in *Piers Plowman*, then, will be an uneasy tension between certainty and instability, between 'confort' and 'wo,' the one available only within the other. This is not because of weakness in argument or structure, but because the subject of the poem, its substance, is the experience of faith which is such a tension. Although another world is promised within its passages, we and Will, in *this* world whose experience the poem 'plays,' cannot get away from the 'pouerte,' instability, and 'nede' of human life, though we can find 'an hope hangyng þerInne' (XII.292). We cannot choose between the poem's 'care' and its 'confort,' its instability and stability.[18] They exist only together, like the meanings of a pun, and there, too, Langland tells the truth in a rare and powerful way.

Word play is therefore a key to the structure and style of *Piers Plowman* as well as to its richness of meaning. Although it is only one small element in the poem, it shows us how the poet's mind worked and what sort of artistic sensibility underlay stylistic habits which seem inconsistent, confused

knowledge, or *scientia*, . . . [to] the modes appropriate to . . . *sapientia*, . . . which appeal to the will, and which persuade through emotional experience rather than rational argument' ('From Reason' 7–8). This may be so, and may explain why certain sections and speakers of the poem use more word play than others. Simpson describes the last part of *Piers* (from XVI.74 to the end) as 'consistently designed to produce a sapiential, experiential, "kynde" knowledge of God' (14), and this seems to me to be a clear statement of the purpose of the poem.
[18] Spearing speaks of the poem's 'unstable solidity. . . . It feels solid yet it will not stay still'; he also points out that we cannot understand the poem 'without fixing our attention with the greatest closeness on the way he uses words' ('Langland's' 187; cf. 189). Bloomfield comments that 'Langland's style . . . perfectly mirrors the movement of his mind' (*Apocalypse* 40). The pun certainly mirrors the coexistence and interrelationship of ideas and impulses sometimes thought to be antithetical. Peter Dembowski sees all medieval poetry as based on antithetical thinking, not as a conflict to be resolved, but as a situation to be lived (unpublished lecture, Rosary College). Cf. also Robertson who points out the non-dynamic character of medieval dialectic, in which resolution was often achieved 'by showing, for example, that the same word might be used with different significations in different contexts' (11). Schleusener stresses the 'fundamental ambiguity' (79) of *Piers*, the 'unsteady view, which gives place to skepticism and to certainty at the same time' (68).

and confusing: mixture of genres; re-definitions of terms; shifting of time, space, characterization, and symbolism; use of an 'endless' structure marked by regressions, delays, cycles, reversions, conversions; perhaps even textual revisions themselves.[19] Each of these, like the pun, allows two or more elements or meanings (kinds of time, levels of consciousness, genres, states of mind or heart, etc.) to coexist in some meaningful relationship. Many years ago, Nevill Coghill urged readers 'to see it [*Piers Plowman*] as a great and single vision made of many visions, held and harmonized in the mind of the revising poet, and written down so that we can hold it in the same way' ('Pardon' 355). The study of word play newly validates his statement, showing us *how* the poet's writing enables us to 'hold' and harmonize several visions in one: not statically or passively as paper holds an image, but actively, as the air holds light from the sun, or as receivers hold balls passed to them in play. The point of the preceding chapters is that the truth of the poem *can* be found and held only by play, by fidelity to the playfulness of its language. Even the simple words and clauses which seem to sum up the poem's argument with great clarity, like 'treuþe,' 'loue,' 'do wel,' '*Ego sum ueritas et uita*,' 'Lerne to loue,' are all polysemous; their multiple meanings are part of their truth. Understanding them or any other aspect of this 'shape-shifter'[20] of a poem requires the sort of mental dancing or play of mind which the foregoing chapters have sought to demonstrate, and which the pun models. Adding such play of mind in attentive reading to our other approaches to *Piers Plowman* will enable us to discover its 'secrets' and thus to be 'trewe' to the 'game of heuene.'

[19] Muscatine notes that the style is 'peculiarly harmonious. Even the poem's seemingly most disparate traits have a common basis,' and he quotes Donaldson (*Piers* 78–79): 'There is a consistency in the [poem's] very lack of consistency' (*Poetry* 105).
[20] Gordon Gerould applied this term to the figure of Piers Plowman (75). It seems also to apply to the entire poem. Its 'shifting' quality is generally noted, e.g., recently by Allen, *Ethical* 299, Simpson, 'Transformation' 171, and Carruthers: 'Things within the poem are not seen as coherent entities but are constantly in the process of changing into something else' (*Search* 23). Bowers speaks of an 'acute sense of uncertainty' (3–4) caused by the poem's 'multiplication of alternatives' (37).

List of Works Cited

Primary Sources and Reference Works

Piers Plowman:

Bennett, J. A. W., ed.   *Piers Plowman: Prologue and Passus I–VII of the B-Text*. Oxford: Clarendon Press, 1972.

Kane, George, ed.   *Piers Plowman: the A Version*. London: Athlone Press, 1960.

—— and E. Talbot Donaldson, ed.   *Piers Plowman: the B Version*. London: Athlone Press, 1975.

Pearsall, Derek, ed.   *Piers Plowman*. York Medieval Texts, 2nd Series. London: Edward Arnold, 1978.

Salter, Elizabeth, and Derek Pearsall, ed.   *Piers Plowman*. York Medieval Texts. Evanston: Northwestern University Press, 1969.

Schmidt, A. V. C., ed.   *The Vision of Piers Plowman: a Complete Edition of the B-Text*. Everyman's Library. N.Y.: Dutton, 1978.

Skeat, W. W.   *The Vision of William Concerning Piers the Plowman* 2 vol. London: Oxford University Press, 1886; repr. 1969.

Goodridge, J. F.   *Piers the Ploughman translated into Modern English*. Baltimore: Penguin, 1959.

Williams, Margaret, trans.   *Piers the Plowman*. N.Y.: Random House, 1971.

Other Primary Sources:

Alanus de Insulis.   *The Complaint of Nature (De Planctu Naturae)*. Tr. D. M. Moffat. N.Y.: Holt, 1908.

——.   'Liber in Distinctionibus Dictionum Theologicalum.' *Patrologia Latina*. Ed. J.-P. Migne. Paris, 1855, 210: 686–1012.

Aquinas, St Thomas.   'De Veritate.' *Quaestiones Disputatae* I. Turin: Marietti, 1949.

——.   *Summa Theologica*. Tr. Fathers of the English Dominican Province. 1st complete American edn 3 vol. N.Y.: Benziger, 1948.

Augustine, St.   *Confessions.* Tr. Frank Sheed. N.Y.: Sheed and Ward, 1943, 1951.

_____. 'Enarrationes in Psalmos.' *Patrologia Latina.* Ed. J.-P. Migne. Paris, 1861, 36.

Bernard, St.   *Ausgewählte Sermone ... über das Höhelied.* Ed. Otto Baltzer. Freiburg i B and Leipzig: Mohr, 1893, repr. Frankfurt: Minerva, 1968.

Bernardus Silvestris.   *Cosmographia.* Tr. Winthrop Wetherbee. N.Y.: Columbia University Press, 1973.

Bonaventura, St.   *The Mind's Road to God (Itinerarium Mentis ad Deum).* Tr. George Boas. N.Y.: Liberal Arts Press, 1953.

Chaucer, Geoffrey.   *The Riverside Chaucer.* Ed. L. D. Benson. Boston: Houghton Mifflin, 1987.

Dante Alighieri.   *La Divina Commedia.* Ed. N. Sapegno. 3 vol. Firenze: La Nuova Italia, 1957.

Glossa Ordinaria. Patrologia Latina. Ed. J.-P. Migne. Paris: Garnier, 1879, 113–114.

Hopkins, Gerard Manley.   *Poems.* 3rd edn N.Y.: Oxford University Press, 1948.

Hugh of St Victor.   'De Sacramentis.' *Patrologia Latina.* Ed. J.-P. Migne. Paris: Garnier, 1880, 176: 174–618.

Isidore, St.   'Differentiarum.' In *Patrologia Latina.* Ed. J.-P. Migne. Paris, 1862, 83: 1–98.

Julian of Norwich.   *A Book of Showings to the Anchoress Julian of Norwich.* Ed. Edmund Colledge and James Walsh. Studies and Texts 35. 2 vol. Toronto: Pontifical Institute of Mediaeval Studies, 1978.

Merton, Thomas. *The New Man.* N.Y.: Farrar Straus and Cudahy, 1961.

Missale ad usum ... Herfordensis. Ed. W. G. Henderson. Farnborough: Gregg, 1969 (facs. repr. of 1st edn, 1874).

Missale ad usum ... Sarum. London: Stewart, 1861.

The Pearl. Ed. Sara de Ford. Northbrook, IL: AHM Press, 1967.

Robbins, Rossell Hope, ed.   *Secular Lyrics of the XIVth and XVth Centuries.* Oxford: Clarendon Press, 1952.

St. Erkenwald, ed. Ruth Morse. Cambridge: Cambridge University Press, 1975.

Shakespeare, William.   *The Tempest,* ed. Frank Kermode. The Arden Shakespeare, 6th edn Cambridge, MA: Harvard University Press, 1958.

'Sir Orfeo.'   In *Fourteenth Century Verse and Prose,* ed. Kenneth Sisam. Oxford: Clarendon Press, 1921, repr. 1978, 13–31.

'The York Play "Harrowing of Hell" BM MS. Addit. 35290 f. 193b.'   In *Fourteenth Century Verse and Prose,* ed. Kenneth Sisam. Oxford: Clarendon Press, 1921, repr. 1978, 171–184.

Reference Works:

Anthon, Charles. *Latin-English and English-Latin Dictionary*. N.Y.: Harper, 1873.

Apperson, G. L. *English Proverbs and Proverbial Phrases*. London: Dent, 1929.

Attwater, Donald, ed. *A Catholic Dictionary*. N.Y.: Macmillan, 1958.

Cassell's Latin Dictionary. J. R. V. Marchant and J. F. Charles, rev. N.Y.: Funk and Wagnalls, 1938.

DuCange, D. *Glossarium Mediae et Infimae Latinitatis*. Paris: Didot, 1840–.

Middle English Dictionary. Ed. Hans Kurath, S. M. Kuhn. Ann Arbor: University of Michigan Press, 1956–.

Oxford English Dictionary. Ed. J. A. H. Murray et al. 13 vol. Oxford: Clarendon Press, 1933.

Webster's Third New International Dictionary. Springfield, MA: Merriam, 1961.

Critical and Historical Works:

Adams, Robert. 'The Nature of Need in "Piers Plowman" XX.' *Traditio* 34 (1978): 273–301.

———. 'Piers's Pardon and Langland's Semi-Pelagianism.' *Traditio* 39 (1983): 367–418.

Aers, David. *Piers Plowman and Christian Allegory*. London: Arnold, 1975.

Alford, John A. 'The Grammatical Metaphor: A Survey of Its Use in the Middle Ages.' *Speculum* 57 (1982): 728–760.

———. 'Literature and Law in Medieval England.' *PMLA* 92 (1977): 941–951.

———. 'The Role of the Quotations in *Piers Plowman*.' *Speculum* 52 (1977): 80–99.

Allen, Judson Boyce. *The Ethical Poetic of the Later Middle Ages: A Decorum of Convenient Distinction*. Toronto: University of Toronto Press, 1981.

———. 'Langland's Reading and Writing: *Detractor* and the Pardon Passus.' *Speculum* 59 (1984): 342–362.

Ames, Ruth. *The Fulfillment of the Scriptures*. Evanston: Northwestern University Press, 1970.

Anderson, Judith. *The Growth of a Personal Voice*. New Haven: Yale University Press, 1976.

Arthur, Ross G.   *Medieval Sign Theory and Sir Gawain and the Green Knight*. Toronto: University of Toronto, 1987.

Baker, Denise N.   'From Plowing to Penitence.' *Speculum* 55 (1980): 715–725.

———.   'The Pardons of *Piers Plowman*. *Neuphilologische Mitteilungen* 85 (1984): 462–472.

Baldwin, Anna.   'The Double Duel in *Piers Plowman* B XVIII and C XXI.' *Medium AEvum* 50 (1981): 64–78.

Barfield, Owen.   *Poetic Diction*. London: Faber and Gwyer, 1928.

Barney, Stephen.   *Allegories of History, Allegories of Love*. Hamden: Archon, 1979.

———.   'The Plowshare of the Tongue: the Progress of a Symbol from the Bible to *Piers Plowman*.' *Medieval Studies* 35 (1973): 261–293.

Barthes, Roland.   *Image – Music – Text*. Tr. Stephen Heath. N.Y.: Hill & Wang, 1977.

Baum, Paull F.   'Chaucer's Puns.' *PMLA* 71 (1956): 225–246.

Bennett, J.A.W.   'Appendix: Natura, Nature and Kind.' *Parlement of Foules: an Interpretation*. Oxford: Clarendon Press, 1957: 194–212.

———.   *Poetry of the Passion*. Oxford: Clarendon Press, 1982.

Benson, C.D.   'The Function of Lady Meed in *Piers Plowman*.' *English Studies* 61 (1980): 194–205.

Benson, Larry D.   *Art and Tradition in Sir Gawain and the Green Knight*. New Brunswick: Rutgers University Press, 1965.

Bertz, Douglas.   'Prophecy and Apocalypse in Langland's *Piers Plowman*, B-Text, Passus XVI to XIX.' *JEGP* 84 (1985): 313–327.

Birnes, William J.   'Christ as Advocate: the Legal Metaphor of *Piers Plowman*.' *Annuale Mediaevale* 16 (1975): 71–93.

Blake, Norman. *The English Language in Medieval Literature*. Totowa, N.J.: Rowman and Littlefield, 1977.

Bloomfield, Morton W.   'The Allegories of Dobest.' *Medium AEvum* 50 (1981): 30–39.

———.   *Piers Plowman as a Fourteenth-Century Apocalypse*. New Brunswick, N.J.: Rutgers University Press, [1961].

———.   'The Present State of *Piers Plowman* Studies.' *Speculum* 14 (1939): 215–232.

———.   Review of G.L. Bursill-Hall works. *Speculum* 49 (1974): 102–105.

Boitani, Piero.   *English Medieval Narrative in the Thirteenth and Fourteenth Centuries*. Tr. Joan K. Hall. N.Y.: Cambridge University Press, 1982.

Boman, Thorleif.   *Das hebräische Denken im Vergleich mit dem griechischen*. Göttingen: Vandenhoeck u. Ruprecht, 1952.

Borroff, Marie.   *Sir Gawain and the Green Knight: a Stylistic and Metrical Study*. 1962. Repr. Hamden: Archon, 1973.

Bourquin, Guy.   *Piers Plowman*. 2 vol. Université de Lille III. Paris: Champion, 1978.

Bowers, John M.   *The Crisis of Will in Piers Plowman*. Washington, D.C.: Catholic University of America, 1986.

Brewer, Derek.   *English Gothic Literature*. N.Y.: Schocken, 1983.

Britton, G. C.   'Language and Character in Some Late Medieval Plays.' *Essays and Studies* 33 (1980): 1–15.

Brown, J.   'Eight Types of Puns.' *PMLA* 71 (1956): 14–26.

Brown, Laura M.   'The Role of Book in *Piers Plowman* B XVIII.' Unpublished paper, 22nd International Congress on Medieval Studies, Western Michigan University, 7 May 1987.

Burnley, David.   *A Guide to Chaucer's Language*. Norman: University of Oklahoma Press, 1983.

Burrell, David.   *Analogy and Philosophical Language*. New Haven: Yale University Press, 1973.

Burrow, John A.   'The Audience of *Piers Plowman*.' *Anglia* 75 (1957): 373–384.

——.   *Ricardian Poetry*. New Haven: Yale University Press, 1971.

——.   'Words, Works, and Will: Theme and Structure in *Piers Plowman*.' In S. S. Hussey, ed. *Piers Plowman*. London: Methuen, 1969, 111–124.

Bursill-Hall, G. L.   *Speculative Grammars of the Middle Ages*. The Hague: Mouton, 1971.

Bynum, Caroline W.   *Jesus as Mother*. Berkeley: University of California Press, 1982.

Caird, G. B.   *The Language and Imagery of the Bible*. Philadelphia: Westminster, 1980.

Carruthers, Mary.   *The Search for St. Truth*. Evanston: Northwestern University Press, 1973.

——.   'Time, Apocalypse, and the Plot of *Piers Plowman*.' In Mary Carruthers and Elizabeth Kirk, ed. *Acts of Interpretation*. Norman, OK: Pilgrim, 1982, 175–188.

Cassirer, Ernst.   *The Platonic Renaissance in England*. (1932) Tr. J. P. Pettigrew. N.Y.: Nelson, 1953.

Cecchi, Emilio, and Natalino Sapegno, ed.   *Storia della Letteratura Italiana* II. Milan: Garzanti, 1965, repr. 1976.

Chamberlin, John.   'Nature of the Redundancies in the Surface Structure of *Piers Plowman*: The Opening Passage of the Third Vision.' Unpublished paper, 22nd International Congress of Medieval Studies, Western Michigan University, 8 May 1987.

Chambers, R. W.   'Long Will, Dante, and the Righteous Heathen.' *Essays and Studies* 9 (1924): 50–69.

——.   *Man's Unconquerable Mind*. London: Jonathan Cape, 1939.

Clutterbuck, Charlotte. 'Hope and Good Works: *Leaute* in the C-Text of *Piers Plowman.' RES* 28 (1977): 129–140.

Coghill, Nevill. 'The Pardon of Piers Plowman.' *Proceedings of the British Academy* 30 (1944): 303–357.

Coleman, Janet. *Medieval Readers and Writers 1350–1400.* N.Y.: Columbia University Press, 1981.

——. *Piers Plowman and the Moderni.* Rome: Edizioni di Storia e Letteratura, 1981.

Courtenay, William J. *Schools and Scholars in Fourteenth-Century England.* Princeton: Princeton University Press, 1987.

Crane, William G. *Wit and Rhetoric in the Renaissance.* N.Y.: Columbia University Press, 1937.

Crenshaw, James L. *Studies in Ancient Israelite Wisdom.* Library of Biblical Studies, ed. H.M. Olinsky. N.Y.: Ktav Publishing House, 1976.

Curtius, Ernst. *European Literature and the Latin Middle Ages.* Tr. Willard R. Trask. N.Y.: Pantheon, 1953.

Davlin, M.C. 'A Genius-Kynde Illustration in Codex Vaticanus Palatinus Latinus 629.' *Manuscripta* 23 (1979): 149–158.

——. '*Kynde Knowyng* as a Major Theme in *Piers Plowman* B.' *RES* 22 (1971): 1–19.

——. '*Kynde Knowyng* as a Middle English Equivalent for "Wisdom" in *Piers Plowman* B.' *Medium AEvum* 50 (1981): 5–17.

——. '*Piers Plowman* and the Books of Wisdom.' *Yearbook of Langland Studies* 2 (1988): 23–33.

Dawson, Christopher. *Medieval Essays.* London: Sheed and Ward, 1953.

Debs, Mary Beth. 'Of Bryddes and of Bestes: Patterns of Animal Imagery in *Piers Plowman.*' Unpublished M.A. thesis, Rosary College, River Forest, IL, 1973.

Dembowski, Peter F. 'Vocabulary of Old French Courtly Lyrics – Difficulties and Hidden Difficulties.' *Critical Inquiry* 2 (1976): 763–779.

Didron, Adolphe N. *Christian Iconography* (1843). Tr. E.J. Millmaton; comp. M. Stokes. N.Y.: Ungar, 1965.

Dillon, Janette. '*Piers Plowman*: a Particular Example of Wordplay and its Structural Significance.' *Medium AEvum* 50 (1981): 40–48.

Donaldson, E.T. 'Apocalyptic Style in *Piers Plowman* B XIX–XX.' *Leeds Studies in English* n.s. 16 (1985): 74–81.

——. 'The Grammar of Book's Speech.' In Robert Blanch, ed. *Style and Symbolism in Piers Plowman.* Knoxville: University of Tennessee Press, 1969, 264–270.

------. 'Langland and Some Scriptural Quotations.' In L. D. Benson and Siegfried Wenzel, ed. *The Wisdom of Poetry*. Kalamazoo: Medieval Institute, 1982, 67–72.

------. *Piers Plowman: the C-Text and its Poet*. New Haven: Yale University Press, 1949.

Donna, Sister Rose Bernard. *Despair and Hope: A Study of Langland and Augustine*. Washington: Catholic University of America, 1948.

Ducháček, O. 'Les jeux de mots du point de vue linguistique.' *Beiträge zur Romanischen Philologie* 9 (1970): 107–117.

Dunning, T. P. 'Langland and the Salvation of the Heathen.' *Medium AEvum* 12 (1943): 45–54.

------. *Piers Plowman*. Dublin: Talbot, 1937; 2nd rev. edn, ed. T. P. Dolan. Oxford: Clarendon Press, 1980.

Economou, George. *The Goddess Natura in Medieval Literature*. Cambridge, MA: Harvard University Press, 1972.

------. 'Self-consciousness of Poetic Activity in Dante and Langland.' In Lois Ebin, ed. *Vernacular Poetics in the Middle Ages*. Studies in Medieval Culture XVI. Kalamazoo, MI: Medieval Institute Press, 1984, 177–198.

Evans, W. O. 'Charity in *Piers Plowman*.' In S. S. Hussey, ed. *Piers Plowman*. London: Methuen, 1969, 245–278.

Ferster, Judith. *Chaucer on Interpretation*. Cambridge: Cambridge University Press, 1985.

[Finnegan], S. Mary Jeremy, O.P. '"Leggis a-lery" *Piers Plowman* A VII.115.' *ELN* 1 (1964): 250–251.

Fish, Stanley. *Is There a Text in This Class?* Cambridge: Harvard University Press, 1980.

Fowler, David C. *The Bible in Middle English Literature*. Seattle: University of Washington Press, 1984.

------. *Piers the Plowman*. Seattle: University of Washington Press, 1961.

Frank, Robert W., Jr. 'The Art of Reading Medieval Personification-Allegory.' In Edward Vasta, ed. *Middle English Survey*. Notre Dame: Notre Dame University Press, 1968, 217–231.

------. *Piers Plowman and the Scheme of Salvation*. New Haven: Yale University Press, 1957; repr. Archon, 1969.

Frost, William. 'A Chaucerian Crux.' *Yale Review* 66 (1976–1977): 551–561.

Gerould, Gordon. 'The Structural Integrity of *Piers Plowman* B.' *Studies in Philology* 45 (1948): 60–75.

Godden, Malcolm. 'Plowmen and Hermits in Langland's *Piers Plowman*.' *Review of English Studies* 35 (1984): 129–163.

Goldsmith, Margaret E. 'Piers' Apples: Some Bernardine Echoes in *Piers Plowman*.' *Leeds Studies in English* n.s. 16 (1985): 309–325.

Gradon, Pamela. 'Langland and the Ideology of Dissent.' *Proceedings of the British Academy* 66 (1980): 179–205.

——. '*Trajan Redivivus*: Another Look at Trajan in *Piers Plowman*.' In Douglas Gray and E. G. Stanley, ed. *Middle English Studies*. Oxford: Clarendon Press, 1983, 93–114.

Gray, Douglas. *Themes and Images in the Medieval English Lyric*. London: Routledge and Kegan Paul, 1972.

Griffiths, Lavinia. *Personification in Piers Plowman*. Cambridge: D. S. Brewer, 1985.

Guillet, Jacques. *Themes of the Bible*. Tr. Albert J. LaMothe, Jr. Notre Dame: University of Notre Dame Press, 1960.

Hahn, Thomas. 'Money, Sexuality, Wordplay, and Context in the Shipman's Tale.' In *Chaucer in the Eighties*, ed. J. Wasserman and R. J. Blanch. Syracuse: Syracuse University Press, 1986, 235–249.

Hala, James Paul. 'For She is Tikel of Hire Tale.' Unpublished paper, 1985.

——. '*Signum et Res*: Wordplay and Christian Rhetoric.' *Michigan Academician* 16 (1984): 315–328.

Hamilton, A. C. 'The Visions of *Piers Plowman* and *The Faerie Queene*.' In *Form and Convention in the Poetry of Edmund Spenser*. Ed. Wm Nelson. English Institute Essays. N.Y.: Columbia University Press, 1961, 1–34.

Hanning, Robert W. 'Poetic Emblems in Medieval Narrative Texts.' In Lois Ebin, ed. *Vernacular Poetics in the Middle Ages*. Studies in Medieval Culture XVI. Kalamazoo: Medieval Institute Press, 1984, 1–32.

Harwood, Britton. '"Clergye" and the Action of the Third Vision in *Piers Plowman*.' *MP* 70 (1973): 279–290.

——. 'Imaginative in *Piers Plowman*.' *Medium AEvum* 44 (1975): 249–263.

——. 'Langland's *Kynde Knowyng* and the Quest for Christ.' *MP* 80 (1982–1983): 242–255.

——. 'Langland's *Kynde Wit*.' *JEGP* 75 (1976): 330–336.

——. '*Liberum-Arbitrium* in the C-Text of *Piers Plowman*.' *PQ* 52 (1973): 680–695.

Hatzfeld, Helmut. 'Linguistic Investigation of Old French High Spirituality.' *PMLA* 61 (1946): 331–378.

Hausmann, Franz J. *Studien zu einer Linguistik des Wortspiels*. Beihefte zur Zeitschrift für romanisches Philologie 143. (Bib. 136–151). Tübingen: Niemeyer, 1974.

Heffernan, Carol. '*Piers Plowman* B. I.153–158.' *English Language Notes* 22 (1984): 1–5.

Heger, K. 'Homographie, Homonymie u. Polysemie.' *Zeitschrift für Romanisches Philologie* 79 (1963): 471–491.

Heraucourt, Will. 'What is Trouthe or Soothfastnesse.' In *Englische Kultur in Sprachwissenschaftlicher Deutung: Festschrift für Max Deutschbein*. Leipzig: Quelle u. Meyer, 1936.

Hieatt, Constance. *The Realism of Dream Visions*. The Hague: Mouton, 1967.

Hill, Thomas D. 'Seth the "Seeder" in *Piers Plowman* C. 10. 249.' *Yearbook of Langland Studies* 1 (1987): 105–108.

Hoffman, Richard L. 'The Burning of "Boke" in *Piers Plowman*.' *MLQ* 25 (1964): 57–65.

Hort, Greta. *Piers Plowman and Contemporary Religious Thought*. N.Y.: Macmillan, [1936].

Howard, Donald. *The Three Temptations*. Princeton: Princeton University Press, 1966.

Huizinga, J. *Homo Ludens*. Boston: Beacon Press, 1955.

Huppé, B. F. '"Petrus, id est, Christus": Word Play in *Piers Plowman*, the B-Text.' *ELH* 17 (1950): 163–190.

Hussey, S. S. 'Introduction.' In S. S. Hussey, ed. *Piers Plowman*. London: Methuen, 1969, 1–26.

James, Stanley B. *Back to Langland*. London: Sands, 1936.

Johnson, Wendell Stacy. 'The Imagery and Diction of *The Pearl*.' *ELH* 20 (1953): 161–180. In Edward Vasta, ed. *Middle English Survey*. Notre Dame: Notre Dame University Press, 1965, 93–115.

Jones, H. S. V. 'Imaginatif in *Piers Plowman*.' *JEGP* 13 (1914): 583–588.

Joseph, Gerhard. 'Chaucer's Coinage: Foreign Exchange and the Puns of the *Shipman's Tale*.' *Chaucer Review* 17 (1983): 341–357.

Josipovici, G. D. 'Fiction and Game in *The Canterbury Tales*.' *Critical Quarterly* 7 (1965): 185–197.

Kane, George. *Middle English Literature*. London: Methuen, 1951.

——. 'Music "Neither Unpleasant nor Monotonous."' In P. L. Heyworth, ed. *Medieval Studies for J. A. W. Bennett*. Oxford: Clarendon Press, 1981, 43–63.

——. 'The Perplexities of William Langland.' In L. D. Benson and Siegfried Wenzel, ed. *The Wisdom of Poetry*. Kalamazoo: Medieval Institute, 1982, 73–90.

Kaske, R. E. 'Gigas the Giant in *Piers Plowman*.' *JEGP* 56 (1957): 177–185.

——. 'Holy Church's Speech and the Structure of *Piers Plowman*.' In Beryl Rowland, ed. *Chaucer and Middle English Studies*. Kent, Ohio: Kent State University Press, 1974, 320–327.

——. 'Langland's Walnut-Simile.' *JEGP* 58 (1959): 650–654.

——. 'The Speech of "Book" in *Piers Plowman*.' *Anglia* 77 (1959): 117–144.

———. 'The Use of Simple Figures of Speech in *Piers Plowman.*' *SP* 48 (1951): 571–600.

Kaulbach, Ernest. '*Piers Plowman* B IX: Further Refinements of Inwitte.' In M. A. Jazavery et al, ed. *Linguistic and Literary Studies in Honor of Archibald A. Hill.* The Hague: Mouton, 1979, 103–110.

———. 'The "Vis Imaginativa" and the Reasoning Powers of Ymaginatif in the B-Text of *Piers Piowman.*' *JEGP* 84 (1985): 16–29.

Kean, P. M. 'Justice, Kingship and the Good Life in the Second Part of *Piers Plowman.*' In S. S. Hussey, ed. *Piers Plowman.* London: Methuen, 1969, 76–110.

———. 'Langland on the Incarnation.' *RES* 16 (1965): 349–363.

———. 'Love, Law, and Lewte in *Piers Plowman. RES* 15 (1964): 241–261.

Kellogg, Alfred. *Chaucer, Langland and Arthur.* New Brunswick: Rutgers University Press, 1972.

Kermode, Frank. 'Secrets and Narrative Sequence.' In W. J. T. Mitchell, ed. *On Narrative.* Repr. of *Critical Inquiry* 7 (1980–81). Chicago: University of Chicago Press, 1980–81, 79–97.

Kirk, Elizabeth D. *The Dream Thought of Piers Plowman.* New Haven: Yale University Press, 1972.

———. '"Who Suffreth More than God?"' In Gerald J. Schiffhorst, ed. *The Triumph of Patience.* Orlando: University Presses of Florida, 1978, 88–104.

Klubertanz, G. P. 'Analogy.' *New Catholic Encyclopedia* 1: 461–465. 17 vol. Washington: Catholic University Press, 1967; repr. 1981.

Knight, S. T. 'Satire in *Piers Plowman.*' In S. S. Hussey, ed. *Piers Plowman.* London: Methuen, 1969, 279–309.

Knowles, David. *The Evolution of Medieval Thought.* Baltimore: Helicon, [1962].

Kökeritz, Helge. 'Rhetorical Word Play in Chaucer.' *PMLA* 69 (1954): 937–952.

Kolve, V. A. *The Play Called Corpus Christi.* Stanford: Stanford University Press, 1966.

Lawlor, John. 'Christian Tradition and Social Revolution in *Piers Plowman.*' Unpublished paper delivered at 14th Congress of International Federation for Modern Languages and Literatures, 1978.

———. 'The Imaginative Unity of *Piers Plowman.*' *RES* 8 (1957): 113–126.

———. *Piers Plowman: an Essay in Criticism.* London: Arnold, 1962.

Lawton, David. 'The Subject of *Piers Plowman.*' *Yearbook of Langland Studies* 1 (1987): 1–30.

Leclercq, Jean. *The Love of Learning and the Desire for God.* Tr. Catherine

132

Misrahi. 2nd rev. edn N.Y.: Fordham, 1974; repr. 1977.

——, et al.   *The Spirituality of the Middle Ages.* Eng. tr. by Benedictines of Holme Eden Abbey, Carlisle. London: Burnes and Oates, 1968.

Leff, Gordon.   *William of Ockham.* Totowa, N.J.: Rowman and Littlefield, 1975.

Lewis, C. S.   *The Discarded Image.* Cambridge, Eng.: Cambridge University Press, 1964.

——.   *Studies in Words.* Cambridge, Eng.: Cambridge University Press, 1960.

Leyerle, John.   'The Heart and the Chain.' In L. D. Benson, ed. *The Lerned and the Lewed.* Cambridge, MA: Harvard University Press, 1974, 113–145.

Longo, Joseph.   *'Piers Plowman* and the Tropological Matrix: Passus XI and XII.' *Anglia* 82 (1964): 291–308.

Lotto, Edward.   'The Function of Wit in Passus IX of *Piers Plowman.'* Unpublished paper delivered at 17th International Congress on Medieval Studies, Kalamazoo, MI, 1982.

Mahood, Molly M.   *Shakespeare's Wordplay.* London: Methuen, 1957.

Mander, M. N. K.   'Grammatical Analogy in Langland and Alan of Lille.' *N and Q* 26 (1979): 501–504.

Mann, Jill.   'Eating and Drinking in *Piers Plowman.' Essays and Studies* 32 (1979): 26–43.

Manning, Stephen.   *Wisdom and Number.* Lincoln: University of Nebraska Press, 1962.

[Martin], Priscilla Jenkins.   'Conscience: The Frustration of Allegory.' In S. S. Hussey, ed. *Piers Plowman.* London: Methuen, 1969, 125–142.

Martin, Priscilla.   *Piers Plowman: The Field and the Tower.* N.Y.: Barnes and Noble, 1979.

Mazzeo, Joseph A.   'Dante and the Pauline Modes of Vision.' *Harvard Theological Review* 50 (1957): 275–301.

McAlindon, T.   'The Ironic Vision.' *RES* 32 (1981): 129–141.

McNabb, Vincent, O. P.   *Faith and Prayer.* Westminster, MD: Newman Press, 1953.

[Mendillo], Louise Dunlap.   'Vegetation Puns in Pearl.' *Mediaevalia* 3 (1977): 173–188.

Mendillo, Louise Dunlap.   'Word Play in *Pearl*: Figures of Sound and Figures of Sense.' Unpublished dissertation. Berkeley: University of California, 1976.

Middleton, Anne.   'The Idea of Public Poetry in the Reign of Richard II.' *Speculum* 53 (1978): 94–114.

——.   'Narration and the Invention of Experience: Episodic Form in *Piers Plowman.'* In L. D. Benson and Siegfried Wenzel, ed. *The Wisdom of Poetry.* Kalamazoo: Medieval Institute, 1982, 91–122.

———. 'Two Infinites.' *ELH* 39 (1972): 169–188.

Miles, Josephine. *The Continuity of Poetic Language.* N.Y.: Octagon, 1965.

———. *Renaissance, 18th Century, and Modern Language in English Poetry.* Berkeley: University of California Press, 1960.

Mills, David. 'The Role of the Dreamer in *Piers Plowman.*' In S. S. Hussey, *Piers Plowman.* London: Methuen, 1969, 180–212.

Minnis, Alastair. *Chaucer and Pagan Antiquity.* Cambridge: D. S. Brewer, 1982.

———. 'Langland's Ymaginatif and late-medieval theories of imagination.' *Comparative Criticism* 3 (1981): 71–103.

———, A. J. *Medieval Theory of Authorship.* London: Scolar, 1984.

Mondin, B. 'Analogy, Theological Use of.' *New Catholic Encyclopedia* 1: 465–468. 17 vol. Washington: Catholic University Press, 1967; repr. 1981.

Moske, Birgit. *Caritas.* Abhandlungen zur Kunst, Musik u. Literaturwissenschaft 193. Bonn: Bouvier, 1977.

Muir, Kenneth. 'The Uncomic Pun.' *Cambridge Journal* 3 (1950): 472–485.

Murtaugh, Daniel. *Piers Plowman and the Image of God.* Gainesville: University Presses of Florida, 1978.

Muscatine, Charles. 'The Locus of Action in Medieval Narrative.' *Romance Philology* 17 (1963): 115–122.

———. *Poetry and Crisis in the Age of Chaucer.* Notre Dame: University of Notre Dame Press, 1972.

Norton-Smith, John. *William Langland.* Medieval and Renaissance Authors 6. Leiden: Brill, 1983.

Oberman, Heiko. 'Fourteenth-Century Religious Thought: a Premature Profile.' *Speculum* 53 (1978), 80–93.

O'Brien, Timothy D. 'Word Play in the Allegory of King Horn.' *Allegorica* 9 (1982): 110–122.

O'Driscoll, Philomena. 'The *Dowel* Debate in *Piers Plowman* B.' *Medium AEvum* 50 (1981): 18–29.

Oliver, Raymond. *Poems without Names.* Berkeley: University of California, 1970.

Olmert, Michael. 'Game-Playing, Moral Purpose, and the Structure of *Pearl.*' *Chaucer Review* 21 (1987): 383–403.

———. 'The Parson's Ludic Formula for Winning on the Road [to Canterbury].' *Chaucer Review* 20 (1985): 158–168.

Olson, Glending. *Literature as Recreation in the Later Middle Ages.* Ithaca: Cornell University Press, 1982.

Ong, Walter, S. J. 'Wit and Mystery: a Revaluation in Medieval Latin Hymnody.' *Speculum* 22 (1947): 310–341.

――――. 'The Writer's Audience is Always a Fiction.' *PMLA* 90 (1975): 9–21.

Paull, Michael R. 'Mahomet and the Conversion of the Heathen in *Piers Plowman.' ELN* 10 (1972): 1–8.

Payne, D. F. 'Characteristic Word-Play in "Second Isaiah": a Reappraisal.' *Journal of Semitic Studies* 12 (1967): 207–229.

Pearsall, Derek. 'The "Ilchester Manuscript of *Piers Plowman."' Neuphilologische Mitteilungen* 82 (1981): 181–193.

Peverett, Michael. '"Quod" and "Seide" in *Piers Plowman.' Neuphilologische Mitteilungen* 87 (1986): 117–127.

Prior, Sandra. 'Routhe and Hert-Huntyng in the Book of the Duchess.' *JEGP* 85 (1986): 3–19.

Quilligan, Maureen. *The Language of Allegory.* Ithaca: Cornell University Press, 1979.

――――. 'Langland's Literal Allegory.' *Essays in Criticism* 28 (1978): 95–111.

Quinn, Arthur. *Figures of Speech.* Salt Lake City: Gibbs M. Smith, 1982.

Quirk, Randolph. 'Langland's Use of *Kind Wit* and *Inwit.' JEGP* 52 (1953): 182–188.

Rahner, Karl. 'The Theology of the Symbol.' *Theological Investigations* IV. London: Darton, Longman and Todd, 1974: 221–252.

Reiss, Edmund. *The Art of the Middle English Lyric.* Athens: University of Georgia Press, 1972.

Riach, Mary. 'Langland's Dreamer and the Transformation of the Third Vision.' *Essays in Criticism* 19 (1969): 6–18.

Richardson, Janette. *Blameth Nat Me.* The Hague: Mouton, 1970.

Ricks, Christopher. *The Force of Poetry.* N.Y.: Oxford University Press, 1984.

Robertson, D. W., Jr. *A Preface to Chaucer.* Princeton: Princeton University Press, 1962.

Robertson, D. W., Jr. and B. F. Huppé. *Piers Plowman and Scriptural Tradition.* Princeton: Princeton University Press, 1951.

Rousse, Jacques. 'Lectio Divina et Lecture Spirituelle.' *Dictionnaire de Spiritualité* 9. M. Villeretal, ed. Paris: Beauchesne, 1976.

Rousseau, M. I. J. '*Victimae Paschali Laudes*'. *New Catholic Encyclopedia* 14: 645–646. 17 vol. Washington: Catholic University Press, 1967; repr. 1981.

Rupp, Henry. 'Word Play in *Pearl.' Modern Language Notes* 70 (1955): 558–559.

Russell, G. H. 'The Salvation of the Heathen.' *Journal of the Warburg and Courtauld Institute* 29 (1966): 101–116.

Ryan, William M.   *William Langland.* Twayne's English Authors Series 66. N.Y.: Twayne, 1968.

———. 'Word Play in Some OE Homilies and a Late ME Poem.' In E. B. Atwood and A. A. Hill, ed. *Studies in Language, Literature and Culture of the Middle Ages and Later.* Austin: University of Texas, 1969, 265–278.

St. Jacques, Raymond.   'Conscience's Final Pilgrimage in *Piers Plowman* and the Cyclical Structure of the Liturgy.' *Revue de l'Université d'Ottowa* 40 (1970): 210–223.

———. 'Langland's Bells of the Resurrection and the Easter Liturgy.' *English Studies in Canada* 3 (1977): 129–135.

———. 'Langland's Christ-Knight and the Liturgy.' *Revue de l'Université d'Ottowa* 37 (1967): 144–158.

———. 'Middle English Literature and the Liturgy: Recent Research and Future Possibilities.' *Mosaic* 12 (1979): 1–10.

Salter, Elizabeth.   *Fourteenth-Century English Poetry.* Oxford: Clarendon Press, 1983.

———. 'Langland and the Contexts of "Piers Plowman."' *Essays and Studies* 32 (1979): 19–25.

———. 'Medieval Poetry and the Figural View of Reality.' *Proceedings of the British Academy* 54 (1968): 73–92.

———. *Piers Plowman: an Introduction.* Cambridge, MA: Harvard University Press, 1962.

Schleusener, Jay.   'Langland's Inward Argument: the Poetic Intent of "Piers Plowman" B, XV–XVIII.' Unpublished dissertation, Columbia University: 1978.

Schmidt, A. V. C.   *The Clerkly Maker.* Cambridge: D. S. Brewer, 1987.

———. 'A Covenant More than Courtesy: a Langlandian Phrase in its Context.' *N and Q* n.s. 31 (1984): 153–156.

———. 'The Inner Dreams in *Piers Plowman.*' *Medium AEvum* 55 (1986): 24–40.

———. 'Langland and the Mystical Tradition.' In Marion Glasscoe, ed. *The Medieval Mystical Tradition in England.* Exeter: University of Exeter, 1980, 17–38.

———. 'Langland, Chrysostom and Bernard: a Complex Echo.' *N & Q* 30 (1983): 108–110.

———. '*Lele Words* and *Bele Paroles*: Some Aspects of Langland's Word-Play.' *RES* 34 (1983): 137–150.

Scholes, Robert.   *Semiotics and Interpretation.* New Haven: Yale University Press, 1982.

Sellert, Friedrich.   'Das Bild in *Piers the Plowman.*' Dissertation. Rostock: University of Rostock, 1904.

Shoaf, Richard A.   *Dante, Chaucer, and the Currency of the Word.* Norman, OK: Pilgrim Books, 1983.

——. '"Speche þat Spire is of Grace": a Note on *Piers Plowman* B.9.104.' *Yearbook of Langland Studies* 1 (1987): 128–133.

Silverman, Albert H.   'Sex and Money in Chaucer's Shipman's Tale.' *PQ* 32 (1953): 329–336.

Simpson, James.   '"*Et Vidit Deus Cogitaciones Eorum*': a Parallel Instance and Possible Source for Langland's Use of a Biblical Formula at *Piers Plowman* B. XV.200a.' *N and Q* n.s. 33 (1986): 9–13.

——.   'From Reason to Affective Knowledge: Modes of Thought and Poetic Form in *Piers Plowman*.' *Medium AEvum* 55 (1986): 1–23.

——.   'The Transformation of Meaning: a Figure of Thought in *Piers Plowman*.' *RES* 37 (1986): 161–183.

Smith, Barbara Herrnstein.   *On the Margins of Discourse*. Chicago: University of Chicago Press, 1978.

Smith, Ben.   *Traditional Imagery of Charity in Piers Plowman*. The Hague: Mouton, 1966.

Smith, Macklin.   'B. 16. 183: The Sense of *Don*.' Unpublished paper, 22nd International Congress of Medieval Studies, Western Michigan University, 9 May 1987.

Spearing, A. C.   *Criticism and Medieval Poetry*. 2nd edn London: Arnold, 1972.

——.   'Langland's Poetry: Some Notes in Critical Analysis.' *Leeds Studies in English* 14 (1983): 182–195.

——.   'The Development of a Theme in *Piers Plowman*.' *RES* 11 (1960): 241–253.

——.   'Verbal Repetition in *Piers Plowman* B and C.' *JEGP* 62 (1963): 722–737.

Speyser, Suzanne.   'Dramatic Illusion and Sacred Reality in the Towneley *Prima Pastorum*.' *SP* 78 (1981): 1–19.

Stock, L. K.   '"Making It" in the *Merchant's Tale*: Chaucer's Signs of January's Fall.' *Semiotica* 63 (1987): 171–183.

——.   'The Meaning of Chevyssaunce: Complicated Word Play in Chaucer's *Shipman's Tale*.' *Studies in Short Fiction* 18 (1981): 245–249.

Stokes, Myra.   *Justice and Mercy in Piers Plowman*. London: Croom Helm, 1984.

Stubbs, Charles William.   *The Christ of English Poetry*. London: Dent, 1906.

Szittya, Penn R.   *The Antifraternal Tradition in Medieval Literature*. Princeton: Princeton University Press, 1986.

——.   'The Trinity in Langland and Abelard.' In Arthur Groos et al., ed. *Magister Regis: Studies in Honor of R. E. Kaske*. N.Y.: Fordham, 1986, 207–216.

Tatlock, J. S. P.   'Puns in Chaucer.' *Flügel Memorial Volume*. Stanford: Stanford University Press, 1916, 228–232.

Tavormina, M. Teresa. 'Bothe Two Ben Gode: Marriage and Virginity in *Piers Plowman* C 18.' *JEGP* 81 (1981): 320–330.

——. 'Kindly Similitude: Langland's Matrimonial Trinity.' *MP* 80 (1982): 117–128.

Tierney, Brian. '*Natura id est Deus*: A Case of Juristic Pantheism?' *Journal of the History of Ideas* 24 (1963): 307–322.

Tkacz, Catherine B. 'Chaucer's Beard-Making.' *Chaucer Review* 18 (1983): 127–136.

Tompkins, Jane P. 'The Reader in History: the Changing Shape of Literary Response.' In Jane P. Tompkins, ed. *Reader-Response Criticism*. Baltimore: Johns Hopkins, 1980, 201–232.

Traver, Hope. *The Four Daughters of God*. Bryn Mawr College Monographs. Bryn Mawr, PA: Bryn Mawr College, 1907.

Traversi, Derek. 'Langland's *Piers Plowman*.' In Boris Ford, ed. *The Age of Chaucer. A Guide to English Literature I*. Baltimore: Penguin, 1954, 129–147.

Tristram, Hildegard. 'Intertextuelle "Puns" in *Piers Plowman*.' *Neuphilologische Mitteilungen* 84 (1983): 182–191.

Tristram, Philippa. *Figures of Life and Death in Medieval English Literature*. N.Y.: New York University Press, 1976.

Turville-Petre, Thorlac. *The Alliterative Revival*. Totowa, N.J.: Rowman and Littlefield, 1977.

Vance, Eugene. *Mervelous Signals*. Lincoln: University of Nebraska Press, 1986.

Vasta, Edward. *The Spiritual Basis of Piers Plowman*. The Hague: Mouton, 1965.

——. 'Truth the Best Treasure in *Piers Plowman*.' *PQ* 44 (1965): 17–29.

Vinaver, Eugene. *Form and Meaning in Medieval Romance*. The Presidential Address of the MHRA, 1966. Leeds: MHRA, 1966.

von Rad, Gerhard. *Wisdom in Israel*. N.Y.: Abingdon Press, 1972.

von Soden, Hans Freiherr. *'Was ist Wahrheit?'... vom geschichtlichen Begriff der Wahrheit*. Marburger Academische Reden 46. Marburg: 1927.

Weber, Sarah. *Theology and Poetry in the Middle English Lyric*. Columbus: Ohio State University Press: 1969.

Wellek, Rene and Austin Warren. *Theory of Literature*. 3rd edn N.Y.: Harcourt Brace and World, 1956.

Wells, H. W. 'The Construction of *Piers Plowman*.' *PMLA* 44 (1929): 123–140.

Whately, Gordon. 'Heathens and Saints: *St. Erkenwald* in its Legendary Context.' *Speculum* 61 (1986): 330–363.

——. '*Piers Plowman* B 12. 277–94: Notes on Language, Text, and Theology.' *MP* 82 (1984): 1–12.

——. 'Uses of Hagiography: the Legend of Pope Gregory and the Emperor Trajan in the Middle Ages.' *Viator* 15 (1984): 25–63.

White, Hugh. 'Langland's Ymaginatif, Kynde and the *Benjamin Major*.' *Medium AEvum* 55 (1986): 241–248.

Williams, James G. *Women Recounted: Narrative Thinking and the God of Israel.* Bible and Literature Series, ed. David M. Gunn. Sheffield: Almond Press, 1982.

Wilson, Edward. 'Word Play and the Interpretation of *Pearl*.' *Medium AEvum* 40 (1971): 116–134.

Wimsatt, James I. *Allegory and Mirror.* N.Y.: Western, 1970.

Wittig, Joseph. 'The Dramatic and Rhetorical Development of Long Will's Pilgrimage.' *Neuphilologische Mitteilungen* 76 (1975): 52–76.

——. 'The ME "Absolute Infinitive" and the "Speech of Book".' In Arthur Groos, et al., ed. *Magister Regis: Studies in Honor of R. E. Kaske.* N.Y.: Fordham, 1986, 217–240.

——. '*Piers Plowman* B, Passus IX–XII: Elements in the Design of the Inward Journey,' *Traditio* 28 (1972): 211–280.

Woolf, Rosemary. *The English Religious Lyric in the Middle Ages.* London: Oxford University Press, 1968.

——. 'Some Non-Medieval Qualities of *Piers Plowman*.' *Essays in Criticism* 12 (1962): 111–125.

——. 'The Tearing of the Pardon.' In S. S. Hussey, ed. *Piers Plowman.* London: Methuen, 1969, 50–75.

Index

141